KISS ME, CHUDLEIGH

William Cook is the author of *Ha Bloody Ha* (Fourth Estate), *The Comedy Store* (Little, Brown), *Morecambe & Wise Untold* (HarperCollins) and *Twenty-five Years of Viz* (Macmillan). He edited *Eric Morecambe Unseen* (HarperCollins) and *Tragically, I Was An Only Twin* and *Goodbye Again* (Century), two biographical collections of the work of Peter Cook and Dudley Moore.

KISS ME, CHUDLEIGH

The World According to Auberon Waugh

EDITED BY WILLIAM COOK

CORONET

First published in Great Britain in 2010 by Coronet
An imprint of Hodder & Stoughton
An Hachette UK company

1

A CIP catalogue record for this title is available from the British Library.

Hardback ISBN 978 1 444 71149 3

Typeset in Garamond MT Std by Palimpsest Book Production Limited, Falkirk, Stirlingshire

Printed and bound in the UK by Clays Ltd, St Ives plc

Hodder & Stoughton policy is to use papers that are natural, renewable and recyclable products
and made from wood grown in sustainable forests. The logging and manufacturing processes are
expected to conform to the environmental regulations of the country of origin.

Hodder & Stoughton Ltd
338 Euston Road
London NW1 3BH

www.hodder.co.uk

This book is dedicated to Teresa Waugh and
Alexander Waugh

'Writing an autobiography is rather like opening your house to the public, and you cannot complain too much if one or two members of the public shit on the carpet. They have not had our advantages, after all.'

Auberon Waugh, *Spectator*, 9 November 1991

Contents

Doctors do not drop off their Victims when they are Sated (*Oldie*); Why the Advantages of Wealth are Exaggerated in the Popular Mind (*Oldie*); Why Young People Wish to Murder Us (*Oldie*)

Acknowledgements

This book is the result of the trust and generosity of two people: Teresa Waugh and Alexander Waugh. Lady Teresa gave me permission to compile this collection of her husband's writing. Alexander gave me access to his unique archive of his father's work. It would have been impossible to produce this book without them, and this book is dedicated to both of them, Auberon Waugh's widow and his eldest son.

My grateful thanks are also due to the following publications for kindly allowing me to reproduce the work that they first published: *Business Traveller*, the *Catholic Herald*, the *Daily Mail*, the *Daily Telegraph*, the *Evening Standard*, the Folio Society, the *Independent*, the *Literary Review*, the *New Statesman*, the *Oldie*, the *Spectator*, the *Sunday Telegraph* and *Tatler*. The material in Chapter Seventeen ('Way of the World') owes its journalistic origins to the discreet genius of Michael Wharton. The material in Chapter Seven ('Street of Shame') is reproduced by kind permission of *Private Eye* magazine (www.private-eye.co.uk).I must also thank my agent, Gillon Aitken for all his support and guidance, his colleagues Andrew Kidd and Ayesha Karim, Charlotte Haycock at Hodder and my editor, Mark Booth, who, as editor of Waugh's autobiography (*Will This Do?*) and several other collections (*Another Voice*, *Way of the World*) has done more than any other publisher to keep Waugh's writing alive. Special thanks also to Amanda Alcock, Mark Caswell, Luke Coppen, Jason Cowley, Paul Dacre, Jonathan Derbyshire, Nicola Doherty, Charles Garside, Julian Gregory, David Haydon, Ian Hislop, Simon Kelner, Ruth Marsh, Sheila Molmar, Fraser Nelson, Hazel Orme, Tom Otley, Gerald Scarfe, Alida Smith,

Boyd Tonkin, Danielle Wall, A. N. Wilson, Andrew Wylie and, in particular, Naim Attallah, Richard Ingrams and Nancy Sladek.

I am grateful to my wife, Sophie, and my children, Edward and Thea, for enduring the domestic chaos that every book invariably brings – and to Alexander's wife, Eliza, and their three children, Mary, Sally and Bron, for making me so welcome in their home, while I waded through Waugh's dusty files, trying to find a way of fitting all the best bits in. I couldn't, of course. This book is merely a small selection. An unexpurgated Waugh would run into millions of words and dozens of volumes. There's easily enough material for a second volume, and a third.

My selection process was entirely subjective. Rather than relying on previous compilations, I went back to the original cuttings and chose the pieces that interested and amused me most. It was like munching through a huge box of chocolates. I didn't want to stop. The chronology jumps about a bit, but within each chapter I've generally tried to keep the articles in date order. I've also kept the original titles wherever possible, only changing them when I thought they'd become too obscure, or referred to some passage I'd excised. Most of these excerpts have been cut somewhat – partly to remove oblique references to events which I thought most readers would have forgotten, but mainly to try and squeeze in as many treasures as I could.

Ten years before he died, Lynn Barber called Waugh the hardest-working journalist alive, but what's remarkable about his output is the quality, not just the quantity. Lots of hacks can churn it out, but his writing was always first rate. He could write a shopping list and make you want to read it. My only problem was deciding what to leave out. When I began to compile this book, I was mindful of Waugh's waspish reputation. By the time I finished, I was most impressed by his irrepressible *joie de vivre*.

Introduction

Since Auberon Waugh died, no other writer has replaced him. No writer has matched his way with words, his talent for turning mundane news and everyday events into comic flights of fancy. Waugh didn't merely comment on the world around him. He transformed it, from a dull and dreary place, inhabited by jumped-up bores and bullies, into a rival universe – bizarre, outrageous and far more vivid than our own. His absurdist barbs exposed the pomposity of our political masters, those self-important bossy-boots who love to tell us what to do. He seized on their trite preconceptions and twisted them to destruction. He loved to champion unfashionable points of view. He was fearless, but above all he was funny – wickedly funny. It's this wicked sense of fun that's celebrated in this book.

Auberon Waugh was born at the start of the Second World War, in a historic country house whose routines and rituals had scarcely altered since the reign of Queen Victoria. He died at the start of the new millennium, in the midst of Tony Blair's 'Cool Britannia'. Waugh chronicled this changing scene with withering contempt, tempered with wry detachment. The vanity of our rulers annoyed him, but it amused him even more.

Waugh broke bread and crossed swords with all sorts of fascinating people, and many of these feuds and friendships are recorded in his work. Yet despite his eventful life story, there's been no biography. This book is the closest thing so far, and its focus is his writing. Squeezed into one volume, it confirms what his fans have always known – that Auberon Waugh wasn't just the son of Evelyn Waugh, but a major literary figure in his own right.

The central thesis of this book is that Auberon Waugh was

a philosopher – savage, eccentric, but a philosopher nonetheless. The reason he deserves this unlikely title is that his writing was underpinned by logic. His attitudes were informed by his libertarian convictions,[1] which he followed with academic rigour, even when they led him to the most incongruous conclusions. He was a virtuoso of the vituperative arts, but he was not a controversialist. Even his most scandalous pronouncements contain a smidgeon of common sense. 'If the sexual abuse of children by their parents is half as common as child abuse enthusiasts maintain, it is hard to see what all the fuss is about,' he wrote in the *Spectator*. 'One cannot sustain a high level of moral indignation against something which appears to be more or less standard practice.'[2] No wonder he described his gift as the ability to make the comment, at any given time, that most people least wanted to hear. His genius was to transform these awkward truths into something funny and profound.

More than any writer of his era, Auberon Waugh had a genius for dividing his readers, into the delighted and the infuriated, and he retained the ability to start a squabble, even from beyond the grave. A few days after he died, Polly Toynbee wrote an article in the *Guardian*, describing him as the leader of a clan of writers that was 'effete, drunken, snobbish, sneering, racist and sexist'.[3] Waugh would have been thrilled. 'I enjoy a scrap,'[4] he used to say. This fresh outburst showed he'd achieved what all good writers dream of doing. His writing had outlived him. It had acquired a life of its own.

This was not first time that Waugh had aroused such ire. The *Guardian* had previously described him as 'vicious, backbiting, snobbish, bullying, ignorant, puerile and slightly psychopathic'. The journalist Tony Shrimsley called him a 'liar motivated by malice who does not deserve either to be employed as a journalist or to share the company of decent people'. In Rawalpindi, a group of Orthodox Muslims were so enraged by an article he had written about their style of trousers that they stormed the British Council library and burned it to the ground. Other journalists might have been cowed by such a violent protest. Waugh described this incident as 'the proudest moment of my journalistic career'.[5] Yet what was notable about Toynbee's critique was its timing. Her article was illustrated with a cartoon of Waugh being flushed down the toilet, published when Waugh's body was still not yet in the ground.

'Never in a lifetime spent in this black trade have I read a nastier valedictory for a fellow scribe,' retorted Keith Waterhouse in the *Daily Mail*. Yet Toynbee was not alone. 'My immediate reaction on hearing of Waugh's death was to punch the air and exclaim, "Good riddance!"' wrote one *Guardian* reader, in a letter to the paper. 'Polly Toynbee's reply to all the sickly and sycophantic obituaries put into words exactly how I really felt about this vile man.'[6]

'Blimey,' retorted Francis Wheen a few days later, also in the *Guardian*, citing Waugh's promotion of feminist writers like Angela Carter, and his lifelong friendships with left-wingers like Paul Foot. 'You'd hardly guess that the subject of this hysterical denunciation was the editor of a small-circulation literary magazine, a minor novelist and a humorous journalist. If that's how *Guardian* readers and pundits react to the death of such a figure, what on earth will they do when General Pinochet pegs out?'[7]

There was an equally spirited riposte in the *New Statesman*, for whom Waugh wrote a column in the 1970s. 'Polly Toynbee is wrong,' it began. 'The writer she reviled as a "ghastly man" should be celebrated alongside George Lansbury and Fidel Castro.' In this piece, the journalist Neil Clark recalled how Waugh had denounced NATO's bombing of Yugoslavia in 1999, calling for the arrest of the prime minister, Tony Blair, and his foreign secretary, Robin Cook, for alleged war crimes. Heartened by this protest, Clark and his left-wing friends wrote to Waugh, to tell him they'd formed an Unofficial Auberon Waugh Appreciation Society. 'Thank you for your letter,' Waugh replied. 'Would it give you comfort if I suggest you call yourself the Official Auberon Waugh Appreciation Society? I know of no rivals.' Clark's article was entitled 'Auberon Waugh, hero of the left'.[8]

Actually, Waugh was neither left nor right, an elusive truth that escaped his admirers as much as his adversaries. More of a romantic than a reactionary, he was only conservative in so far as he preferred country houses to council estates and old masters to modern art. He was a man of enthusiasms as well as irritants, of passions as well as hatreds. He adored John Betjeman, P. G. Wodehouse, fine wine and *la belle* France. His idea of happiness was 'a game of croquet played on an English lawn, through a summer's afternoon, after a good luncheon, and with a reasonable prospect of a good dinner ahead'.[9] Yet despite his olde worlde pleasures, Waugh was an anti-establishment figure. He was suspicious of innovation. He had a distaste for legislation. He despised the political status quo, regardless of its ideological hue. 'I am convinced that intelligent, educated and literate Englishmen are neither left wing nor right wing, but are bored by politics and regard all politicians with scorn,'[10] he said, and his own scorn was sublime.

Unlike a lot of journalists, Waugh didn't subscribe to a job lot of preconceptions. His prejudices were instinctive, but they were bespoke, not off the peg. He railed against the 'workers' and all those who claimed to represent them. Once Mrs Thatcher had tamed them, he turned his fire on her free marketeers, be they upper or lower class. 'There is no point or purpose in any form of political idealism,' he declared. 'Not only does socialism do nothing to improve the lot of the poor, making it in fact considerably worse, but capitalism also, by scattering plenty o'er a smiling land, creates as much vileness and havoc as socialism creates poverty and oppression.'[11]

Waugh's writing was marked by a lifelong contempt for cant. When the left was in the ascendant, he attacked the rhetoric of the left. When the right was on the rise, he mocked the mantras of the right. 'At one time socialism might have been a good idea,' he wrote, at the start of Thatcher's reign. 'Its inspiration, in those days, was generous and humane. Nowadays, it can appeal only to those whose social maladjustment might otherwise push them into the criminal classes, or whose intellectual inadequacies make them hungry for a dogmatic system in which they can hide their inability to think for themselves.'[12] He despised the torpor of the welfare state, but once Thatcher had the whip hand, he lampooned the philistinism of the new right. 'If ever the *Sun*'s readers lift their snouts from their newspaper's hideous, half-naked women to glimpse the sublime through music, opera, the pictorial and plastic arts or literature, then they will never look at the *Sun* again,' he wrote. 'It is the *Sun*'s function to keep its readers ignorant and smug in their own unpleased, hypocritical, proletarian culture.'[13] Yet even if he was sincere, he never lost his sense of humour. Clare Short protested about topless models in national newspapers. Waugh proposed a Nipple Tax.

Waugh was an élitist, not a populist. He saw no attraction in mob rule.[14] 'You are either a convinced liberal or a convinced democrat,' he argued, citing the popularity of the death penalty. 'You can't be both.'[15] A born trouble-maker cunningly disguised as an irascible old buffer, he was an iconoclast, a rebel in a tweed suit. He was tireless in his defence of free speech, championing Salman Rushdie, even though his writing bored him. He publicised the plight of prisoners of conscience (especially motorcyclists who refused to wear crash helmets)[16] but he was happy to fight for less heroic freedoms too. He defended smokers, drink drivers and adulterers.[17] He hated all forms of mass control, from television to fast food. 'Nothing is more repugnant to true Britons than the idea of freedom,' he wrote, of our dependence on state hand-outs. 'The idea of liberty will always cause anxiety, dismay and resentment.'[18] He could see that most Britons were quite happy to be mollycoddled by the state.

Waugh welcomed Mrs Thatcher's crusade against the tyranny of the trade unions, but he soon realised she had no sense of humour and lost interest in her thereafter. Rightly, he regarded humourlessness as a fundamental flaw.[19] He was never a Thatcherite, or any sort of 'ite' for that matter. A devout opponent of capital punishment,[20] he was opposed to most forms of punishment, *per se*. Above all, he was guided by Goethe's humane dictum: 'Distrust all those in whom the urge to punish is strong.'

What made Waugh such fun to read was that he always kept you guessing. A constant critic of the police, the prison service and the judiciary, unlike most modern Tories he was a firm fan of the European Union,[21] which he believed to be our best defence against the incoming tide of Americana, and against British politicians, whom he regarded as more stupid than any of their Continental counterparts. His ideal form of government, he said, was a junta of Belgian ticket inspectors — a remark guaranteed to enrage the majority of his right-wing readers. Waugh didn't care. He regarded EU bureaucracy as more benign than the cultural and economic imperialism of the USA, a better safeguard of the English way of life that he adored. He was a bon viveur, a hedonist — at times almost an anarchist. The most incisive columnist of the last half-century, he deserves to stand alongside Samuel Johnson in the pantheon of English letters. Yet part of the fun was trying to work out when he was joking. 'British prostitutes have the reputation for being not only the ugliest and greediest but also the laziest in the world,' he protested. 'Few even pretend to enjoy the job, they make no secret of despising their customers and being in it only for the money. Many will tend to sympathise with them, but that is just part of the English disease.'[22] Much of his best work was mere mischief-making. When Cyril Connolly revealed that he had never masturbated until the age of eighteen, Waugh lobbied the McWhirter brothers to include it in their *Guinness Book of Records*. 'Mr Norris McWhirter doubts whether it is a record,' he wrote. 'Even so, I would have thought it merited a comparative footnote.'[23]

From his salad days on the *Catholic Herald* to his swansong on the *Literary Review*, Waugh wrote about virtually every aspect of his life, treating his readers like friends and confidants.[24] By the time he died, he'd become a familiar presence in millions of other people's lives. Probably the most prolific journalist of his generation (and undoubtedly the most amusing) he was most famous for his columns in the *Daily* (and *Sunday*) *Telegraph* and the *Spectator*, but this was just a small part of his huge output. He also wrote columns for such unlikely organs as the *Sun*, the

News of the World (later the targets of his ire), *British Medicine*, *Business Traveller* and even (on one occasion) the bible of hippie counter-culture, *Oz*.[25] Waugh loathed most modern innovations, but he was no old fogey. From Peter Cook to Tina Brown, he had a keen eye for up and coming talent.[26] He promoted younger writers like Martin Amis in his influential book reviews, published in newspapers as diverse as the *Independent* and the *Daily Mail*.

Waugh's opinions were unorthodox, but his judgement was invariably spot on. He denounced the 'Hitler Diaries' as forgeries before the *Sunday Times* had even published their first instalment. 'I stake my journalistic reputation as a leading British cynic on my conclusion that they are fake,' he wrote. 'The whole story stinks from beginning to end.'[27] Subsequent events soon bore him out. He was an astute judge of popular culture, even though he claimed to detest it. In 1978, he called for a new 'down-to-earth' comic to challenge the 'old-fashioned attitudes' of the *Beano*. 'A downmarket *Beano* for the new generation of non-élitist, comprehensively educated adults would eschew all advice on how to clean their teeth and wash behind the ears,' he predicted. 'Instead it would have brightly coloured "adult" comic strips specialising in lavatory jokes and mild forms of sexual innuendo. Its naked ladies would be fat, middle-aged and copiously endowed with pubic hair.'[28] When such a comic duly appeared, in 1979, he was quick to spot its potential. 'If the future generations look back on the literature of the age, they'll more usefully look back to *Viz* than they would, for instance, the novels of Peter Ackroyd or Julian Barnes,' he said, 'because *Viz* has got a genuine vitality of its own which comes from the society which it represents.'[29] The same could be said of Waugh. Although he regarded his writing as ephemeral, destined for 'the great wastepaper basket of history'[30], his passing observations are far more revealing than the official histories of his time.

Yet Waugh wasn't just an observer. His own life was full of incident. He grew up in the household of the finest English novelist of the last century. He wrote five highly regarded novels of his own. He reported on the murderous civil war in Nigeria.

He stood for Parliament. He was embroiled in some of the most ridiculous libel actions of the last fifty years. However, none of this would have happened without the army surgeon who snatched him from the jaws of death, after a mishap that provides this book's title.

Before he became a writer, Waugh served in the British Army in Cyprus, and very nearly killed himself when, while trying to dislodge a jammed machine gun, he inadvertently fired half a dozen bullets into his chest. Yet even on the brink of death, Waugh never lost his sense of humour. In the immediate aftermath of this accident he was approached by a member of his platoon, a tough corporal called Chudleigh. Waugh was gravely injured but he still had the wit to say, 'Kiss me, Chudleigh.' If he'd died there and then, these would have been wonderful last words, yet we would have lost a unique writer, and Auberon Waugh would be a mere footnote in his father's story. Since he survived, it seems fitting to preserve this heroic quip as the title of this book.

'Chudleigh did not spot the historical reference, and treated me with some caution thereafter,' wrote Waugh, in his autobiography. 'At least I think I said "Kiss me, Chudleigh." This story is denied by Chudleigh. I have told this story so often now that I honestly can't remember if it started as a lie.'[31] That Waugh wasn't sure whether this tale was true or false makes it a particularly suitable title. Waugh loved to blur the boundaries between the real and the surreal. This strange mélange of fact and fiction was his finest achievement, an art form of his own.

Thanks to the surgeon's skill, Waugh lived for another forty-three years, and when he eventually died, of heart disease, at home in Somerset, his death was headline news around the world. Yet in the front-page tributes that spanned several continents he was mainly mourned as a journalist. This was both right and wrong. Journalism was Waugh's main medium and he was happy to call himself a journalist, an unpretentious job description for an unpretentious man. But just because his work appeared in newspapers doesn't mean it was only fit for wrapping fish and chips. Some of the world's greatest writers earned their living as penny-a-line hacks — like Dickens, whose novels were first published in weekly periodicals, a chapter at a time. Though he was scarcely older than the Beatles, Waugh was a curiously Dickensian figure – ageless, timeless, archetypal – not so much a product of the twentieth century, more like a character from *The Pickwick Papers*.

In fact, Waugh's writing, like Dickens's reporting, was only journalistic in a superficial sense. His satiric riffs and rants were usually prompted by public events, but these events were just a starting point. A column might begin with a prosaic news report but it often ended in a world of make-believe. In his *Private Eye* Diary Waugh created a new literary genre, in which reality and fantasy merge. In this regard, as A. N. Wilson said, he was an even more important writer than his father. Evelyn was a brilliant novelist, but Auberon did something new. 'Rather than aping his father by writing conventional novels, he made a comic novel out of contemporary existence,'[32] wrote Wilson, likening him to that great Augustan satirist, Jonathan Swift.

Wilson was right. Like Swift, Waugh revelled in testing received opinions to destruction, so as to reveal their intrinsic cruelty and absurdity. One thinks of Waugh's assertion that watching television gives you cancer, his suggestion that the offspring of divorcees should be put to death[33] or his proposition that Britain should declare war on Sweden. Swift's *Modest Proposal*, in which he advocated eating children to solve the Irish famine, found an echo in Waugh's campaign for a National Smack A Child Week.

Of course Swift meant to infuriate his more dimwitted readers — and he succeeded – but sharper minds could see that the target of his satire was English free-market economics, not Ireland's starving poor. For Swift, read Waugh. Like Swift, Waugh delighted in taking the dictates of those who govern us to their illogical conclusions. Like Swift, his comedy depends in part on the pious reactions of those indignant do-gooders, those po-faced people who simply don't get the joke. Like Swift, his satire is eternal, despite its specific points of reference. 'Timeless journalism is bad journalism,'[34] declared Waugh. This book will prove him wrong.

Auberon Waugh lived and worked through a golden age of journalism. Like all great writers, he gravitated towards the most vibrant medium of his age. His career marks newsprint's last hurrah before the Internet explosion, which has fragmented newspaper readerships and driven down circulation figures. Cyberspace is universal and anonymous. The new media will produce its own new stars but they will be less literary and less distinctive. Ten years on, Waugh's death looks like the end of an era. A voice like his will not be heard in our brave new virtual world.

'There is an intelligent, sceptical England surviving under all the rubbish we see on television,'[35] wrote Waugh in his final 'Way of the World' column, a few weeks before he died. Sadly, part of that intelligent and sceptical England died with him. Yet happily, millions of his words remain — and here are some of them, the best of Waugh in all his shrewd and caustic glory. *Kiss Me, Chudleigh* is a comic novel and Auberon Waugh is its unlikely hero, a cynical yet life-enhancing Everyman, who raged with coruscating wit and candour against the idiotic fads and fashions of our age.

Chapter One
Unwillingly to School

Education is much overrated as a general benefit. Few are
made much happier by it, and many are made miserable
by being confronted with their own ignorance and incu-
riosity. [1]

Auberon Waugh was born on 17 November 1939, the second
of seven children, at Pixton Park in Somerset, the model for
Boot Magna Hall in *Scoop*, Evelyn Waugh's peerless satire of
journalistic life. This grand Georgian house belonged to
Auberon's mother's family, the Herberts, direct descendants of
the Earls of Carnarvon (of Tutankhamun fame). Auberon's
maternal grandfather was even offered the crown of Albania –
twice, in 1924 and 1930 (he declined, which seems a shame).

The Waughs, on the other hand, came from far humbler
stock: Evelyn's father, Arthur Waugh, a publisher, lived in a
modern house in Hampstead; Evelyn's literary success brought
him more fame than wealth. By ordinary standards the Waughs
were pretty well-off, but compared to the Herberts they were
strictly middle class. This difference may account for the social
tensions in Evelyn Waugh's writing, but unlike his father,
Auberon was not class conscious. Evelyn married into the
aristocracy, and did his best to become a part of it. Auberon
was born into the aristocracy, but lived a life free from class
distinction. Like his father he earned his own money, but
unlike his father he felt no reverence for the upper classes.
Like a lot of the best writers, he lived on the cusp between

two castes, an insider and an outsider, able to see the absurdities of both.

Waugh's background was privileged, but privilege did not
constrict his writing – it liberated it. 'Those of us who have the
good fortune to live in ivory towers need attach no particular
importance to whatever the public may think,' he wrote, in later
life. 'I have never been able to understand why views like my
own should be treated with suspicion just because they come
from an ivory tower – they are likely to be more extensive, for
instance, than views to be gained from the bottom of a coal
mine.'[2] Waugh never tried to please his readers. He simply told
them what he thought and felt.

Waugh lived at Pixton for six years. During the Blitz, he had
to share the house with forty toddlers who'd been evacuated
from London. 'Pixton has an enormous well at its centre,
reaching up to the top floor, and the evacuees used to lean over
this well and spit on those who walked below. I got my revenge
on these disgusting people by untruthfully telling their super-
intendent that I had seen one of them eating rat poison. They
were all taken away and stomach-pumped, my first victory of
the class war.'[3]

This early exposure to the proletariat may in fact account for
Waugh's disparagement of the 'workers' in later life (what he
called his jealous hatred of those less fortunate than himself)
but, all other things considered, it was a pretty good place to
spend the Second World War:

> I was five years old when the war ended, and have only
> one war memory, which is of the bombing of Exeter. As
> a great treat, we children were allowed on the roof to watch
> flashes on the horizon from forty miles away. I never heard
> a buzz-bomb in Somerset, never saw a dogfight in a cloud-
> less blue summer sky, although I dare say that as I get older
> I shall begin to remember these things, just as my father,
> in his later years, came more and more round to the view
> that he had fought in the Great War. I have always envied
> those who lived through the war. It may have seemed

disagreeable at the time, but I have the impression that they lived more vividly than my generation has ever lived.[4]

In 1945, with the war won, Evelyn returned from active service (and writing *Brideshead Revisited*) and took Auberon, his elder sister Teresa and their mother Laura to live at Piers Court, a Georgian house in Gloucestershire (modest after Pixton, but still grand by any other yardstick). Auberon didn't have much time to enjoy it. A few weeks after his arrival, he was packed off to boarding school. He was six years old.

Waugh arrived at All Hallows preparatory school in Somerset in January 1946, the youngest (and smallest) boy in the school. From the start of his school career, he displayed an admirable contempt for authority. During his time at All Hallows, he stole the deputy headmaster's ration of Ribena, and shot a fellow pupil in the leg with an air pistol (this injury was not intentional, he protested, before the inevitable beating – he'd merely been attempting to whip up the gravel around the boy's feet). Waugh's subversive flair seems to have been something he was born with, an innate predilection, as natural as sporting prowess or perfect pitch. Yet it was undoubtedly exacerbated by the pedantry of his schoolmasters. Boarding school was the making of him, though maybe not in quite the way that his parents had hoped for:

From earliest youth I noticed how other people often had a passion for making lists, and in those days I ascribed it to a strain of the illness which afflicts a certain sort of teacher, the passion for organising other people's lives and knowing best. Later, one sees it taken to its logical conclusion in politics and sociology, two vast industries dedicated to bossing everyone else around and putting them in categories.

At my prep school there was even a list on which every boy had to disclose every day whether or not he had been to the lavatory. One had to report to the Master on Duty and say either 'I've been, Sir,' or 'I've tried and I couldn't go.' Constipated prigs found themselves horribly dosed with a brown mixture every third day. The rest of us learned the simple lesson – invaluable in a bureaucratic society – that there is no moral or practical obligation to tell the truth when filling in forms.[5]

Waugh's appetite for japes and pranks was reflected in his writing, and several examples of his subversive juvenilia have survived. As well as an ear for parody (Horatio Hornblower and Sherlock Holmes were two of his early targets), these pre-pubescent essays also demonstrate a strong sense of the absurd. Was this comic verve inherited from his father, and honed by his incarceration? Maybe, but there was surely more to it than that. Countless children are sent away to boarding school without developing any way with words, and writing talent isn't usually inherited (literary dynasties like the Waughs are actually relatively rare). No, Auberon was a one-off like (yet utterly unlike) his father, as this precocious piece, written before he reached his teens, so clearly shows.

*

LOST
(*All Hallows Chronicle*)

Captain Slingsby, late of the Royal Horse Guards, had been thinking for the last fortnight that he should go out and visit his vast estate. He had only done so twice before and then as now he took with him his old shotgun, not because he was likely to shoot but because he thought it made the tenants respect him.

So he set out with his gun under his arm, when he saw a particularly large hare running along his path. He brought up his gun and fired it for the first time in fifty years. It would have gone off if his gun had been loaded, but it was not. The Captain, therefore, was either going to miss a most enjoyable luncheon or was going to have a very long run. So, all his schoolboy spirit that he had saved for sixty years getting the better of him, he threw caution to the winds and sprinted as fast as his fat self would allow him. After an hour of painful jogging, he realised that he had lost sight of the hare and had also lost any bearing that he might have had before. He had lost, too, his top hat, his gun, the greater part of his jacket and his dignity. He now sat down to contemplate. Having once given way to his boyish spirit he found it very hard to return to that of a stiff old gentleman. In the distance he heard a man coming towards him. So hiding behind a tree he picked up an acorn and shied it at the surprised gamekeeper who, acting on an impulse, seized the infuriated Captain round the waist and telephoned the nearest lunatic asylum.

This is a warning to all elderly gentlemen never to return to their youth, even for a few minutes.

At the end of his first term away at school, Waugh returned home for the holidays and, keen to interest his father, spun an entirely spurious tale about a ten-shilling note and a boy called Lavery. The memory remained so clear that Waugh could comfortably recount it in vivid detail over thirty years later.

THE TEN SHILLING NOTE
(*Spectator, 16 September 1978*)

'Were you aware, Papa,' I said, 'that every Ten Shilling Note carries a wire filament?'

'Yes. What of it?'

I racked my brains. 'Without this filament, it is of no value,' I ventured.

'Are you sure?' said he.

Inspiration flowered. 'Yes, indeed,' said I. 'At the end of term I had exactly such a ten shilling note which I showed to another boy, who told me it had no filament and was therefore worthless.'

'Where is this ten shilling note?'

'Oh, he kept it.'

'My boy, you have been the victim of an unscrupulous trick. Tell me this other boy's name.'

'Lavery,' I said at random.

Thirty-two years later, I still blush to think what followed: angry letters to Lavery's parents from my father, indignant denials from his father, an anguished letter from Lavery to me saying he remembered my showing him the ten shilling note but assuring me he gave it back.

This was taken as proof of guilt. The day came when my father was to write to the headmaster denouncing Lavery. 'Are you absolutely sure?' he said. I thought hard. Lavery was an older, slightly bigger boy than I was.

'Well, no,' I said. 'Now I come to think of it, I think it may have been a lie.' I often wondered whether the Lavery family has preserved my father's letter of apology.

Despite his prep-school misdemeanours, Waugh won a scholarship to Downside, one of Britain's leading Catholic public schools. Here he cultivated his talent for insubordination. 'I should hate you to be low-spirited and submissive, but don't become an anarchist,'[6] warned his father. This warning fell on deaf ears. Waugh arrived in 1952, aged twelve, and soon broke the record for the most number of beatings in a single term – seventeen. Like his prep-school masters' penchant for lists, this was a formative experience. It didn't make him a sadist or a masochist. On the contrary, it gave him a lifelong aversion to flagellation, and all those who advocate it. 'On no occasion did I experience the slightest pleasure in those beatings, and at no time, since leaving school, have I felt the slightest desire to be beaten again, or to beat anyone else,' he reflected. 'Although I occasionally contemplate physical violence against my fellow citizens – usually bad novelists or illiterate journalists – I do not support the reintroduction of corporal punishment for any crime whatsoever, and regard any form of judicial chastisement with abhorrence.'[7] Brutality brutalises most men, but it liberalised Waugh.

Yet for proponents of corporal punishment, there is no doubt that Waugh's beatings were well earned. He held a satanic black mass in the chemistry lab and started a smoking club in a cottage rented from a local poacher. When prefects broke down the door and caught him red-handed, Waugh telephoned the police to report the head boy and the headmaster for breaking and entering. He also raised a petition against the head. 'I am sorry to say he did not like me much, nor I him,' recollected Waugh. 'He beat me savagely throughout three years, sometimes twice a week, and although none of my elaborate schemes to kill him ever came to anything, I took my revenge in various subtle ways.'[8] His most subtle form of retribution was writing most of the *Rook*, a libellous and obscene parody of Downside's official magazine, the *Raven*. 'I could instantly recognise the pieces you wrote,' the headmaster told him. 'They were so much better written.'

During the school holidays, Waugh's relations with his father were rather distant. Auberon spent much of his time at Pixton. Evelyn spent much of his time in London, or abroad. When they were both at Piers Court, Evelyn ate most of his meals alone, in the library, appearing before his children for 'ten awe-inspiring minutes' (as he used to say) each day. Yet while Auberon was away at Downside he kept up a regular correspondence with his father, and one of his liveliest dispatches concerned a fire that swept through the school in November 1955. 'Please excuse the extreme squalor of this letter,' he begins. 'It is being written in prep and must somehow look like a history essay.' It was an adolescent foretaste of the fantastical diarist to come.

THE GREAT DOWNSIDE FIRE

The Great Fire was immense fun; the circular you got from the headmaster kept just within the bounds of Truth, although it does not give a glimmering of what actually happened. Beside the Gym, which, as it says, is completely destroyed, three dormitories (not two) are left without a stone upon a stone, and one is badly damaged. The Linen room, containing the whole school's sheets etc has been completely destroyed. One classroom has been pulled down because it was unsafe.

The school divided, more or less, into three distinct sections. Those who were confined to their dormitories, not being able to escape at an early stage, then those who gallantly tried to put the fire out, and then the reactionary group who tried to let it burn. More hoses were squirted at the boys than at the fire. The headmaster was equally delighted with both groups – he was torn between conflicting emotion at the thought of the insurance (a claim for £40,000), the love of a bonfire, and his duty to the insurers. The other monks did not attempt to conceal their delight. Father Hubert van Zeller danced in front of the fire singing the Te Deum rather off key. Another monk rushed into Father Wulstan Phillipson's room (some 30 yards from the fire) and started throwing the wireless out of the window, breaking pictures, jumping on gramophone records etc.

I managed to get out of the dormitory while a riot was taking place at the other end; down in the hall I joined a group of other boys who had escaped and were busy throwing their Corps uniforms into the blaze. I managed to grab a hose from a semi-stupefied fireman and was the first (of many) to squirt the headmaster. The flames were now raging some 30 feet above the top of the gym. Among the junior boys there was a general tendency to be heroic, but since there was no one to be rescued and they had no one to practise their Boy Scout training on, they had to content themselves with running everywhere very usefully, and running the gauntlet of our hoses, which knocked them down like ninepins.

I joined the headmaster who was standing with the Abbot instructing the firemen as to which parts of the building they should let burn, and which parts they could squirt so long as they stopped if the fire showed any signs of abating. At 3 a.m. the fire reached its climax. While it roared and hissed some fifty feet above the roof, while iron girders became white hot and crashed in twisted shapes on to the floor, while over 2000 gallons of water were being pumped every minute at enormous pressure from some forty hoses, while all this was happening, boys were still running up and down to the dormitory with tooth mugs full of water.

With that horrible bureaucratic outlook which always prevails in schools, work has been resumed as usual. Boys are sleeping on mattresses in the classrooms, Old House, even Old Chapel, but still things go on. Gym is being held out of doors. The whole of the prefabricated area of the school – about two acres, is now a pile of rubble with twisted bed frames here and there. The fire was definitely a good thing.

No news. All stories in the papers about forty boys being rescued by monks are quite untrue – they were made up by myself for the reporters' benefit. I was televised by the BBC and ITA hunting, distraught, for lost belongings. Actually we were looting the remains of the signals room. I found one charred toothbrush.

Looking back in later life, Waugh remained unsentimental about his time at boarding school. 'It would be absurd to pretend that all prefects at my school were hypocrites, sodomites or criminal psychopaths,' he wrote, 'but enough of them seemed to have tendencies in one or more of those directions to put me on my guard against anyone who retained the uniform and the mannerisms of a public-school prefect in later life.'[9] Unlike a lot of public-school boys, he never believed these privations benefited him in any way. Unlike his father or his grandfather, he never sent any of his children away to school. Reading this account of his schooldays, it's easy to see why.

A WET RAG TO A BULLY
(*Tatler, September 1980*)

'Sir, I wish to report someone to you for bullying.'
   'Who?' said the Master-on-Duty.
   'Pratt-Bingham.'

'Pratt-Bingham? But he's tiny. Who has he been bullying?'

'Me, sir.'

The Master-on-Duty gave me a level stare.

'He's half your size.'

This was unfortunately true, but he was disconcertingly free with his fists. I was taking a fine moral stand in reporting Pratt-Bingham and thus breaking the schoolboy code of *omerta*. It had been debated at great length and the whole of the Classical Sixth was on my side, or said it was. Nearly all the worst bullies at my prep school were rather small. They usually had double-barrel names, too, although sometimes they had foreign ones. But the Master-on-Duty's objection unnerved me.

'No he's not,' I said, 'and anyway he has been bullying other people, too.'

The entire Classical Sixth denied that Pratt-Bingham had been bullying it, or that it had seen him bullying anyone else, although the biggest boy of all said he might have been bullied a little bit, but not so much that he really noticed or minded.

'I think, Waugh, you had better sort out your own problems with Pratt-Bingham,' said the Master-on-Duty.

Accordingly, I became a member of the Pratt-Bingham gang and terrorised the rest. In due course I was promoted to be 'Biggy's' chief lieutenant, and was taken out to a cream tea by Brigadier Pratt-Bingham (or possibly he was a Wing Commander) and his tiny, mouse-like wife.

Violence lies about us in our infancy, but in my childhood it was always the violence of the gang or the mob which was to be feared. Individual threats of violence could generally be appeased or outmanoeuvred. Goodness knows what has happened to Pratt-Bingham now. Whatever people may say about it, the modern world is not designed for him, nor for any of the other gang leaders who terrorised my childhood. Perhaps the shades of the prison house have closed upon them all. More likely these Princes and Emperors of old occupy some humble position in middle management, manufacturing plastic tea-trays or travelling in cellophane. Their best times came first, unless there is to be a great Fascist Reorganisation, or World War, or

After-the-Bomb period when they will have another opportunity to deploy their particular talents.

Most of the violence, as I say, was gang violence, but all the worst and most terrifying forms of bullying were sanctioned by the whole society of schoolboys. Sligger Two regularly wet his bed and smelled like a badger. For that reason, it was most unpleasant to sit next to him, or even to be in the same classroom. On one occasion, Pratt-Bingham accused Sligger Two of pushing him in the queue for milk and buns during mid-morning break. Sligger Two denied this, but there was a general feeling that his proximity was quite offensive enough. Pratt-Bingham decided to put the matter to trial by combat. Within seconds, the whole school formed itself into a cheering ring. Nobody cheered Stinker Sligger. 'Bash him up, Pratt. Go on, slosh him one. Phew, what a pong. You could smell him in Moscow.'

Poor Sligger Two. He and Pratt-Bingham were dragged away to the Headmaster and made to shake hands before being beaten. They had to take their trousers down before being assaulted by a tattered carpet slipper called the Furry Object. Pratt-Bingham was the school hero for a week.

Others remembered appalling acts of cruelty inflicted by one boy on another, but all the greatest cruelties in my experience were inflicted by a mass of boys on one unfortunate individual who had aroused their disapproval. Gangs operated either openly, as a group of boys who strung themselves in a line across the corridor, hands in pockets and with a hideous scowl on their faces, refusing to make way for anyone else – or as secret societies. These usually had bloodcurdling initiation ceremonies and appalling penalties for anyone who broke the rules of the society, so that their effect was usually to terrorise their own members, rather than the world at large. The fact that boys voluntarily submitted to such tortures suggests an element of masochism in the public school make-up. Quite possibly former members of the Lotus Eaters, the Red Snake Gang and the Inner Circle are now to be found walking gingerly out of Soho of an afternoon, pinstripe trousers hiding the bright red weals on their bottoms.

But of all initiation ceremonies I ever attended at prep or public school, the worst was imposed by the school authorities. The practice has long since been discontinued, I hear, but in my day at Downside, recruits to one particular house had to appear before the whole House, including the Housemaster and Prefects, sing a song of his choice under the shower and then run a sort of gauntlet around the swimming bath while the older boys threw buckets of cold water over him. It may seem inconceivable that such institutionalised brutality could exist as recently as 1953, but in those days it was all thought good, clean fun. If, in the judgement of a number of boys, you had not sung adequately, you were made to swallow a mug of soapy water. Mysteriously, it was generally the prettier small boys who attracted this punishment. No doubt all that has changed now, too.

The essence of the gang, as opposed to the secret society, was that it generally consisted of a group of lesser mortals fawning on some lout. The lout himself seldom had any need to use his gigantic strength. A reputation for toughness and recklessness was all he needed to be treated as a God. The worst reputation to get was of someone who could be baited, and all the greatest cruelties were inflicted on these people – not by a handful of sadists, but by the whole society of their fellows. There were form-baits, house-baits and, on at least one occasion, a school-bait, when all 450 boys joined in tormenting an individual who had displeased them.

The unfailing victim of form-baits, in my day, was a boy called Goyle. He had a temper such as I have never come across before or since. To get him in a bait we would lock the door of the Classics Library where we did our prep and throw books at him from a safe distance, shouting 'Baity, baity', 'Goyle-bait' and other provocative remarks. Another way of baiting him was simply to remove his spectacles, but this was thought to lack subtlety as it involved physical contact. Goyle-baits were always conducted in a spirit of great good-humour, not to say glee, among everybody except the unfortunate victim. The art of a Goyle-bait was to let it peak about five minutes before the beginning of a class, when he would be screaming and throwing himself at his tormentors. Then the class would begin, with Goyle simmering quietly. In order to arouse him again one simply had to point a finger at him in such a way that the Master in charge of the form could see nothing. All he would know about it was when he heard a piercing scream and saw Goyle throwing books and bottles of ink at his tormentor . . .

Sometimes the bait could be conducted under the Master's nose, in the summer term when a wasp came into the classroom. Then work would stop while we pretended to deal with the wasp, which meant that we all threw our books at Goyle. I hope he has forgiven us now, but I rather fear he won't have. Perhaps, one day, I will find myself drowning and see the spectacled face of Goyle grinning at me over the side of a lifeboat . . .

House-baits were usually directed against a boy called Garlick who flew into a violent rage if ever it was suggested he was slightly duskier than anyone else. The whole House would beat time with text books on the table in the day-room, singing this unpleasant ditty to the tune of Jingle Bells:

> 'Nig-nig-nig, nig-nig-nig, nigger colony.
> Oh what hell it is to smell the nigger colony.'

Oh dear. The only occasion of school-baits came at the end of term, when departing school prefects had to make a valedictory speech to the whole school. An unpopular school prefect was given a very unpleasant time indeed . . .

But I never roasted a fag or inflicted any physical pain, honestly. That was all done by the school authorities, with beatings and punishment parades in the school gymnasium. It should never be said that these things did us no harm. I am convinced that we were all irreparably damaged, and that is why Britain is such a screwed up, hopeless country today. There may be less bullying in public schools now – the pupils all look incredibly wet and pious when I visit – but the grand old tradition has obviously been taken up in our new Comprehensive schools, where teachers join with working-class louts on wreaking vengeance against any pupil who is cleverer than the others, or talks with a middle-class accent. Never mind. Our time will come again.

Waugh's experiences left him with an enduring disdain for formal education. Yet there was one aspect of schooling about which he felt passionate, and that was the efforts of Labour politicians to do away with grammar schools, and replace them with comprehensives. 'Comprehensive schooling has removed any prospect the working-class child might ever have had of improving himself, escaping from the miserable proletarian rut which the "workers" create for themselves wherever they have the upper hand,'[10] he protested. 'Personal experience was enough to convince me that a stupid boy is held up by being put in a clever class every bit as much as a clever one is held up being put in a stupid class.'[11] Waugh's distaste for Labour's education policies never wavered. Years later he looked back on Shirley Williams's comprehensive strategy and saw its baleful results not just in the classroom, but throughout society at large.[12]

SHIRLEY WILLIAMS'S ACHIEVEMENT
(*Spectator*, 7 May 1983)

Many middle-aged men nowadays must dream of revenging themselves on the young. It is not just that the young are so ignorant and rude. Their worst crime is to be so conceited. For two decades it has been fashionable to talk about the generation gap as if it sprang from some failure on their part. Weighed down by bourgeois and materialistic considerations, if not by simple snobbery, the middle-aged were unable to make the great imaginative leap necessary to communicate with the young.

Young people were by definition idealistic, uninterested in materialistic things, untouched by colour or clan prejudice. Their attitude to sex was healthy and natural, uncoloured by hypocrisy or religious guilt. They were interested in employment which gave them an opportunity to help other people – the old, or kiddies, or deprived folk generally – but they were definitely not interested in joining the wage slave rat race, buying themselves a semi or equipping it with labour-saving devices. Wages were less important than fulfilment. If they drank at all, it was only in moderation. They preferred the subtler, more peaceful satisfaction of cannabis. Young people ruled the earth, and anybody over thirty must cringe before them.

As for the kids, they were if anything even better. They were never happier than when redecorating the home of some senior citizen, voluntarily, in their spare time. Of course they were too intelligent to be impressed by older people and, being naturally classless, they were sometimes slightly impatient of snobbery when they met it. But, by and large, kids were wonderful. Then Shirley Williams arrived on the scene – or, to be more exact, the first Harold Wilson government arrived, with a huge apparatus of educational theory which had largely been thought up by Anthony Crosland.[13] The primary purpose of state education was no longer to inculcate the rudiments of reading, writing and arithmetic in those whose natures made them unreceptive to anything more advanced. Still less was it to introduce a finer taste of the discipline necessary for any sort of social existence. The purpose of education was not even to prepare children for a classless society where nobody could look down their noses at anybody else – it was to create such a society. At whatever cost to the conventional values of education, the joys of engineering came first. Every valley must be exalted at whatever cost to the hills and mountains.

When Mrs Shirley Williams arrived at the Department of Education and Science it was already perfectly plain that the great Comprehensive experiment had been a disaster. Like socialism, it simply did not work. Huge schools, with little or no supervision of the teachers, let alone the pupils, were open invitations to truancy and violence. In the four years since the Labour government was defeated there has been plenty of time to take stock of the havoc which was wrought on an entire generation by this silly woman's opinions. For at least seven years I have been pointing out that a substantial proportion of young Britons – I would put it at about a third overall, perhaps a quarter in the south and a half in the north – are completely unemployable. They not only lack the discipline necessary to acquire the most rudimentary skills, they also lack the necessary will to please. They are a lost generation, without even the resources to amuse themselves.

Chapter Two
Arms and the Man

The whole purpose of a public school education is to teach
a chap to accept injustice like a man. It should leave no
mark on him beyond a certain resolve to get his own back
on the next generation.[1]

'You have a sense of humour and a good gift of self expression,' Evelyn told his wayward son. 'On the other hand you are
singularly imprudent and you have a defective sense of honour.
These bad qualities can lead to disaster.'[2] He might have been
talking about the *Private Eye* diarist to come. After this astute
and sombre warning, his eldest son finally buckled down. Despite
his schoolboy scams and his heroic disregard for discipline, in
1957 he won an exhibition in English to Christ Church College,
Oxford. However, this was the era of National Service, so he
decided to defer his place for two years, and do his stint in
uniform before he went up to university, rather than after he
came down. It was a fateful choice. National Service was abolished just a few years later, in 1960, so if he'd waited until after
he'd graduated, like a lot of his contemporaries, he might have
avoided it altogether, and his life might have taken an entirely
different turn.

Auberon had hoped to fail the medical – he had bad eyesight,
and had been a dedicated smoker since the age of twelve – but
to his regret he was passed fit and enlisted in his father's old
regiment, the Royal Horse Guards. His first stop was the Guards
Depot, Caterham, where he reported for basic training. It was

an experience that shaped him, though not quite in the way the army had intended.

Although there were officers at Caterham we hardly saw them. The place was run to all intents and purposes by NCOs and by a figure of authority which existed nowhere else in the British Army, so far as I know, called the Trained Soldier. Trained Soldiers were senior Guardsmen judged too stupid or too venal even for the single stripe of a lance corporal, but given enormous power, almost of life or death, over the recruits in their barrack rooms. It was an early and somewhat unfortunate taste of what is the reality of workers' power: brutal, sometimes sadistic, often vindictive but invariably – and most terrifyingly of all – bottomless in its stupidity.[3]

Much to his surprise, Waugh was commissioned as a second lieutenant, and flown out to Cyprus as part of the British effort to keep the peace between warring Greek and Turkish Cypriots. At first, he found it rather fun (certainly a lot better than Caterham), as he wrote in this chirpy letter to his father. Evelyn proudly told his friend Ann Fleming that 'Cornet Waugh is enjoying Cyprus top hole.'[4] His assessment was to prove somewhat premature.

Life is immensely exciting and unbelievably comfortable. Nearly every day we are out on some raid, roadblock, search or patrol. The only boring day was spent waiting outside a village in the sweltering heat for Dr Kuchuk, the Turkish leader, to arrive, which he never did. The troopers spent the time waving to motorbicyclists – we are meant to fraternise with these people – and seeing how many fell off in their anxiety to wave back.
Politics here are very involved and quite interesting. One always associated politics with Auberon's[5] boring, ineffectual discussions but here it is quite different. For instance a bomb in a petrol station will mean quite clearly that the

moderate Left nationalist faction is preparing to make an amnesty for a time with the ethnarchist Right wing extremists, whereas a bomb elsewhere will mean something quite different.

Waugh's National Service probably would have continued in this cheerful, inconsequential vein if his comrades had not taken about thirty Greek men in for questioning and dropped them off on the main road between Kyrenia and Nicosia, leaving them to find their own way home. Unfortunately, the British Army left these suspects outside a Turkish village called Guenyeli. The Turks assumed they were under attack, and hacked the poor men to bits. Nine were killed and many more were mutilated. After the army had cleared up the dismembered bodies ('one officer wandered around, rather green in the face, holding a head and asking if anyone had seen a body which might fit it'),[6] Waugh's troop was ordered to take up a position on the road, to keep the Greeks and Turks apart. It was an order that changed his life.

*

THE GHASTLY TRUTH
(*New Statesman*, 27 September 1974)

The date was 9 June 1958. I was a slim, suntanned eighteen-year-old national service officer in a famous cavalry regiment. The morning of 9 June 1958 found me posted on the Kyrenia–Nicosia road between a Greek village called Autokoi (or something like that) and a Turkish village called Guenyeli (or something like that) with three or four armoured cars, hoping to discourage the villagers from massacring each other, if I had read my map correctly and was in the right place.

I had noticed an impediment in the elevation of the Browning machine gun in the turret of my particular armoured car and, having nothing else to do, resolved to investigate it. Seizing hold of the end with quiet efficiency, I was wiggling it up and down when I noticed it had started firing. Six bullets later I was alarmed to observe that it was firing through my chest, and got out of the way pretty sharpish.

It may encourage those who have a fear of being shot to learn that it is almost completely painless, at any rate from close range with high velocity bullets. You feel a slight tapping and burning sensation and (if shot through the chest) a little winded, but practically no pain for about three-quarters of an hour after-wards when, with luck, someone will have arrived with morphine, if you are still alive. My first reaction to shooting myself in this way was not one of sorrow or despair so much as mild exhil-aration. I lay down behind the armoured car and explained what had happened in words of a few syllables, to incredulous murmurs of 'coo' and 'cor', while an enterprising corporal climbed into the turret and tried to stop the machine gun. That then is my memory of the incident, although there is no partic-ular reason to prefer it to others.[7] The incident deprived me of a lung, a spleen, several ribs and a finger but nothing else.

What sort of a man would Waugh have been if he hadn't given that machine gun a little jiggle? What would have become of him if he hadn't been shot to bits that day? Maybe this acci-dent was what made him a writer. The stuff he wrote before was fluent, but it had no real attitude. As his father wrote to him, in hospital, on his nineteenth birthday, 'to have looked into the throat of death at 19 is an experience not to be sneered at'. That near fatal mishap gave him a perspective, a point of view. 'For the first time I managed to watch Trooping the Colour without a lump in my throat,' he wrote in middle age. 'This may have been because I now have coloured television and was able to see the guardsmen's faces in all their brutal stupidity at close range – a sight I had forgotten since my days at the Guards Depot, Caterham, over twenty years ago.'[8]

Waugh spent nine months in hospital where he underwent twelve operations. Initially, he was not expected to survive. When he finally went up to Oxford in 1959, he was a war veteran on a disability pension, a man apart, and not only on account of his (self-inflicted) war wounds. During a six-week convalescence in Italy, he had written a novel, loosely based on his schooldays at Downside. Evelyn advised him to get it typed up and send it to his literary agent, A. D. Peters, but Auberon didn't feel so confident. Instead, he simply stuffed it away in the proverbial desk drawer. It was only another near fatal accident that prompted him to dig it out again.

At the end of his first term, en route to a student party, the car in which he was a passenger had a head-on collision with a lorry. He woke up in hospital two days later with a fractured skull. Fortunately he endured no lasting damage, but something upstairs had shifted. Returning to his parents' house for Christmas, he reread his literary debut, found it rather better than he'd recalled, and sent it to his father's publishers, Chapman & Hall. In the first week of the spring term, he received a telegram, accepting *The Foxglove Saga* 'with delight, horror and deepest admiration'.

For the rest of his time at Oxford, Waugh did virtually no work at all. The spring term was a boozy blur, and at Easter he failed his first-year exams. He did pass one paper (on a French book he hadn't read) but his main tests were in logic and economics, and he flunked them both. At the end of the summer term, he failed them again and that was that. He could have applied for re-admission, by resitting them a few months later, but he declined to do so. After less than a year, his student days were over.

Intriguingly, one of the few relics of Waugh's abortive spell at Oxford is an opera review from the university's student journal, *Isis*:[9]

To many it has been a source of regret that the English language does not lend itself to the expression of noble or dramatic sentiment in song, and a few have exerted themselves to remedy the gap by the translation of the Italian and German masters in English [wrote Waugh, in

May 1960]. But the truth remains that foreigners have a very imperfect sense of the ridiculous, and while Englishmen are very happy and often much moved to watch their performances so long as they do not understand a word of what is being said, as soon as it is translated, the poignancy seems to lose its sting.

Several factors contributed to Waugh's early exit from Oxford. Things might have turned out very differently if he'd read English (his original intention) or history (his father's choice). Yet in an impetuous moment he'd chosen to read PPE, mainly because it sounded grown-up and important, only to discover he had no real interest in philosophy or economics, and little understanding either (his economics tutor, Sir Roy Harrod, said he would never make an economist because he was reluctant to believe anything that he was told)[10]. He also fell in love, with a fellow first-year student, but lost her to another undergraduate, Grey Gowrie.[11] Waugh was still awkward with women, the legacy of a decade spent in single-sex boarding schools. With a novel due for publication in the autumn (and an advance of £150 to spend) the prospect of cramming for re-sits in a subject that bored him – merely to return to the scene of his romantic humiliation – held scant appeal. The experience left him with a dim view of universities, and students, as this piece clearly shows:

HATRED OF STUDENTS
(New Statesman, 11 July 1975)

Hatred of students stretches across the whole political spectrum in Britain, through every age group and social class, and I often wonder why no politician has thought of harnessing it to his own ends. No doubt blacks arouse stronger feelings in some parts of the country, but hatred of students is nearly universal. The traditional explanation for working-class hatred of students was that they outraged ordinary social values: they didn't work. But nor do many other people nowadays and work has lost much of its kudos. Next there was an element of implied superiority: man is born equal, but some of them pass their O levels and some of them don't. But money is the only accepted criterion here, and coalminers already earn more than many headmasters. Finally, of course, there was and remains the element of sexual jealousy which may always have existed between the generations but which is made particularly bitter nowadays by the apparently endless sexual opportunities available to young people, something *we* never knew. Oh dear, I feel a twinge of it even now as I write. And the truth is that many of these students are rather prettier than we are, an awkward fact from which we may need protecting.

So, in the popular mind, we have the stereotype Essex University or North London Polytechnic freak. He is hideous to behold; what little intellectual vitality he ever possessed has been destroyed by drugs, bombarded by mindless revolutionary jargon to inhibit any awareness of his own ignorance and social parasitism. Ingratitude, lust, idleness, hypocrisy and self-right-eousness are the main characteristics of this horrible cancer in our midst which we call higher education. But what can the honest politician do with all this popular resentment? To close down the North London Polytechnic and Essex University would be to kill the geese which lay the golden eggs. Besides, every time an outlet for public expenditure is closed we are all diminished, are we not?

The trouble is that fewer and fewer people nowadays are prepared even to pretend that they like working, or think it a useful thing to do. Why should we, after all? Hypocrisy may be the essential glue which binds all human society together, but other people seem only too anxious to assume responsibility for holding society together nowadays and it is really none of our business. On the other hand, as we watch these students sauntering down to collect social security in their tight jeans and nipple-flaunting shirts, we may start remembering the days gone by when people used to say they took a pride in their work, believing in a good day's work for a good day's wage, etc., etc., etc. When our hypocrisy is finally exhausted, only the labour camps will remain.

'There are only two possible careers for a man who has been sent down from Oxford,' Evelyn Waugh told his son. 'You must become either a schoolmaster or a spy.' Strictly speaking, he hadn't been sent down, only rusticated, but he took his father's advice. He applied unsuccessfully for MI6 and successfully for a teaching post in a prep school. Yet when he joined the headmaster at the top table in the school dining room, the memories of his own schooldays came flooding back, and he fled for ever. Instead, he got a job as a picture researcher at *Queen* magazine, edited by Quentin Crewe.

In his first week at *Queen*, Waugh's novel was published to rave reviews. 'I don't want constructive criticism,' he told a friend, who offered him some helpful tips. 'I want praise.'[12] The papers obliged. 'Most enjoyable,' wrote the *Observer*. 'A remarkable performance,' concurred the *Listener*. The book was also lauded by several of his father's literary friends. 'Deserves to sell in thousands,' declared John Betjeman.[13] 'Superb,' agreed Graham Greene. Malcolm Muggeridge[14] called it brilliant, but not everyone was so impressed. An especially withering review appeared in the *Sunday Express*. 'One of the most heartless, disagreeable books I have ever read,' it said. 'Contempt reeks from every page.' The reviewer was Quentin Crewe, Waugh's new editor at *Queen*.

Like quite a lot of hatchet jobs, Crewe's review was so scathing that it actually served as an advertisement (who could resist a book of which it was said, 'No sadistic, perverted, vulgar trick is missed'?) but this was clearly not Crewe's intention. 'Auberon Waugh is no ordinary author,' wrote Waugh's new boss. 'Because he is the son of his father, the literary establishment has gone to work. Only a son of the literary establishment would have got this book published with so much publicity.' Crewe had a point. Chapman & Hall was very much the family firm (Evelyn was on the board; his father, Arthur, had been a director) and the publicity for *The Foxglove Saga* was extensive. No wonder Evelyn had advised his son (advice that Auberon disregarded) to send his novel to a range of publishers, under a *nom de plume*.

Crewe was quite right that Waugh's connections opened lots of doors, but they would soon have slammed shut again if *The Foxglove Saga* hadn't been any good. Maybe Greene and Betjeman should have known better – their eulogies look rather extravagant in retrospect – but there was no denying *The Foxglove Saga* was an extremely accomplished debut. It was also highly original. Set in a Catholic boarding school, an army barracks and a hospital (no prizes for guessing where Waugh got his inspiration), it was a world away from the kitchen-sink novels that were all the rage in 1960.

THE FOXGLOVE SAGA
(Chapman & Hall, 1960)

Throughout morning church Stoat wondered whether he had made a fool of himself the night before. So great was his preoccupation that he lost eight cigarettes running to O'Connor who knelt beside him and who owned the poker dice which helped to while away the long hours of worship. Eventually one of the dice rolled away and bounced irretrievably down the aisle. There seemed nothing to do but pray, and as he lifted his little black heart and mind in the direction he had been taught he prayed that he might be nicer. It was his only prayer, and it had never yet been answered. He was sharp enough to see how mean, how intolerant, how incredibly nasty he was, but somehow lacked the technical ability to do anything about it. The only thoughts that ever came into his mind were uncharitable, spiteful ones, often quite shrewd in their way, but he knew that they only showed one side of the picture.

Waugh's first novel was an inverted cautionary tale, a dire warning that good deeds rarely go unpunished. It was also an oblique autobiography. At first glance, the book seems gratu-itously cruel, a callous celebration of misfortune and injustice. Its superficial heroes, Julia Foxglove and her angelic son Martin, both come to a bad end. Its apparent villain, Kenneth Stoat, ends up as a monk. Yet a closer reading reveals a complex Christian morality. The Foxgloves are smug and pious, obliv-ious to their own failings. Stoat is a repentant sinner, mindful of his many faults. As he winds his way from trespass to redemp-tion, it's not too hard to picture him as Waugh, wrestling with his conscience, battling to suppress an urge to be bad.

Stoat began to realise that he had gone too far. It had happened several times in his career before, when, without warning, his entire world had seemed to collapse about his ears, leaving him just a shade more lonely and spiteful, and not a jot wiser than before. When his first Nanny, called Freda, to whom he was passionately attached, had suddenly been teased too much about her boyfriends, and had turned and thrashed him savagely, and given her notice the same evening; when his spaniel puppy, Rollo, had been pushed once too often into the goldfish pond, and had caught a cold and died, and his father had sworn that he would never have another dog; when, at his first prep school, a game of Cops and Robbers had got out of hand, and a boy had nearly lost a finger, and Stoat had been asked to leave.

Chapter Three
Vive La France

Wherever one looks in England one sees wetness and stupidity, whether in the defeatism of the middle class, the brutal opportunism of the unions or the recklessness of the politicians. The French may work harder than we do, which is morally reprehensible, but they also spend their money more intelligently and plainly get more enjoyment from it.[1]

Despite Quentin Crewe's hatchet job (or perhaps even, in part, because of it) *The Foxglove Saga* sold 14,000 hardback copies. Waugh sold the US rights to Simon & Schuster for $2000 and the serialisation rights to the *Daily Express* for £1500 (ten times his original advance). He rented a smart flat in Piccadilly and got a job on 'Peterborough', the diary column of the *Daily Telegraph*. For a short while he was quite a wealthy bachelor, but that all changed in 1961 when he married Teresa Onslow, daughter of the Earl of Onslow. They were both just twenty-one. 'Although extremely young I do not think that celibate existence has many more surprises, lessons or pleasures for me,' he wrote, in a letter to his father. 'I am extremely lucky to have such a charming and lovely girl fond of me, and feel confident it would not happen again.' Happily, Waugh's high opinion of his young wife never wavered. 'When we married, being drawn by face, limbs, laugh, a sympathetic manner and a shared sense of humour,' he recalled thirty years later, 'I had no conception of the strong and virtuous character which would emerge over the years, keeping me within nearly acceptable range of the straight and narrow path.'²

It was Teresa who dragged Waugh away from the *Daily Telegraph* diary, where he reckoned he could quite easily have remained, writing forgettable paragraphs about octogenarian generals for the rest of his working life. As he reflected in middle age, thinking what course his career could have taken, 'A life of placid London existence on a shoestring, with weekends in the houses of people much richer than ourselves, was not for her.'³ And so in 1963, after two utterly uneventful years on 'Peterborough', Waugh and his wife decamped to a modern bungalow on the edge of an obscure village called Labécède-Lauragais, in the Languedoc, in southern France.

Waugh planned to write his second novel in pastoral solitude, while Teresa reared their first child, Sophia, who'd been born the year before. It was a world away from the quaint idyll of cosy books like *A Year in Provence*. As Waugh soon discovered, the nearest town, Castelnaudary, is a byword for the back of beyond in metropolitan France, and Castelnaudary was a teeming metropolis compared to Labécède-Lauragais. Virtually none of the houses in this village had running water. The Waughs' (shared) water supply came from a spring in a nearby field. 'It is hard to imagine now how backward the French countryside was in 1963,' wrote Waugh. 'There was nothing very picturesque about the life of these peasant farmers, and no philosophical conclusions to be drawn about the superiority of simple country ways. The only lesson was that such a life was extremely uncom-fortable.'⁴

Yet this discomfort proved seductive. The Waughs returned to London after six months, but Auberon formed a lifelong attachment to France in general, and Labécède-Lauragais in particular, and he spent virtually every subsequent summer there. He wrote about it often, calling it an alternative panorama of life, 'a soap opera which is still running and will continue to run long after I am dead'.⁵ France became his yardstick, against which he measured the UK, and though he regarded the French as equally ridiculous, he generally found them more sympathetic.

As he said, 'It seems to be self-evident that France is a happier, pleasanter, richer country than our own.'[6]

*

WE DRINK FROM MUSTARD POTS WHILE THE ENEMY CREEPS CLOSER
(*Evening Standard*, 8 June 1974)

La Pesegado, Montmaur, Aude

Britain's Great Debate on the Common Market was followed here with quiet incomprehension. While the fields groan and clink with money around us, nobody can imagine a single reason for wishing to remain outside. At any rate the Great Debate was conducted in Aude with rather more vigour and wit than it was conducted at Westminster, to judge from newspaper reports. Installed at last in the semi-collapsed barn two miles from anywhere which passes for a farmhouse, we have begun to discover some opposition to our brave venture of beating the politicians and joining the Common Market at the receiving end as French farmers.

The main opposition comes from a colony of French spiders. Some are only the size of kittens, others grow to frolic around like spaniel puppies. If one turns one's back on them for half an hour one feels they will come bounding out as large and as frisky as Shetland ponies. So long as they are smaller than me and I have a stick while they have not I think I can hold out against them, but my children are demented by cowardice. It is lucky in many ways that Britain no longer has an Empire to keep in order, as I do not feel that the younger generation would be up to it.

Instead, they spend most of the day in the scorching heat out of doors, hunting for snails. Soon, we will have to make the decision whether to eat them or not. My wife, who will be expected to cook them, feels we may be in danger of taking the Common Market challenge too seriously. Treatment involves starving them for twenty-four hours, parboiling them, removing them from their shells and cutting away the big intestine, putting them back in their shells and baking them in garlic butter. Incidentally, English snails are just as good. The last time we tried it, eight years ago while I was writing a book in the neighbourhood, they escaped and crawled all over my manuscript. The children, of course, become very indignant at any suggestion that we should eat snails, regarding them as pets. The scandal is that even in France you can't eat spiders.

If the charming and beautiful Southerners we have landed among are kinder and more hospitable than their northern neighbours, they are certainly no less complicated. You hear no false heroics about the Resistance down here for the good reason that there was no resistance, although all the village war memorials of 1939–45 carry longer lists of the dead for the last years of the war than for the first years, before the surrender. These are the Frenchmen who were killed in Russia and the Ukraine, fighting with the Germans against the Red Army. They were volunteers in the cruellest and bitterest campaign of modern history. Goodness knows why they volunteered.

There is no suggestion that they were coerced, but few could have been highly educated or highly political. Perhaps if they had been better educated they would have known about Napoleon's retreat from Moscow and stayed at home; but there is no reason to be sure of this as French education, though tough, is highly selective where French history is concerned. In any case, whatever decided these sons of the soil that Stalin was marginally worse than Hitler, whatever drove them to fight it out in the freezing cold of Stalingrad, it certainly wasn't cowardice.

My own family is engaged in a campaign of similar bitterness and intensity at the moment. Although we brought most of the furniture and utensils from Wiltshire, we stupidly forgot to bring any glasses. The Bank of England explains very clearly that although Mr Barber[7] allows you to buy food with your travel allowance (thank you very much, Sir) you are not allowed to buy furniture or household utensils. Glasses are household utensils. For these, you must spend investment dollars, bought at a premium of 25 per cent. But you are allowed to buy food! How wonderful to be an Englishman and enjoy these heady freedoms.

There is a firm of mustard manufacturers in France whose mustard is rather nasty, but who have had the clever idea of putting it into pots which when washed out become drinking glasses. The glass we are engaged on now has a tasteful picture of Babar, King of the Elephants, and Queen Celeste. The next one promises a representation of Snow White, with at least three of her seven dwarfs. By the time we have finished seven pots of this really most unpleasant mustard, we will have a glass each, not allowing for breakages. Quite apart from a fixed determination not to give Mr Barber a penny more of our hard-earned money than we need, we find our supply of investment dollars dwindling. But one begins to understand how these Frenchmen from the Lauragais must have felt, fighting another country's war and starving to death in twenty feet of snow, 4000 miles from home.

Of course, this is not an entirely accurate picture of life at La Pesegado. The heat is so intense that it makes you gasp whenever you set foot outside, and food is dangerously abundant. The name of La Pesegado is patois for a place where mud is weighed. Apparently the inhabitants of my farm spent all their time in this diverting and harmless occupation, before the French Revolution came, destroying all idea of harmony, social order and traditional values. Nowadays, there is not even any mud around, so one could not weigh it even if one had the time, inclination and necessary machinery.

The ancient patois of the Languedoc survives among the older peasants. This means that they can communicate only with each other, since no Frenchman understands them, and they understand no French. It solves the generation gap in the most marvellous way, and to everybody's complete satisfaction. The few old timers who are sufficiently evolved to have learned a little French seldom have anything very interesting to say, in my experience, and no doubt my conversation bores them as much as theirs bores me. With monoglot patois speakers, we merely exchange smiles of exaggerated delight, before going our separate ways, fortified by a general feeling of benevolence. What a good idea it would be if British teachers, instead of filling their pupils' heads with a lot of boring, outdated rubbish about contraception, abortion, and how to masturbate, could teach each generation an entirely different language. Only those who wish to promote strife for their own sinister purposes can seriously pretend that there is anything to be gained at this stage of our nation's history by the generations talking to each other.

ME AND MY MOBYLETTE
(*New Statesman*, 5 September 1975)

Not far from where I live in southern France there runs a small canal called La Rigole. It is a tributary of the great Canal du Midi linking the Atlantic with the Mediterranean, and its pine-fringed towpaths make an ideal place to ride on a Mobylette or French autocycle when one has nothing better to do. Phuttering along it last week I noticed for the first time a public notice on its banks:

INTERDICTION FORMELLE
DE JETER DANS LA RIGOLE ET SUR SES
DÉPENDANCES DES ANIMAUX MORTS
(volailles comprises) ET DES ORDURES –
Décret du 6–2–32 ART.59

It had never occurred to me before that it might be fun to throw dead animals into the water but this notice, advertising a formal interdiction, could only be interpreted as an open invitation to join in what was presumably a traditional French sport. It was beyond reasonable hope that I would find a dead chicken or duck – obviously the greatest pleasure of all – but I remembered seeing a dead hedgehog on the road some miles back. Unfortunately, it proved inseparable from the tarmac of which it had already begun to form a part, and it was while I was trying to run over a huge green lizard, the size of a small crocodile, that I fell off my Mobylette and suffered the sort of injuries which would cause any self-respecting British worker to draw sick benefit for a year, if not for the rest of his life.

Nursing my pain, I fell into a sombre mood. It seemed rather irresponsible of those departmental Fathers of the Aude, one February day in 1932, to issue a decree which can still cause grievous injury to visitors more than forty-three years later. Almost certainly the men responsible are now dead, tastefully entombed in great marble sarcophagi all over the Languedoc countryside. Possibly they felt they had done a good day's work when they returned to their wives and families in the evening of 6 February 1932. After all, they had passed a decree, and few people can expect to do that every day.

My point is not that it is a particularly savage or oppressive decree. No doubt there was a good reason why dead cows or chickens should not be put there at that time, although it may seem odd that people had nothing better to do with them than send them floating down the canal like dead Hindus on the Ganges. My argument is simply that there are too many laws in existence. If that piece of business was concluded on 6 February 1932, think how many decrees and articles must have been published since then. Then think how much worse the situation is in Britain. Every other country has had natural breaks in its accumulation of laws: revolutions, new Constitutions, periods of occupation by a foreign power. In Britain, practically no law has ever been repealed except to be replaced by something even more complicated and oppressive over a period of 700 years, and all that time new interdictions have been accumulating.

There may be greater pleasures in life than phuttering around on a Mobylette after a heavy lunch in the heat of the afternoon – perhaps a night of passion with Brigitte Bardot would be one – but I have yet to discover any. Moreover it is one of the few

pleasures that have never, at any stage, been condemned by the
Church – the only other one I can think of is sniffing tangerine
skins. The Mobylette makes very little noise, burns amazingly
little petrol and constitutes no serious danger to one's fellow
citizens. I usually wear a straw hat for these outings which serves
to protect my head from the sun and also as a useful device in
the absence of a speedometer to warn me when I am driving
too fast. As I say, it is the nearest to a glimpse of heaven that
has yet been granted me.

Now let us compare the regulations governing this activity
in England and France. In France, I must have third-party insurance (which costs ninety francs) and I am not allowed to carry
any passengers over the age of fourteen. This is the only formal
interdiction. In England I must also have a driving licence, pay
road tax and have my machine registered with the county council.
In addition, there is a mass of legislation concerning things like
reflectors, brakes and depth of tyre tread which no citizen can
possibly be expected to have read. Its effect is that any policeman
who does not like the look of my face can land me with a
summons, a fine and a licence endorsement whenever he
chooses.

Worse than any of this, I would be required to wear on my
head an absurd metal object against the risk of my falling off
the machine – which, admittedly, I do quite often – and falling
on my head, which I have so far managed to avoid. No doubt
when I say that this law is an odious infringement of human
liberty and freedom of choice, some official from the Royal
Society for the Prevention of Accidents will write in and accuse
me of callous indifference to the suffering and death which
would result from another policy. He is wrong. I quite see that
it would be unpleasant to break my head open, and I sincerely
hope it doesn't happen to me, but it is a risk I prefer to take
rather than wear a metal egg on my head every time I go into
the countryside. And since my straw hat endangers no one else,
it is surely a risk I am entitled to take.

But not in England. As I drive my little Peugeot Mobylette
through the fields of sunflower and vine, the thought that any

government could impose such ridiculous and undignified head-gear on the grizzled peasants, nuns and old women who are my companions on the road is repugnant to every decent feeling. In England, people have accepted it without a whisper of complaint, and the only sign that anyone has resented it must reside in some marginal increase in the hatred for politicians.

Now that Parliament is at last in recess, we should surely ask ourselves if it would not be a good idea for it to stay adjourned. When Simon de Montfort (a man much hated in this part of France for his cruel prosecution of the religious wars) made the great mistake of founding the House of Commons during the ghastly reign of Henry III, even that notorious French bully boy can scarcely have expected the same body to sit adding to its own laws 700 years later. Now it has had 700 years to pass all the laws it can think of, it is surely beyond reason to suppose that many more are needed. It is not just that we have become over-nannied and over-governed but nearly all our recent problems are plainly the result of being exceptionally badly governed in relation to other countries. We all know how pitifully over-worked these MPs are, and I should have thought two weeks a year was quite enough to keep existing laws up to date. At other times they might learn to cultivate wider interest and tastes than this single, unhealthy passion for creating new punishable offences.

THOUGHTS ON THE WEATHER
(*New Statesman*, 29 August 1975)

The Feast of the Assumption was marked in my corner of the Languedoc by terrible storms. As I sat deafened and blinded in the open barn where I work, trying to compose a little sermon for the *New Statesman*, it seemed inconceivable that the end of the world was not at hand. Superstitiously, I began to worry whether it might be anything to do with what I was writing. I had proposed, on the day that many of us celebrate the

Assumption of Our Lady into Heaven, to write a little treatise exposing some errors in the current campaign for the ordination of women in the Church of England. It seemed topical, and I know from my postbag that *New Statesman* readers take a particular delight in topics of this sort.

In the face of this tumult of the elements, I eventually decided it might not be prudent to write on the vexed question of the ordination of women. Perhaps I have saved the world. Certainly, my prudence seems to have been repaid so far as the weather is concerned. As I write now, little green lizards are playing about my feet in the scorching sunshine, glow worms are re-charging their batteries and crickets are limbering up for their evening chorus. Within minutes of my deciding to leave the Virgin Mary out of it the weather cleared and the huddled figures of neighbouring farmers' wives appeared to scour the hedges and ditches for snails. After rain these snails always emerge in their thousands, although only the fat brown ones are thought worth eating. In England, of course, nobody bothers to collect them; just as most butchers throw away their pigs' trotters and marrow bones, fishermen throw spider crabs back into the sea. When harder times come we may have to change some of these luxurious habits, and I look forward to the day when I see snailing parties in the lanes of Somerset.

FOOD FOR THOUGHT
(*Spectator*, 23 August 1980)

Montmaur, Aude
The martyrdom of St Lawrence is celebrated every year in the nearby village of Puginier, of whose parish church he is the patron saint, by dancing in the village square which lasts two days and two nights. On the first evening, a *grillade* is set up selling pieces of Toulouse sausage and other delicacies – possibly because the French seem to need an enormous amount

of food to keep them in high spirits, possibly as a reminder of their patron saint, whose story is told them every year by the *curé* at the sung Mass which opens proceedings on the Sunday morning.

St Lawrence, or Lawrence as he then was, was sent to negotiate with some barbarians besieging Rome, as barbarians tended to do in the fourth century. They told him that if he would deliver all the treasures of the Church, they would go away. Lawrence went back and collected all the blind, the maimed, the simple and the sick. He brought this collection of unfortunates – who were not, I suppose, fit for military service in any case – and delivered them to the barbarians, saying: 'Here are the chief treasures of my church.'

The barbarians were not at all taken with this little joke and proceeded to roast him on a gridiron. When he was half done, he suggested that he should be turned and roasted on the other side. History does not relate what happened to the sickies, blindies and dafties. One rather dreads to think. But the Church took a favourable view of his initiative and canonised him in due course.

With their patron saint's little jokes in mind, said the *curé*, he wished to preach a eulogy on the Folly of God. There were those who described these village fêtes as foolish affairs, when normal standards of behaviour were allowed to slip. They were certainly somewhat gratuitous, he said. But was not the most gratuitous act of all time God's creation of the world? God had created the world purely to amuse Himself. We were all part of a gigantic *divertissement* or entertainment. At other times and in other places, he said, it was normal to hold a *fête des fous* where simpletons were called in to act out, for a time, the roles of bishop, squire and policeman. But was this not, in a sense, the paradigm of all human society? God, in His wisdom, had even given us a contradictory set of rules by which to live, at one moment telling us that anyone who looks with lust on another woman is damned, at the next that he will almost certainly be forgiven for this understandable lapse. Should not the birth, life and death of Christ also be seen as gratuitous?

he asked – sailing rather close to the wind, I thought, on this occasion.

But it did not trouble his congregation. The *curé* of Puginier is famous for miles around for the originality of his sermons and their high intellectual content, no less than for his personal sanctity. There must be worse ways to spend one's life than to amaze the gazing rustics ranged around.

On the second night of the *fête* they cooked an enormous *cassoulet*, prompting further gloomy thoughts about the likely fate of St Lawrence's sickies, blindies and dafties. Long after midnight, a peasant youth whom I know slightly – the nephew of a lady who stuffs geese and ducks for me – tapped my stomach and asked cheekily if I had eaten more than my share of the *cassoulet,* but that was the only social outrage of the evening. I do not think that the Lord of Disorder can have supposed it was a festival held in his honour.

CARE IN THE COMMUNITY
(*Oldie*, August 1995)

Thirty-two years ago, when the Waugh family started taking its summer holidays in the part of agricultural southern France they call the Pays d'Oc, every village in the neighbourhood had its village idiot. In those days, French villages were quite backwards by English standards, and all the village washing was done by hand in a communal cold water tub, fed from a spring. It never occurred to anyone to lock the village idiot away in a special home for the educationally challenged, with idealistic, specially trained young women to talk to them slowly in patronising welfare accents. They just loped around the village, sometimes making a nuisance of themselves and breaking things, sometimes engaging people in conversation of a sort, but always accepted as what is nowadays called part of the community.

A similar fate awaited those who lived too long and became

senile. On sunny days they were pushed out of doors, and anybody who was passing would greet them, receiving a grunt back, or the rolling of an eye, or more probably no acknowledgement at all. In the winter they were kept indoors in the kitchen, wrapped in filthy sacking, and left to dribble quietly in a corner until someone – the daughter-in-law, more often than not — went to spoon in some soup.

It was not tremendously dignified, perhaps, by our modern ideas, but it was a great deal less gloomy than the rows of recumbent forms on drips, lying in a coma, recognising no one, turned once in the morning and once in the evening like newly cut hay. These forms represent our furthest advance in the science of caring for the aged. The point about senility is that it is only distressing if people are prepared to be distressed by it. In the small villages of the Aude, in southern France, they simply weren't prepared to treat it as anything except a fact of life, to be regretted, sworn at or joked about as the spirit moved them. In England, it seems to me that we treat senility as something between a disgrace and an infectious disease, possibly brought on by masturbation in youth. Not only are oldies who begin to show the symptoms whisked away into a home, even if it means ruining the family in the process; once they are in a home, they become a non-person, visited grudgingly and with increasing embarrassment on both sides.

This is not just a reflection on our peculiar family relationships. It is institutionalised in the fabric of the nation. When distinguished oldies become senile, they are immediately withdrawn from view, not left babbling in the sun. Harold Wilson was scarcely seen in his last five years, while he was suffering from Alzheimer's. It seems especially craven to lock a former prime minister away in this fashion when we have a national institution called the House of Lords, specially designed for them to exhibit themselves. This is one of the most humane political initiatives in the world. When I visited the Upper House on business two weeks ago, I was surprised to see a very elderly peer pushed past me in an invalid chair with his jaw tied shut by a bandage over his head. I could not make out whether it had been put there because he had died, or in order to gag him. In either even, it was much more human to wheel him around than to shut him away in a funny farm or a mortuary.

Chapter Four

In My View

The Pope's tirade against sexual laxity among the clergy undoubtedly struck a deep chord among my colleagues in the tabloid press. There is a feeling that however tolerant, or even broad-minded, we might be among ourselves, we do not want the clergy joining in. The great question remains: what is to be done? I wonder if the Pope has studied the habits of the emu. This delicate bird, whose females emit a loud booming sound, is both monogamous and chaste in its habits – to such an extent that, in Western Australia, where it is farmed for meat, all efforts at scientific breeding have failed. The pairs stick together through thick and thin, just as good Christians are expected to. Somewhere, the rot has to be stopped. Pope John Paul decided to attack the clergy, threatening them all with hell. I am not sure enough of them believe in it to make this a useful threat. Instead, he might adopt the emu as the ibis was adopted in ancient Egypt, as a sacred bird and best example to the human family. Every priest should be required to eat an emu's egg every day. It might not work but it is certainly worth a try.[1]

Apart from his army pension, of £7 a week, Waugh's only income while he was in France came from the *Catholic Herald*. His brief was to write once a week, on the leader page, about current affairs. This prestigious appointment was fortuitous, to say the least. As Waugh readily admitted (though, sensibly, not to his new employers) he had few informed opinions about current affairs, and no particular knowledge. Still, with a wife and newborn baby to support, it was a precious lifeline. His salary was eight guineas a week.

'In My View' was Waugh's first weekly column and, like a lot of its successors, it caused no end of fuss. Rereading these pieces today, it's hard to see what people got so worked up about. Despite his lack of prior knowledge (or maybe because of it), his articles were carefully argued, written in the authoritative, judicious tone that journalists adopt when they're not quite sure what they're on about. Compared to his later columns they were models of diplomacy, but what seems mild today was evidently heady stuff back then. Virtually every piece he wrote provoked a flurry of correspondence, as readers wrote in to praise him or to demand that he be fired. 'Any paper that can afford to be made a fool of by Auberon Waugh can do without my subscription,' wrote one indignant reader. 'The whole concept of employing this person is irresponsible and above all deeply stupid.' But he had plenty of supporters too. 'You hired young Waugh in the nick of time,' wrote another. 'I was about to give up the wishy-washy *Catholic Herald*.'

Most modern editors dream of provoking such a heated reaction from their readers, but this was a more deferential age and religious papers have never shared Fleet Street's enthusiasm for poking hornets' nests. Eventually the *Herald* threw the matter open to the readership, asking them to write in and say whether the paper should retain his services. 'Columnists are usually allowed freedom of expression,' wrote the editor, rather limply, 'but not if their policies are consistently at variance with that of the paper.' The readers rose to the bait, filling several pages with spirited letters, both for and against.

'I have admired your paper for many years and am dismayed at your taking on Waugh as a columnist,' wrote one reader. 'He does you no credit.'

'I cast my vote pro-Waugh,' retorted another. 'Please keep him.' There were about as many pros as antis. The *Herald* kept him – for a while.

In the end, Waugh lasted eighteen months – a reasonable innings for a columnist. He continued to write the column for about a year after his return to England, though the political pieces he wrote back in London weren't noticeably better written (or better informed) than those pieces he'd written in splendid isolation in the depths of the French countryside. Waugh's journalism didn't depend on access. It was more a feat of imagination.

Waugh was ploughing his own furrow, indifferent to received opinion, and the reaction of his Catholic readers gave him a useful insight into the minds of his audience. 'The letters which poured in brought my first awareness of an altogether larger circle of hostility outside the circle of those who disliked me because they knew me,' he wrote, in his autobiography. 'To the hatred of progressive Christians for conservatives, I had to add the hatred of large numbers of people for Evelyn Waugh, the hatred of older people for the young, the hatred of the under-privileged for the privileged and the hatred of humourless people for anyone who tries, however unsuccessfully, to make jokes.'[2] It was a valuable lesson, and a taste of things to come.

*

KEEP BRITAIN BLACK
(*Catholic Herald*, 1 March 1963)

A Lincolnshire priest has suggested in his parish magazine that black clothes should be banned at funerals and everywhere else. The normal arguments given to support this rest on two premises, that black clothes are drab and that funerals should be joyful things, celebrating a departure from this vale of tears into the happy abode beyond.

The only reason that black is thought drab is because it is associated with death and the clergy. But if kept clean, which the clergy often can't manage, it can be devilishly attractive. I can also think of several of my acquaintances whose death will leave me with no such happy certainty as to their future abode. One could always modify one's dress at funerals according to one's estimate of the dead man's chances.

The real reason, I am afraid, for many people's objections to black is because they do not like to be reminded that with all the twentieth century's advances in the fields of teenage thought and cosy living, our scientists have not yet abolished the ancient and time-honoured institution of death. For myself, if anyone attending my funeral is not dressed in black, I shall haunt him through all his waking nights, dressed in South Sea Island shirt and Bermuda shorts and howling like a banshee.

CRITICS ON THE MAT
(*Catholic Herald*, 2 August 1963)

'We may not be living in a great age of literature, but it is sometimes said to be a great age of literary criticism,' says an advertisement for *The Times Literary Supplement* currently appearing in intellectual monthlies. Certainly, as the advertisement points out, the names of leading critics on both sides of the Atlantic are as famous as the authors they criticise. I look forward to the time when literary criticism is finally recognised for what it is, the supreme pinnacle of letters, to which creative writing is no more than a humble support.

Such creative writers as remain, weary of being shown to the back door of the critic's opulent residence, are rapidly taking to criticism. Soon we may be left with a new art form, literary criticism *in vacuo*. Just as other artists in their gropings towards a more profound abstraction, whereby pictures represent nothing, sculpture confirms to no known shape, music is tuneless and hideous to hear, writers are always confounded by the fact that whatever degree of meaninglessness they achieve by the juxtaposition of unconnected words and phrases, there is always a critic who will claim to understand and distil its meaning. Plainly, the next step, when critics have exhausted their comparisons between Chaucer and Jane Austen, Trollope and James Joyce, their treatises on modern trends in literature and literary criticisms, their treatises on trends in criticism of trends in criticism, is that they must be left with the abstract form itself.

NO POETS
(*Catholic Herald*, 31 January 1964)

The news that there is to be no Poets' Conference at this year's Edinburgh Festival will be welcomed by anyone who has a regard for poetry, but deplored, of course, by those who believe in conferences as an alternative art form. I have never been able to understand why poets should need to confer. Of all methods of expression, poetry is the most personal. If a poet finds himself stuck for something to rhyme with 'disarmament' or 'apartheid', there are excellent rhyming dictionaries available. No worthwhile movement in art has ever resulted from a conference. So long as artists are encouraged to assemble and posture before the public, deriving a spurious sense of their own importance from activities quite unrelated to their calling, we can be sure the arts will be neglected.

One solution might be to recognise the Conference as an art form in its own right. It would be heavily subsidised by the state, and all those people whom we now uncharitably think of as charlatans because they are forced to claim some implausible connection with the other arts could come out in their true colours as Conference Artists. Then we could have Conferrers' Conferences to discuss latest trends in this medium, historical precedents – Athens, Trent, Potsdam – and any other business. Only then could our misunderstood poets retire to their cottages and try writing some poetry.

Chapter Five
The ABC of Beauty

The material advantages of a very good education over a reasonably good one are easy to exaggerate. A few years ago I was trying to write captions for a pin-up series in the *Sunday Mirror* called 'The ABC of Beauty' when my editor, Hugh Cudlipp, sauntered past my desk smoking a large cigar. 'Wonderful thing it must be to have a good education, Auberon,' he remarked sententiously. I might have translated my perky, gloating captions into Homeric Greek, but I would never earn a tenth of his salary, and he knew it very well.[1]

Waugh returned to London in the autumn of 1963 for the publication of his second novel, *Path of Dalliance*, which he'd written that summer in France. He'd already plundered his schooldays for his first novel. This one drew on his abortive year at Oxford, inviting inevitable (and invidious) comparisons with his father's masterpiece, *Brideshead Revisited*. John Betjeman likened Auberon's new novel to Dickens, but most of the reviews were more modest. So were the sales. Auberon's uncle Alec – a fellow writer, whose early career had eclipsed his brother's – was full of praise, but Evelyn was more cautious. He'd been enthusiastic about *The Foxglove Saga* ('original, lively and well written,' he'd noted, in a letter to Auberon, 'far better than I or your uncle Alec wrote at that stage') but he'd always doubted whether his son would be able to make a living out of fiction. *Path of Dalliance* confirmed his fears. He found some parts of the book very funny, but he thought other bits were boring. Auberon's attitude to the book suggests he felt similarly uneasy. He refused to show it to his father before publication. In his autobiography he dismissed it as 'a novel of Oxford life which I have not read for twenty-five years and do not propose to re-read now',[2] so it's a nice surprise to find that this neglected novel is really rather good. The book's main target is the earnestness of student socialists, but there are plenty of other deft assaults, including this acute critique of abstract art.

*

PATH OF DALLIANCE
(Chapman & Hall, 1963)

Goyle contemplated the first picture. It was a thing of greens and browns, with here and there a hint of orange. He put his head close to it, as if inspecting some minutiae of the brushwork. Goyle was not a person to form rash judgements but he could see that this painting was quite exceptional. As he later said, it was one of the most exciting moments of his life. There was a pulsing harmony, a kind of inner activity to which no words could do justice. It was as if the artist was living inside the picture, occasionally pushing out and jabbing one in the eye with the end of his paintbrush. He moved to the next one. It was decorative, pleasant, excellent of its sort, but no more. It was the work of an accomplished artist who had said, 'Let us now rest and produce not a potboiler but some light entertainment, something to divert and titillate. This is my *Midsummer Night's Dream*. The last was my *King Lear*.' The next painting was sombre in the extreme. Occasionally it jarred. Perhaps the artist had not yet found his legs, perhaps he had been crossed in love. It was of historical interest, but no aesthetic movement. The next, more ambitious, was magnificent, but did it achieve an integral tonality? Goyle would not have liked to rely on his judgement on that point, particularly when so much money was involved.

But the fun really starts when Jamey tries to enter the world of journalism, applying for a job on a left-wing periodical called the *Reserver*. Its editor suggests Jamey should write an article about cricket.

'Query: why is cricket so peculiarly British and what is the explanation for such a pointless activity in the first place? Answer: cricket sublimates the aggressive urges of class and siphons them into innocuous activity. When a bowler throws the ball at a batsman, he is not just throwing a ball at a batsman. He is trying to kill that batsman, who represents, in his pads and gloves and with his hard, impervious bat, all the entrenched privilege of the upper and upper middle class. When the wickets fly, that is a real victory. It is a victory for the worker against his capitalist overlord, for the other rank sergeant against his weak-chinned young officer. Then, of course, when the game is over, the capitalist overlord and his menial return to their respective positions, and the menial has lost the urge to destroy, overthrow and put aright. Don't you think that is what cricket is about?'

Jamey had never thought about it like that. 'You mean so that the working classes will go on working and won't have to vote Socialist?'

'Exactly.'

'I think it's an excellent idea. Of course, I always thought cricket was a capital game, and enjoyed it immensely. Now I see why.'

In later life, Waugh was pleased to find that a passage from *Path of Dalliance* had been selected as a comprehension text in the English language O level exam. Eventually, his second novel achieved a sort of immortality, after all. Yet although this book's muted reception didn't put an end to his ambitions as a novelist, it taught him what his father had always suspected: that he would not be able to earn a living from fiction alone.

Like the hero of *Path of Dalliance*, Waugh stumbled into Fleet Street, where he was hired by Hugh Cudlipp as a 'special writer' for the *Daily Mirror* on £1600 a year. In fact, there was precious little for him to do, but he was wise enough not to rock the boat. 'The secret of success on the *Mirror* was never to try to get anything into the paper,' he recalled. 'That stirred up endless resentments among your fellow scribes.'[3] During his three and half years there, Waugh worked on just four major projects, including a three-part series on sexual morals (which gave his father much amusement) and surreptitiously wrote another novel, about a thwarted writer on a women's magazine, called *Who Are the Violets Now?*.

WHO ARE THE VIOLETS NOW?
(Simon & Schuster, 1965)

Arthur Friendship sat down and scanned the current number of *Woman's Dream*. His own contributions were there, so lucid and beautifully written that they seemed to stand out from the paper. Every euphonious syllable contained the essence of poetry, without actually being constructed in verse form. Beside them, the pullout knitting supplement and cooking hints appeared shoddy in the extreme. He found he remembered every word of his criticism, and read it anxiously to see what had been cut out. All editorial matter was delivered to the offices nine weeks before it appeared on the bookstalls, but words which are born from the agony of creative travail are not quickly forgotten. Sure enough, a sub-editor had cut out the last sentence.

Critic's Column was the only one of Arthur's contributions which appeared under his own name, and the only one in which he took a personal pride. Industry, artifice and all the learning to be derived from an expensive education had been behind his

elbow when he wrote his account of an Englishwoman's life
with her kangaroo in the South of France, as described in
'Jacquetta & I' by Elsie Peartree. The punch had been saved for
the end, when Arthur revealed that Jacquetta was, in fact, a
kangaroo. But the sub-editor knew better. Whether for reasons
of good taste, libel or shortage of space, there was to be no
mention of kangaroos.

Evelyn Waugh liked his son's third novel a lot better than the
second. 'I spent a very happy day in reading it,' he wrote to
Auberon. 'I congratulate you on the best constructed and
controlled work you have yet done and am very proud that it
should be dedicated to me. I hope it achieves the success it
deserves.' Sadly, though the critics were kinder than they'd been
to *Path of Dalliance*, the sales were no better. For the time being,
at least, Waugh was stuck with journalism, a fate he'd antici-
pated in his novel.

Under his superficial veneer of cynicism, Arthur knew in
his heart of hearts that he was an artist. He had once read
a book about Michelangelo by an American writer, and it
had touched a deep chord. He knew all about the agony
and ecstasy of creative travail at first hand. He reviewed
the book for *Woman's Dream*, but the review never appeared,
being superseded at the last minute by an advertisement
for dog food. Perhaps that was why he did not like animals.
He was a warm-hearted person by nature, but for some
reason animals did not touch a chord. Or perhaps dislike
of animals was just another fascinating clue to his many
sided genius. The review hinted that he, Arthur Friendship,
was just such a one as Michelangelo. And so he was.

How often he had wished he could be like other men,
taking pleasure in the simple things which seemed to keep
them happy. Whenever he heard two labourers conversing
in their stumbling, unaffected way about the weather, or
football, or television, or some other subject of general
working-class interest he yearned to be able to participate.

But his occasional attempts had been uniformly disastrous. He wished he could enjoy the television serials which so diverted the entire working class of Great Britain, and were enjoyed by those blessed with an inferior intelligence in every class. There could be no doubt about it, stupidity and a low level of sensitivity were the greatest levellers of all, and the most precious assets in the modern world.

Like Jamey in *Path of Dalliance*, Waugh had swapped Oxbridge for Fleet Street and found the going rather slow. The apotheosis of his tabloid travails was writing corny captions for the *Mirror*'s 'ABC of Beauty', featuring such alliterative monstrosities as P for Pert and A for Allure. These pin-ups were tame by modern standards — the models wore swimsuits at the very least. What's more revealing is the torpid prose Waugh was required to write alongside them. 'Allure seldom wears a bikini,'[4] he declared, beside a photo of Raquel Welch in a two-piece bathing costume — hardly the best use of his novelistic skills. Waugh's 'ABC of Beauty' epitomised the talent that lay dormant at the *Mirror*, but between writing pin-up captions and moonlighting on a couple of novels, he did pen a few substantial articles, ranging from po-faced pieces like 'The Pill – and the Pope's Dilemma' to a photo-shoot with Mandy Rice-Davies taken in Israel during the Six Day War. Best of all was his series of premature obituaries, of famous personalities still living, prompted by his review of his father's obituaries in the *Spectator* (which we'll come to later). Waugh kicked off with Malcolm Muggeridge, whose obituary of his father had not been as generous as he would have liked. He went on to mourn the passing of David Frost, Jean Shrimpton and the Duke of Edinburgh (all happily still with us). These pieces weren't just polemics. They contained an element of the absurd. 'Many people will have been saddened as they read of Malcolm Muggeridge's sudden death at the age of 150,' wrote Waugh, in the first (and finest) of his mock obits, surmising that millions of mourners would feel as if they had lost a beloved budgerigar, 'or a dog which had given many years of faithful service'.[5]

Finally, Waugh was beginning to spread his wings, but it was on an even more unlikely paper that he really found his voice, as a columnist for the *Sun*. Back then, before Rupert Murdoch bought the paper, it was still a left-wing broadsheet, supposedly more upmarket (though far less popular) than the *Mirror*, and supposedly more independent (though still allied to the Labour Party). 'I think there may have been a certain amount of dismay among the writers in what was, after all, a newspaper of the left, if the price of calling themselves independent was to print my own reactionary Catholic burblings,'[6] recalled Waugh. He was too modest. His columns, though right wing, wouldn't have looked out of place in today's *Independent*. And they were written in a style that was recognisably his own. 'Murder is still, on the whole, something to be discouraged,'[7] he wrote, in a piece on capital punishment. And his solution to the Miss World debate? 'Let them parade in the nude.'[8] In a jubilant letter to his father, Waugh wrote, 'I have found a new metier in journalism. A newspaper called the *Sun* prints a weekly sermon, rather on the lines of my old *Catholic Herald* pieces, but pays 25 guineas a time . . . Money for jam.'

Chapter Six
HP Sauce

Political motivation is psychotic in origin. People enter politics or the civil service out of a desire to exert power and influence events; this, I maintain, is an illness. It is only when one realises that great administrators and leaders of men have all been at any rate slightly mad that one has a true understanding of history.[1]

Still spectacularly under-employed by the *Mirror* on a series of increasingly unlikely and inconsequential assignments, Waugh wrote another novel, *Consider the Lilies*, which he regarded as his best. The critics agreed, and they were right. Waugh's previous novels had had their moments, but this one was all of a piece, and for the first time it spoke with a voice that was entirely his. It was about a reticent man on the edge of middle age, rather than a brash young man on the make. It was much more intimate, and a lot less arch. Its hero is a shrewd and cynical vicar, infatuated with the daughter of the local squire, yet shackled to a sexless, godless wife. Full of dangerous jokes and dark wit, this bitter black comedy was about his futile attempts to get rid of her, without straying too far from the dictates of his Christian calling: 'Thou must not kill; but need not strive officiously to keep alive.'

*

CONSIDER THE LILIES
(Michael Joseph, 1968)

It is true that the role of the Church has changed. We used to provide comfort to people living wretched, undernourished lives, and we fulfilled a useful social purpose: by assuring them of a real or imaginary paradise ahead we accustomed them to accepting a miserable existence in this world without creating further unhappiness for themselves by trying to change it. Nowadays, in the age of affluence, we are just one more luxury offered in the already glutted consumer market. So, of course, is Oxfam. People actually derive more satisfaction from giving sixpence to Oxfam than from buying an extra packet of chocolate flavoured potato crisps. The Church teaches you why it is better to give the sixpence to the starving millions. Oxfam merely knows what people like, and caters for their tastes, like a cynical prostitute. We still have a purpose – to fill that aching void left in the consciousness of even the most affluent which might be called spiritual and aesthetic awareness. Oxfam has none. People might as well eat their revolting potato crisps and die with a nasty taste in their mouths.

This was brilliant writing, and Waugh knew it. However, his sales remained modest, and so did the reviews. As a novelist, he was condemned to remain his father's son for ever. His father's praise would have been some consolation but, sadly, Evelyn didn't live long enough to read his son's best novel. He died on Easter Sunday 1966 at the age of sixty-two. Nigel Lawson, editor of the *Spectator* (and subsequently Margaret Thatcher's chancellor), invited Auberon to review his father's obituaries, many of which were rather grudging. Waugh rose to the challenge, and lacerated his father's foes with scorn sharpened by grief.[2] It was a requiem for an admired father, and a mission statement from his admiring son. As a novelist, he'd been unable to escape his father's shadow. He would have to do it as a journalist instead.

In fact, it was no more than a surrender to economic pressure [reflected Waugh, a few years later]. I could not possibly afford to take six months off from journalism to write a novel unless I was prepared to live like a tinker. A few writers are prepared to live like tinkers, but there is no reason to suppose they make better novelists. In any case the novelist has rather lost his place in society, if the truth be told. I attribute this to the fact that he is so poor – where once he was the lion at any cocktail party, now he is to be seen furtively pocketing the canapés after the last guest has gone.[3]

But money was not the only reason that Waugh turned his back on fiction:

I gave up writing novels for various reasons. One of them was undoubtedly depression at the appalling standard of reviewers, who were and remain a novelist's chief contact with his reading public. In those days the critical orthodoxy was that novels should concern themselves with the struggle and ancient disabilities of the working class. It was a waste of time to suggest that the vast majority of novels, since the form was invented, had been written by the middle classes about the middle classes for the middle classes to enjoy. Anything written by, about or for the middle classes was obscurely judged 'escapist'.[4]

Wearied by this class prejudice and the invidious comparisons with his father, Waugh made the great escape into journalism. It was the defining decision of his working life.

DEATH IN THE FAMILY
(*Spectator*, 6 May 1966)

There was a time when obituary notices used to list the dead person's achievements and express polite regret at his death. In

the case of notorious war criminals, voluptuaries or enemies of
society perhaps a hint of disapproval would be allowed, coupled
with charitable assumptions of repentance. No doubt there was
something hypocritical in the convention – and hypocrisy, of
course, to our literary jackals is what cowardice would be to a
lion – but it sprang from the belief that few people are totally
contemptible and that death is not an opportune moment to
remind wife, family and friends of whatever shortcomings
existed or were imagined to exist.

The new fashion is to attempt a portrait 'in the round'.
Nobody can reasonably object to that if the writer has any idea
of his subject. The *Sunday Times* printed an eloquent and moving
tribute to my father by his close friend Christopher Sykes.[5] *The
Times* obituary was the work of another old friend, Christopher
Hollis. Douglas Woodruff wrote a longish piece in the *Tablet*.
All the others, whether laudatory or primly disapproving, had
in common that they were written by people whose acquaintance with my father, if any, was of the very slightest. Roundness
was achieved either by dredging up unfavourable book reviews
or by raising fatuously uninformed judgements on his private
life and attitudes.

Time magazine announced: 'In the last ten years of his life
he was a flabby old Blimp with brandy jowls and a menacing
pewter complexion . . . he lived in an eighteenth-century country
house 140 miles from London where he played the country
squire with a conservatism that soon became simply amniotic
[*sic*] . . . And then last week on Easter Sunday, home from a
Mass sung (to his crusty satisfaction) in Latin, he climbed the
stairs to his study and died of a heart attack.'

If the purpose of this advanced style is to inform the public,
they have been cheated. My father did not die of a heart attack,
nor did he die in his study which is on the ground floor. The
Mass he attended was not sung. He never at any stage played
the country squire, having no interest in local affairs or rustic
pastimes, and probably never spoke to more than half a dozen
people in the neighbourhood. It is true that he lived in the
country, as do many writers, and in a large house because he

had a wife and six children to accommodate. Those who saw him in the last ten years will know that they were probably the most mellow and tranquil of his life – certainly much more so than the preceding ten. In the final years he worried about some work he had undertaken and was distressed by the extraordinary simple-mindedness of Catholic bishops, but to me he was never so benign or gentle.

Like the sneer that he acted the part of a country squire, the charge of Blimpishness is familiar. It is true that he thought socialism nasty, stupid and wrong. Many of his friends were socialists, and for the most part they respected each others' views. But there is a recognisable need among less intelligent socialists to fit their adversaries into a mould – the crafty capitalist, the obsequious peasant, the half-mad racialist or the Colonel Blimp. They cannot believe that anybody who does not share their prejudices and muddled reasoning is either intelligent or humane. By one remove, any book which does not explicitly state that its author accepts Clause Four of the Labour Party constitution[6] cannot be a good book – it lacks compassion; it has withdrawn from the twentieth century. Well, we shall see which survives – my father's writing or the memory of these smart young men on television who *have* got compassion and who *are* part of the twentieth century.

The *Daily Telegraph* printed a full and generous tribute by David Holloway (so did the *Express*, by Robert Pitman, and the *Mail* by A. E. W. Parsons) beside an obituary of such niggling ineptitude that it is difficult to believe it was the work of human hand. Describing him as 'a prolific writer of high literary merit', it added: 'As his other books appeared it became obvious that Mr Waugh adored blue blood and affected to despise the common man. Yet he sprang from the modest middle class of whom he wrote so scornfully, being born in Golders Green in 1903, son of a publisher.'

What paradox! What insight! Since there was nothing affected about his dislike of the common man – a sociologist's way of conjuring every mediocrity the flesh is heir to – and since he never wrote in terms of anything except the greatest affection about the kind of intelligent, educated professional background from which he came, the purpose of this can scarcely be instructive. It is to suggest that he was a snob and a social climber who turned his back on his own kind. This is the theme song taken up by Alan Brien[7] – who, compassionately, found it in his heart to forgive him – and Malcolm Muggeridge, who compassionately saw my father's entire inner life as a tortured class struggle.

It is true that he conceived a romantic attachment to the aristocratic ideal, and nurtured it when he discovered how much it annoyed people. His politics, in fact, were far closer to the Manchester School anarchists than to the Conservative right wing, but he took no interest in the subject, and I never once heard him discuss politics seriously. He despised all English politicians since 1832, most particularly the Conservatives, just as he despised television personalities, but it was his unfashionable interest in pedigree which the jackals really seized on. In his life, it played a much smaller part than his interest in nineteenth-century chromo-lithography, his collection of Victorian narrative pictures, stone eggs, carved animals, his interest in wine, the peacocks on which he lavished so much affection. If interest in architecture were to become unfashionable, the jackals could show that his books are obsessed by the subject.

The charge of snobbery is easy to explain. My father's life was largely spent in the avoidance of boredom and of people who were likely to bore him. He occupied the social position which his talents commanded, and although he punctiliously answered all letters except those from obvious lunatics or Americans, he saw no reason why his time should be spent in the company of those he had not chosen. Many people who pushed themselves on him were rebuffed. Understandably reluctant to accept that they were bores, they attributed his avoidance of them to some genetic inadequacy on their part for which they could not be held responsible and which might even win a little sympathy. When Mr Muggeridge noticed that my father had stopped listening to his speech at a Foyles lunch, he naturally assumed that it was out of dissatisfaction with his lineage. It did not occur to him that he was making a boring speech. Equally, when my father was eventually driven mad by the jackals snarling and whining around his ankles, Mr Muggeridge sees this madness as the moment of truth. It was certainly Mr Muggeridge's moment of triumph. All the malicious sneers which the Muggeridges and Briens had been directing at him in his lifetime came home to roost until, by an iron effort of the will, he sent them back to Fleet Street and the obituary columns.

Another triumph for the jackals was that my father died unhonoured by the country to whose literature he had contributed so much. Once, the prime minister of the time – an infinitely depressing publisher some years his senior[8] – wrote offering him the CBE – or perhaps it was the BSc – and he wrote back proudly that he would wait until he had earned his spurs. Often he would pat his corporation with its heavy gold watch chain and say to my mother, 'You will be Lady Waugh before I die.' This was not, Mr Muggeridge, evidence of class conflict. It was a joke. Although one may doubt whether anything coming from the present troupe of clowns would have caused him much pleasure, he certainly would have liked recognition, and it was a modest enough ambition.

The main point about my father, which might be of interest to people who never met him, is not that he was interested in pedigree – it was the tiniest part of his interests. It is not that he was a conservative – politics bored him and his interest was confined to resentment at seeing his earnings redistributed among people who were judged more worthy to spend them than he. It is not that he was tortured by class aspirations – he was not. It is not that he had a warm and compassionate heart – warm and compassionate hearts are two a penny. It is not even that he was a Catholic – there are 550 million of them and a fair number must be Catholics by conviction. It is simply that he was the funniest man of his generation. He scarcely opened his mouth but to say something extremely funny. His house and life revolved around jokes. It was his wit – coupled, of course, with supreme accuracy of expression, kindness, loyalty, bravery and intelligence – which endeared him to every-body who knew him or read his books. Wit is something indefinable and absolute. Can one ever hope to explain this to the mean and humourless prairie dogs who prowl around in our literary desert? Is it even worth the effort?

But the new-style obituary notice is with us yet, lest we forget, lest we forget. Alan Brien, I fear, will scarcely merit more than a two-line mention, unless he dies in particularly dramatic circumstances. As he observed, he has little to lose. I think I can leave it to the news desks to concoct some variation on the from-rags-to-a-terrace-house-near-Tufnell-Park theme should he choose to immolate himself in Trafalgar Square.

But Mr Muggeridge is another kettle of fish. I am twenty-six, and have a reasonable chance of surviving him. Reading through his contribution in the *Observer*, I see that he claims to have met my father first at a picnic party given by the Duff Coopers in North Africa during the war. I wondered rather about that, since I seem to remember being present at the first meeting between Mr Muggeridge and Lady Diana Cooper – at Portofino in 1955. A small point, of interest only to those like myself who are obsessed by class attitudes. But my pencil will be out, my throbbing compassionate heart in my hand, when the unhappy event occurs.[9]

After this robust review of his father's obituaries, Lawson[10] asked Waugh to write more articles for the *Spectator*, and the following year, in 1967, he made him the magazine's new polit-ical correspondent. Waugh was happy to admit he knew next to nothing about politics, but he soon found his feet. 'My only qualification for the job was a certain scepticism about anything I was told and an unbudgeable suspicion of political motives,'[11] he recalled. In fact, this made him far better qualified to do a decent job than most political reporters — those so-called 'Westminster Insiders' who often end up being far more chummy with the people they're supposed to be writing about than the people they're supposed to be writing for:

The reason political writers regale us with speculation about political reshuffles, despite the fact that nobody is remotely interested in them, is that they live their lives among these wretched politicians, who are interested in nothing else.[12] Newspapers should refuse to talk to politicians. They are nothing but liars and gourmandisers. Political reporting should be confined to accounts of parliamentary speeches and election manifestos, Green and White Papers and Bills, commentary on them and satirical parliamentary sketches. There is nothing to be gained by talking to the brutes.[13]

In 1968, after a year spent reporting from Parliament for the *Spectator*, Lawson sent Waugh to Biafra to report on the Nigerian civil war. In 1966 Nigeria's Ibo tribe had staged a coup in an attempt to usurp the national government. The coup had failed, resulting in retributive massacres, which prompted the Ibos to secede from the Nigerian federation, setting up their own state in Biafra, the eastern heartland of their tribe.

By the time Waugh arrived in Biafra in July 1968, this break-away republic had already lost a good deal of territory, including several of its most important conurbations, and its people were being systematically starved to death by the federal government's blockade. Waugh flew in at no small risk, landing at dead of night on an ancient plane from Lisbon full of crates of ammunition (several of these planes were shot down by the federal air force during the war). In Biafra, he witnessed the starvation of the civilian population at close hand, and became convinced of the Biafran cause.

Unlike most Nigerians, who were Muslims, the Ibos were mainly Catholic, but there was more to Waugh's support than Christian kinship. More than any religious fellow feeling, his fury was ignited by his natural sympathy for the underdog, and the knowledge that the British government was aiding and abetting this brutal blockade. 'It was quite an unpleasant thing to see children dying of starvation, and then back in London I'd meet people like Roy Jenkins[14] and think, These are the buggers who're actually doing this.'[15]

Waugh campaigned tirelessly to publicise the unseen plight of the Biafrans. He demonstrated outside Downing Street, held rallies in Trafalgar Square and stood as a Save Biafra candidate in the Bridgewater by-election. He even named his fourth child, born in 1968, Nathaniel Thomas Biafra. The most lasting legacy (apart from his second son's middle name) was *Biafra: Britain's Shame*, published by Michael Joseph in 1969, a passionate denunciation of the UK role in the conflict, co-written with the South African Suzanne Cronje.

This new-found zeal added fresh zest to his old bile and bite, but Waugh soon became uncomfortable with this high moral tone. 'There is something suspect about it,' he told Lynn Barber. 'You suddenly start thinking what a wonderful person you must be to be so morally indignant.'[16] And so he dropped it. Biafra finally fell while he was campaigning as a Save Biafra candidate. He resigned his candidature and advised his supporters to vote Liberal instead — the only party, he believed, who'd behaved honourably in the affair.

AVENGE O LORD
(*Spectator*, 3 June 1978)

I became involved in the Nigerian civil war at a fairly late stage, in the summer of 1968, when I was sent as the *Spectator*'s political correspondent to report on conditions inside Biafra, already reduced to an enclave of the heartland around Aba, Owerri and Umuahia. My trip was a brief one, ten days all told, just long enough to convince me that the place had been unjustly treated by Britain, that they were determined to fight and that reports of mass starvation had not been exaggerated. Thereafter I covered the story, and watched the unfolding pageant of events, exclusively from the Westminster and Whitehall end.

It would be idle to pretend that my interest was not coloured by the things I had seen and heard in Biafra, or by my admiration for the Biafrans. One could not listen to the well-rehearsed

arguments for continuing British policy in the Nigerian civil war
with quite the same equanimity having once seen its results and
knowing that the results were growing more severe with every
week that passed. Having said that, and making every allowance
for a certain failure of imagination among the British official
and political classes (many of whom came from humble homes
and poor educational backgrounds) whereby one or two million
Africans dead might represent no more than a statistical concept,
something to be played around with on a computer, a tribute,
in some way, to their own responsibility and importance in the
world – making every allowance, as I say, for all of that – I can
only testify that the episode has burned itself into my memory.
It has entirely shaped my subsequent attitudes to politics and
politicians, journalism and journalists, the House of Commons,
British democracy, the British people and its suitability to have
any particular role in the world.

Waugh's job as Lawson's political correspondent only lasted
for a few years. In 1970, to wile away an idle hour at the printers,
he altered one of the names on the contents page, from George
Gale[17] to Lunchtime O'Gale (Lunchtime O'Booze was a stock
character in *Private Eye*, an archetypal drunken hack). Lawson
fired Waugh, and Waugh sued him for wrongful dismissal.
Bizarrely, by the time the case came to court Lawson had left
the paper, Gale had been appointed editor, and had rehired
Waugh as the *Spectator*'s literary critic. 'Lawson, as a sacked editor,
had to defend himself for sacking me, who had since been re-
employed, for insulting the man who had since re-employed
me,'[18] recalled Waugh, marvelling at the absurdity of it all. Waugh
won £600, and continued writing for the *Spectator* throughout
his life. Wisely, Gale refused to give evidence for either side.

'The only important discovery I made as the *Spectator*'s political correspondent between 1967 and 1970 was that very few
British people are in the slightest bit interested in politics,'[19]
concluded Waugh. After three years at the parliamentary coal-
face, he could see their point of view. 'The problem with
democracy is that it is not democracy at all but a zealotocracy

or rule by enthusiasts,' he argued. 'It may be lovely for bossy people who like deciding how the rest of us should live, but it is hell for those at the receiving end.'[20] Half a lifetime after Lawson hired (and fired) him, this attitude endured. 'The last thing we want from MPs is greater productivity,' he declared. 'They should be offered half the pay for half the hours, with an open invitation to go on strike for the rest of their natural lives.'[21]

LET'S ALL LIE DOWN AND DIE
(*New Statesman*, 21 June 1974)

Whenever a political speaker talks about 'the frustrations of ordinary people excluded from the process of decision-making', I tend to raise my eyebrows. Obviously politicians suffer from extreme frustration when excluded from the process of decision-making – but ordinary people? This phrase seems to sum up one aspect of the political illness which I write about so frequently on this page: the refusal of people who suffer from the desire to impose political decisions on their fellow men to believe that everybody else is not similarly afflicted.

In my days as a political correspondent I was constantly asked – usually by backbench MPs but sometimes by quite senior ministers – what plans I had to secure myself a constituency and which party I reckoned would offer the best opportunities nowadays. My slightly priggish rebuttals were usually met with polite disbelief and always with plain incomprehension that there can ever be anyone who does not wish to have a say in decision-making and exerting power over his fellow men. Yet I believe that I am in the majority. Ordinary people, if such there be, want more money for less work, better conditions, better housing and all the rest. To the extent that they are unable or unwilling to secure these benefits for themselves they will very properly blame the politicians. But few of us have any very clear idea of what needs to be done and most are quite happy to leave that side of things to the poor boobies who think they know best, sacking them from time to time when they fail.

Which is why, whenever I see political zealots trying to advance their own power urges by exploiting the supposedly frustrating power urges of everybody else, my reaction is a belly-laugh. It is not lumpish proletarian apathy which prevents most good journalists from having the slightest desire to be editors. It is simple distaste for the power urge. Until politicians can realise that, they will never understand why they are so much disliked.

WE ARE NOT AMUSED
(*New Statesman*, 25 July 1975)

Try as I will – and I really have tried very hard – I can't see the squabble over MPs' pay as anything except a sublime joke. It is a joke of such exalted and lofty proportions that it dwarfs every other aspect of contemporary life and sums up anything that can usefully be said about the state of the nation, Britain's role in the world, the basic patriotism and moderation of the British, our sense of fair play, our wonderful parliamentary system, our concern for the underdeveloped, our marvellous feelings for old people and the compassion which underlies everything we say, do, write or think. It is an Armageddon among jokes, a joke to end all jokes.

The joke would have been subtler if a week or two had been allowed to elapse between the announcement of a tough new limit on wage settlements and discussion of an enormously bigger award to the legislators themselves. MPs could have filled the weeks with patriotic appeals for restraint, mentioning the heroic efforts of the British people at Dunkirk and assuring us that the issue today is exactly the same: parliamentary democracy against a vicious dictatorship. But the trouble with subtle jokes is that they are liable to be missed by 95 per cent of the population. As likely as not, the public would have joined the patriotic mood, agreed wholeheartedly that the new limit was essential and a week or two later have listened to the arguments that MPs are a special case without seeing any connection.

For the first time I find myself really growing rather fond of our politicians. Of course they are mentally ill, or they would not feel this terrible urge to be important and boss other people around in the first place. But there is something rather endearing about the way they blink their eyes when you tell them how horrible they are, and say anything else would be worse; the way they have absolutely no idea how they are despised and hated by their fellow citizens; the way they put their heads on one side whenever you tell them this and say that such opinions should not be encouraged as they undermine the fabric of democracy. In the Middle Ages there was a special affection for simpletons and the mentally disturbed on the grounds that they were God's children: by their innocence and lack of concern for worldly affairs they afforded a glimpse of the holy vision enshrined in the Sermon on the Mount.

THE POWER URGE
(Spectator, 15 December 1984)

Taken by a friend to a performance of Peter Hall's[22] magnificent *Coriolanus* at the Olivier theatre, I have since spent my time urging as many people as possible to go and see it, even buying tickets for them. It was not a play I had thought about much since studying it for A level nearly thirty years ago, when it seemed tremendously boring. One could not sympathise with the hero, or find his mother anything but disgusting, his wife irritating, his best friend a fool. Although it contained some fine polemic against the working classes, such people did not threaten one's life or comforts in those days as they do now; in fact, to the extent that they infringed at all, they appeared as friends and supports in life's struggle. It was inappropriate to describe them as 'common cry of curs' – and also rather rude when, in many cases, they had not enjoyed one's own advantages.

Although I passed the examination, and have the certificate to prove it, I never understood the play until seeing Ian McKellen's[23] memorable performance. The play's message is very simple, and even more relevant to modern democratic society than it was to Tudor England, that politics is not a suitable occupation for a gentleman. If that message could be generally accepted by all intelligent people in the country it would have a profoundly beneficial effect, not so much in discouraging gentlemen from dabbling in politics, since very few are tempted to do so nowadays, but in giving the rest of us a more accurate perspective of politics and politicians.

In fairness to the great British public, it has never shown a tendency to put any exaggerated trust in politicians. But until it accepts that the urge to power is a personality disorder in its own right, like the urge to sexual congress with children or the taste for rubber underwear, there will always be a danger of circumstances arising which persuade ordinary people to start listening to politicians and would-be politicians, and taking them seriously. It happened in Russia, of course, and in Germany, and may even now be happening in Central America for all I know or care. The important thing is to prevent its happening in England.

Politics, as I never tire of saying, is for social and emotional misfits, handicapped folk, those with a grudge. The purpose of politics is to help them overcome these feelings of inferiority and compensate for their personal inadequacies in the pursuit of power. Power, I imagine, is all that democratic politicians have ever been interested in. Those who do not suffer from this urge may have difficulty in understanding it: they may even be reluctant to believe in its existence. Among the lower classes it is generally supposed that politicians are in it for the money, but I believe that they are wrong, and we should all study this phenomenon of the power urge. It seems to cause far more unhappiness than happiness.

The yells and animal noises which the nation listens to on the radio programme *Today in Parliament* have nothing to do with disagreements about the way the country should be run, or how much fuel should be given to old age pensioners at Christmas time. They are cries of pain and anger, mingled with hatred and envy, at the spectacle of another group exercising the 'power' which the first group covets; alternatively, they are cries of alarm as the group in 'power' sees its territory threatened. Old age pensioners are mad if they think anyone actually cares about their wretched coal. Until one understands this one will never understand the confrontational nature of democratic politics. The only thing that any of them is really interested in is the chance to make decisions and see them put into effect – to press a button and watch us all jump.

THE BEST NEWS I HAVE HEARD FOR A LONG TIME
(Sunday Telegraph, 21 May 2000)

When I first became a full-time political correspondent in 1967 the House of Commons was exactly the same as it is today. Members of the Press Gallery felt they belonged to an exclusive club dedicated to keeping the secret of how awful the Commons were: how gross their attitudes, how affected their manners, how transparent their motives. But this was how democracy seemed to work in Britain, and it wasn't such a bad country to live in.

When Parliament decided to televise itself in 1989 I thought it was making an obvious and possibly catastrophic mistake. Its motives were easy to perceive. While a few Members waffled about their sacred duty to promote an informed democracy, to bring politics to the people, the rest quite simply wished to see themselves on television. They wanted a slice of our celebrity culture, bringing them closer to the glory enjoyed by football stars, actors, pop singers and the occasional athlete. This may seem a harmless enough ambition, but those who admired the system and marvelled that it seemed to work were worried that greater exposure would bring it crashing down. People would be so appalled by the pretentiousness and mediocrity of the participants that they would demand a more forceful expression of the various half-baked political ideas floating around.

In the event, this did not happen, partly as the result of stringent editing, partly because practically nobody watched these dismal programmes. But now we learn that they have had a powerful effect on the young. The first generation to have grown up with Parliament being televised has been made the subject of a study by the Joseph Rowntree Foundation. Its report, *Young People's Politics*, has just been published. It reveals that young people reaching the voting age of eighteen this year take an 'extremely negative' attitude to politics in general and politicians in particular. They were seven when Parliament was first televised in 1989. The feeling among fourteen-to-twenty-five-year-olds is that politicians are 'untrustworthy, boring, remote and self-serving'.

After nearly twenty years as a political correspondent – first for the *Spectator*, then for *Private Eye* – I find this criticism rather harsh. By no means all politicians are boring. As for their being remote, the more important thing about them, which these young people failed to spot, is that they are all ill. Perhaps this is a euphemistic way of saying they are all mad: they are driven by a sick compulsion to be on top, to organise and boss us all around.

Be that as it may, the important thing to emerge from the survey is that British young people are not interested in politics. They may take an interest in some local cause, or adopt some absurd campaign like 'animal rights', but politics leave them cold. So far as they are concerned, the House of Commons can go droning on. We already knew that practically no eighteen to twenty-five-year-olds vote, but I always feared this might be because they could not find their way to the polling booths, or got the dates wrong. If they genuinely reject politics, that is some of the best news I have heard for a long time. Democracy can work as a form of government only in conditions of general apathy. Where there is a greater commitment, it is a recipe for conflict, not to say civil war. Why should ten voters abandon their fondest wishes just because eleven voters have a different preference? Democracy works perfectly well in an atmosphere of indifference and cynicism, but only so long as practically nobody is interested in politics. In the same way, politicians would be well advised not to push themselves forward. If they want celebrity like David Beckham or Martin Amis, they should forget about exerting power and start writing novels or playing football.

Chapter Seven
Street of Shame

The role of journalists is to ridicule, humiliate and generally torment politicians, pour scorn on everything they
propose to do and laugh at them when they do it. We
should never, never, never suggest new ways for them to
spend money, or taxes they could increase, or new laws
they could pass. There is nothing so ridiculous as the
posture of journalists who see themselves as part of the
sane and pragmatic decision-taking process.[1]

Waugh's dismissal from the *Spectator* was a blessing in disguise.
Upon being sacked by Nigel Lawson, he walked around the
corner to the offices of *Private Eye*, and was thrilled to be
appointed their political correspondent instead. The result was
'HP Sauce', a column that poked fun at parliamentary hacks as
much as politicians. However, Waugh soon discovered that journalists can be even more prickly than MPs. They were happy
to give him disparaging stories about one another, but when he
wrote them up they were just as happy to go to law, knowing
that *Private Eye* would pay them off rather than risk a long and
costly libel case. Only one such case came to court, but there
were numerous complaints and settlements, and although the
column was required reading for insiders, after two years Waugh
decided it was more trouble than it was worth. In any case,
Waugh was disenchanted with politics. 'In several years' sitting
through every important debate in the House of Commons, I
never consciously heard anyone tell it a word of truth,' he wrote.

'I never once checked on an answer to a Parliamentary Question without finding it either gravely misleading or a straight lie.'[2]

The replacement was 'Auberon Waugh's Diary', which ran for thirteen years and became, by common consent, Waugh's most inspired piece of writing. Its genius was to marry fact and fiction, and Waugh began to think he might have invented a new art form. 'The essence of the diary was that it was a work of pure fantasy, except that the characters in it were real,' explained Waugh. 'Its success was partly because there was a slight suspicion in the back of people's minds that I might indeed be very rich and grand, and they could never be absolutely sure when I was pulling their legs.'[3] In fact, many of the events Waugh described were gleaned from the society pages of the newspapers, with Waugh assuming the starring role as confidant of popes, prime ministers and presidents. The reality was more prosaic:

*

9 November 1977

A typical day. I rise at five forty-five, take my dear Wife some coffee in bed, and give the children their breakfast. I then retire for a few minutes to a small, private room where, among other things, I read the Bible. I then prepare sandwiches for my Wife to take to university, drive the children to school and return home to work throughout the day. At six o'clock I have my first drink and go to bed, drunk, at about midnight, having written my Diary for the day. Jolly interesting.

The inspiration for this new art form was a column in the *Sunday Times* called 'Alan Brien's Diary'. Brien, a prolific journalist, had provoked Waugh's ire by saying that his 'HP Sauce' column in *Private Eye* wasn't funny (Brien's obituary of Evelyn Waugh may also have played a part). 'Auberon Waugh's Diary' started out as a parody, in the same format, complete with a photograph of Waugh wearing a false beard. Brien's diary also bore a photo of the author, and, at that time, Brien also wore a (real) beard. Brien's beard only lasted a few years, and so did his diary – but Waugh's diary ran on and on.

Private Eye soon dropped Waugh's bearded picture byline, but it made occasional comebacks, as a useful space filler in the event of last-minute legal cuts, to the bewilderment of readers who'd long forgotten Brien's diary, even if they'd known about it in the first place. 'All characters and incidents are fictitious,' read a nervous disclaimer below Waugh's byline. 'No resemblance intended to real persons or events whatever.' And later, 'This column is entirely jocular. It contains no serious allegations whatever and everything in it is untrue.'

This was not quite true. Amid the surreal flights of fancy were snippets of straightforward reportage and sincerely held opinion, and it was this inspired blend of truth and falsehood that made it unique.

2 October 1972

The English Country Cheese Council has allocated £500,000 to promote British cheeses against foreign ones from the Common Market. At a special press reception, the Cheese Council had the amusing idea of wrapping each piece of cheese in a £5 note. Journalists were given whisky, and encouraged to keep the wrappings as a souvenir.

We were also given an off-the-record briefing by Mr Pinkerton from the Foreign and Commonwealth Office, who told us that many foreign cheeses are suspected of causing cancer, syphilis, St Vitus's Dance and other diseases of the brain, skin and central nervous system. Foreign Office analysts suspect that the unconventional behaviour of Uganda's General Idi Amin may be due in part to immoderate eating of foreign cheeses.

I must say, I'd quite forgotten how good English cheese can be. You can keep your Camembert and your goat cheeses from the Alps. Give me scrumptious, mumptious, cheesy Cheddar every day! I sometimes imagine that Wensleydale is not a cheese at all, it is a poem, an intricate symphony of diverging yet mutually dependent clusters. It is a song, a celebration of life's ultimate source. It is the sperm which runs through the veins of our primitive post-bourgeois tribal taboos like a needle through a haystack. I have never eaten so much cheese before.

12 October 1972

To get into the Women of the Year lunch at the Savoy Hotel I was forced to dress up in drag and give my name as Miss Glenda Slag, first lady of Greek Street. I disliked doing this, as it seemed to cheapen everything the Women's Freedom Movement stands for. I also thought my beard might excite ribald comment, but in this I underestimated the sisterhood. As Jill Tweedie[4] of the *Grauniad*[5] (who happened to be with me) points out, it is time people recognised that women have the fundamental right to grow beards if they want to. Men have taken it for granted for too long that theirs is the only sex capable of an act which is, fundamentally, as natural as going to the lavatory.

I found myself hypnotised by the shimmering patterns on Princess Anne's dress. Although I stared at her throughout the whole meal and although she must have been aware of the effect she was having on me, she refused to meet my eye, or indeed have anything to do with me. Normally, of course, I don't give a fig for the Royal Family, having spent my childhood in the reeking slums of Jericho, but there was something about the lift of her young bosoms, the haughty aristocratic neck and the deep, horsy voice which really tickled my fancy for a moment. It is a pity she would not take advantage, as I feel I could have given her a much better time than any of the double-barrelled chinless wonders she is used to.

3 November 1972

Spent the day in court.[6] My eye was caught by one of the plain-tiff's junior counsel, a most delightful creature with her little barrister wig perched demurely over what looked like a pony tail. There was a sweet frown of concentration on her face as she listened to all the sonorous denunciations and pregnant pauses of judge and senior counsel. This was altogether love-lier than anything my solicitors had chosen and I felt a pang of sorrow that circumstances had put her on the other side.

For one delicious moment our eyes met and I gave her a friendly wink. It seemed to make her at the same time happy and confused. She blushed and lowered her beautiful eyes with perhaps the faintest hint of a smile on her generous lips. I thought of following up my initiative with a Peace sign, but judged it imprudent under the circumstances.

Yet in that moment it seemed to me we had brought a touch of beauty into the four grey walls of the courtroom, accus-tomed as they are to tales of heartbreak and distress: reputations unjustly besmirched, fathers of families reduced to penury; tales of pomposity, spite, avarice and iniquity in every form. For one brief moment the light shone in that dingy corner of our capital city. If the young lady concerned would like to get in touch with me, I am to be found here on many mornings of the week.

3 December 1972

Tea-time walk-around talk-around in Soho to give ordinary people a chance of meeting me. I must admit I find the friend-liness and informality of ordinary people quite delightful, even though some of them, I believe, are terribly poor. A coloured lady kindly asks me into her house. It is not furnished in my sort of taste, but I suppose she likes it. She absolutely insists we have a drink before she can show me upstairs. I suppose this is some native custom, and sip watery beer while she drinks four tiny glasses of fruit juice, mysteriously thanking me each time. Suddenly she says I must pay six pounds for the drink, and if I want to go upstairs I must pay £25 more. Giving her all the money I have, I hastily make my excuses and leave. I wonder how Their Majesties avoid this sort of embarrassment on their walk-arounds among ordinary people.

12 December 1972

George Best[7] is up for sale, I see, priced at £200,000. By an odd coincidence, I happen to have this sum available at the moment as the result of a small legacy. It occurred to me as possibly quite an agreeable idea to buy the young man for a companion on my occasional visits to the night club scene of our metropolis. On the other hand I believe he is rather off-hand with his employers, and I might have a certain amount of difficulty in understanding his conversation. Perhaps I shall buy a little Filipino servant instead.

14 March 1973

Delighted to see they have burned down the British Council Library in Rawalpindi again – this time in protest against the shooting of two Pakistani youths in London. The last time they burned down this particular library was in February 1970, in protest against an article I had written in *The Times*, telling a joke about Allah which I had heard in the army. This burning remains the only public recognition my jokes have ever received.

21 March 1973

The first time I was taken to tea with Ivy Compton-Burnett[8] must have been in 1945 or 1946 when I was about six. She had expressed a desire to meet me, but at that age I had a particular taste for jam tarts, and Miss Burnett neglected to serve them – whether from incompetence or deliberate malice I was never able to discover. To make matters worse she placed me on a high chair like a two-year-old and proceeded to feed me by hand with scones dipped in milk, much to the amusement of Sir Max Beerbohm[9] and Bernard Shaw.[10]

Understandably annoyed by this, I bit her finger and proceeded to be violently sick all over the tablecloth and into the lap of H. G. Wells,[11] to whom I had also taken a dislike. Wells died soon after, and Miss Burnett never asked me to tea again, which I can't help thinking a pity, as I am sure we could have got along quite well and had some good fun together once she learned the simple rules of hospitality.

22 July 1973

'I am an old age pensioner aged 84 and live in a bedsitter. I find my NH pension ample for lunch out every day, postages, newspapers, occasional bus fares and 50 pence for the Offertory on Sunday,' writes a correspondent in the *Sunday Telegraph*. With more careful stewardship, he could probably run a string of race horses, too. Congratulations to the *Sunday Telegraph* for finding this courageous man. So many old age pensioners are in fear of their lives if they mention how happy they are, or how embarrassed by the enormous sums of money the government pours into their pockets. Stupefied by food and drink, they can just stagger from their restaurants to church where they hope to secure forgiveness for their indolent, luxurious lives on earth by extravagant bribes to the clergy.

26 August 1973

The most appalling thing about football hooligans is the discredit they bring on that superb game. Mr Len Shipman, President of the Football League, has suggested a return of the birch. Other suggestions include closing all pubs on match days, declaring a state of emergency or martial law and the use of paralysing gas on football crowds as soon as the match starts. My own suggestion for football hooligans is that after their arms and legs have been cut off their trunks should be covered with HP Sauce and sent to relieve the famine in West Africa. This would be a small gesture of concern for an area which is being pitifully neglected by the British people.

26 September 1973

My son at Eton writes to tell me that bodyguards are now being provided for Eton boys at the weekends. The headmaster, Mr Michael McCrum, has employed a security firm to protect his pupils after complaints from worried parents about a series of attacks by local guttersnipes. The bodyguards are, of course, drawn from the poorer classes themselves, so now Etonians will be treated to the diverting spectacle of the lower orders bashing each other up at every street corner while they saunter past into a carefree, protected future. The whole purpose of an Eton education is to prepare boys for such a world. I telephoned McCrum to congratulate him but of course today is the Jewish New Year so the whole place has closed down.

1 November 1973

Reckless chauvinism will never find a place in this column. We have all grown to accept the need for a German Royal Family, and even for their odious Protestant religion. But they, too, should learn a little tact. It is announced today that Princess Anne has chosen the refrain to greet her on arrival at Westminster Abbey to marry her hideous young tradesman – Haydn's well-known ditty 'Deutschland Deutschland Über Alles'. A pretty tune, you will say, but when I reflect on how many people died in two World Wars to prevent exactly this sort of thing, I, for one, propose to boycott the whole proceedings.

5 November 1973

Fireworks night, so we join the citizens in their fawning celebration of a brave and good man's death. In our family we always let off fireworks in celebration of the attempt to blow up Parliament, rather than its failure, and we have never had an accident. If ever the Vatican requires evidence of divine intervention before raising Guy Fawkes, Soldier and Martyr, to the celestial company of canonised saints, it has only to look at the hundreds of men, women and children blinded and disfigured every year in their attempts to mock him.

27 January 1974

The Chinese are quite right to denounce Beethoven as a class enemy seeking to reverse the decisions of the Great Cultural Revolution and undermine the dictatorship of the workers by encouraging certain 'spontaneous tendencies towards capitalism', especially in the rural areas. I confess that I seldom find my warm admiration for the working class much enhanced by listening to Beethoven.

We should all be on our guard against any middle-class backlash. Already I have found three Fascists under my bed and had to whip them soundly before they would agree to be dosed with

Syrup of Figs – although I disapprove of corporal punishment in principle, of course. For my own part, I shall listen to nothing but the pop group called Slade while the present uncertainties pass.

17 February 1974

To the Palace to receive my CBE from a smiling Queen Mother – the Queen is apparently in Uganda or somewhere. It is a very handsome bauble and becomes me rather well. Thank you, Grocer. A disadvantage of these agreeable things from many people's point of view is that they can only be worn with full evening dress, that is to say, white tie and tails. This does not worry me particularly, because of course in Somerset we still do wear the more formal evening dress for dinner unless we are dining with the middle class. But it occurs to me that as these awards are increasingly made to people from quite ordinary backgrounds (quite rightly, in my view), many of the recipients may only possess a dinner jacket, and will never have an opportunity of wearing them unless they hire evening dress at considerable expense to themselves and some risk of contagious disease.

If Labour wins the election on the sort of left-wing ticket which they have shown so bravely throughout the campaign, they might pluck up the courage to introduce legislation allowing Commanders of the British Empire to wear their insignia with an ordinary dinner jacket. At any rate, I pass the idea to Mr Wedgwood Benn,[12] who seems the most anxious to get things done. But if past experience is anything to go by, they will forget all their radicalism as soon as they're in office and we'll have to wait until Paul Foot[13] comes to power for this sensible and humane reform.

30 April 1974

Artists should not be required to take O levels, argues John Bratby, on the grounds that creative geniuses are 'driven to make pictures compulsively' and as a result are frequently unable to pass exams. It is true that no education is required to produce paintings nowadays. On the other hand, we can be sure that if artists are not made to take exams every little kiddie in the country will announce it is driven to make pictures compulsively; the slow national slide into illiteracy will accelerate and professional writers like myself will all be out of a job. The answer is surely that everybody should still take O levels as now, and those who would normally be said to have failed should instead be declared Artists. They should be given a hopelessly inadequate pension and encouraged to slosh around producing works of genius out of everybody's way.

25 July 1974

The death at ninety of Dame Sibyl Hathaway, the Dame of Sark, removed the only person in the British Isles whom I still wanted to meet. Unfortunately, she rejected all my advances. She was a model ruler for our times, forbidding not only cars and aircraft on her island, but also trade unions, taxation, female dogs, divorce, and most of the troublesome manifestations of our age. I had always hoped to persuade this admirable lady to take England under her rule when our parliamentary system finally disintegrates. Now she is dead I think I shall leave the country for a time – probably for a very long time. I can see no hope.

16 October 1974

What a miserable election it has been. In the new spirit of austerity I take an Underground train from Islington to Tottenham Court Road. One would have thought that at least the lower classes would look happy to have won again, but they look absolutely wretched. Perhaps they always do, but in that case the whole thing seems a waste of time.

11 November 1974

Old people are becoming more of a menace every day. Sugar workers can't even go on strike like ordinary self-respecting British workmen without promising that 'emergency' supplies of sugar will be made available to old age pensioners. British sentimentality about old age pensioners has always struck me as the most sickening of our national hypocrisies, springing from the cruel British practice of sending old people away instead of keeping them in the family. The applause which greets any public expression of concern for the old always reminds me of the compassionate noise one hears at a bullfight when a bull is being incompetently killed.

28 November 1974

Services in the Roman Catholic Church have become so inane and so repulsive that I am seriously thinking of joining the Church of England. Perhaps it is just that we have a particularly ghastly set of priests in the Taunton area, but visits to church are now occasions of sin, tempting one to anti-Christian frenzies of the sort which once led to Nero's excesses in the Roman Coliseum. Obviously the history of the Church of England is totally abject, rooted in cowardice, servility and doctrinal error. On the other hand, it seems to have acquired a certain dignity over the years, while the present countenance of the Roman church is transcendentally ignoble and reptilian in every aspect. I would welcome guidance in this moment of darkness and doubt.

16 January 1975

A visit from Miss Angela Levin, of the *Observer* colour section, who is interviewing the nation's top workers to discover the source of their exceptional energy. My secret is very simple. For breakfast I touch nothing except a couple of young partridges (in season) or a fat capon, washed down with a quart of barley wine. I never eat aubergines, Scotch broth or shellfish at breakfast. For lunch I prefer to sit in a convenient church (or in the church-yard, if the weather is fine) to eat my cheese sandwiches with a bottle or so of whisky to help them down, while I ponder the eternal verities – life and death, beauty and pain, *yin* and *yang*, etc. After April I will probably have to make do with a bottle of methylated spirits.

In the afternoon, if my work involves heavy intellectual strain (VAT accounts, for instance, or an important game of bridge) I may drink a bottle of crème de menthe, frappé, on crushed ice. Tea is not taken seriously in any of my houses (thin cucumber sandwiches, followed by a hot meat or eel pie – even sausage and mash, at a pinch – and ice cream). Dinner is the most important meal for the intake of energy and essential food supply. Here one tries to be as varied as possible, but a typical meal might start with pigs' blood pudding followed by demoiselles of goose, cold lobster or stuffed carp, roast suckling pig in honey, redcurrant leaf sorbet, roast beef or venison, artichoke soufflé, orange or raspberry tart, snipe's entrails on toast, fruit jelly with cream and nuts. Brown rice and sesame seeds are available as a small contribution to world problems. I think my agreeable complexion comes from the fruit jellies, while nuts are well known to be good for sexual performance.

6 March 1975

Rather unexpectedly I find myself in Kathmandu with Prince Charles and a party of fourteen other Etonians for the coronation of King Bihendra. I never knew Bihendra at Eton, where he was a junior boy when I was Captain of Oppidans, but he seems to think he knew me.

Before we left London we were given a briefing by a man from the Foreign and Commonwealth Office, who strongly advised us to be careful during the celebrations on the grounds that a staggering 94 per cent of Nepalese women suffer from hepatitis and related disorders. Can it really be true? Misconceptions of this sort have plagued British foreign policy from the earliest times and probably account for the loss of our Indian empire. But I confess that what little I have seen of Nepalese women has not encouraged me to delve for the salubrious six per cent.

Instead the British party spends an agreeable evening dancing together in the Royal Guesthouse. With typical British improvisation some of us dress up as girls – the Prince of Wales looks particularly fetching in a yashmak with blue paint on his eyelids. We all have to call him Omyhla, which means Daughter of the Moon.

8 March 1975

On its return journey our plane refuels in Tehran and I lose no time in securing an invitation to tea with the Shah. He is a disconcerting man with an abrupt way of speaking which many may find unsympathetic. When I suggest (for this is the purpose of my call) that he uses the opportunity of the Queen Mother's visit to Persia on 14 April to propose marriage, his first question is: 'What makes you think she will have anything to do with a dirty old wog like me?'

As a matter of fact, this was exactly the aspect of the affair which had been most troubling me. He might almost have read my thoughts. Under the circumstances, I didn't feel I could give him an entirely straight answer, but thinking it over afterwards I am confident that our doughty and magnificent royal lady will not fail in her duty at the hour of her country's need. I also happen to know that the Shah has some very nice necklaces and other pieces of jewellery.

20 April 1975

Tougher penalties for sexual offences are urged by the Police Superintendents Association in a report to the Law Commission today. They propose a maximum fine of £400 for flashing against the present maximum of £100. This depresses me rather, because although I have never yet been tempted to expose myself I can see that as I get older it might have its attractions as a way of passing the time. The new rate will mean that only the very rich can afford this pleasure, and it could easily be reduced to a form of status symbol or financial boasting.

23 July 1975

Going on holiday is much more hazardous than it used to be. Squatters have discovered they have an absolute right in law to occupy your house, sleep in your bed, drink all your wine, sodomise your cat and insult the goldfish. If you try and get back into your house, the police will beat you up with truncheons, pull your fingernails out and arrest you under the Vagrancy Act of 1203.

Today I have been busy preparing the house for our departure. I have poisoned the water supply, set lethal booby traps on most of the doors and windows, backed up by a 'second strike' battery of unpleasant practical jokes in every room. Last year, on our return, we found the bodies of two German students, a Norwegian au pair girl and a Birmingham artisan, all hideously disfigured by the guard dogs which must have been feeling hungry. I buried them unceremoniously under a willow tree after dark.

31 August 1975

To Scotland, where I have missed the opening of the grouse season by nearly four weeks and find there are practically no birds left. I had thought that with Parliament sitting so long the birds would be practically untouched. But the days are past when moors were trodden by fat *nouveau riche* Conservative MPs in tweeds. Now they are left to Japanese, who come with eight-barrelled automatic shotguns and never miss, or to Arabs who are even worse with their hawks and flashing scimitars and horrible oaths.

An old keeper tells me he had great difficulty preventing one Japanese from eating the nests after he had slaughtered all the grouse inside. At any rate, that's what I think he said, although to tell the truth I can scarcely understand a word the man utters. My first day on the moors I bag a brace of motorbike manufacturers from Hamamatsu and a dealer in electronic components from Toyama.

18 December 1975

For Christmas shopping in London I go by force of habit to Harrods. The toy department is still full of loud-voiced Englishwomen, all rich, all claiming to have highly intelligent six-year-olds, and all damned. But I do not see a fellow Englishman anywhere until I chance upon the Women's Underwear Department. To these unhappy people, Christmas is no more than a pretext for buying female underwear. As I pass, I hear a Major of the Household Brigade ask for some knickers with pussy fur; another man, almost certainly from the Treasury, asks in a hoarse whisper for some crotchless briefs. They all look like rats, they're all going mad, and they're all damned. To those who ask what I was doing in the Women's Underwear Department, I can only say – no, I am not planning any unseemly celebration for the end of International Women's Year. I had simply lost my way to the Food Hall.

26 December 1975

Still no newspapers, but I find I can understand practically nothing which is said on television nowadays. Today it is full of comedians with incomprehensible accents imitating other comedians I have never heard of. In desperation we turn to *The Magic Flute* sung in Swedish – a very good joke to play on the lower classes for Boxing Day. At least I can recognise a few of the tunes.

20 April 1976

In my first meeting with Jim Callaghan since his promotion I mention that I've been invited to the private dinner party at Windsor Castle before the Queen's Birthday Ball. Noticing his look of sick rage, I explain that it is only for family and personal friends: I doubt if I shall stay long for the ball itself, as I hear all sorts of riff-raff have been asked.

I did not tell him that it was my idea that he should not be asked to the dinner party. We both agreed that it was most important he should not grow too conceited after suddenly becoming prime minister. That is what happened to Grocer Heath, with disastrous results for everybody. She did not accept my alternative suggestion, that Callaghan should be asked to a separate party in the butler's pantry, where he would be given tea and sausage rolls. This might have done wonders for his image with Labour voters, but she was frightened of upsetting her butler.

21 April 1976

We are both seriously worried about Princess Margaret. Perhaps I was wrong to joke about her. The main problem appears to be that after so much discouragement of personal initiative in this country, after the attrition of incentives, comprehensive schooling etc., there may be no men left with enough heart for the job. I suggest placing an advertisement in the Personal Columns of *Private Eye*, but the Queen feels this might cheapen the monarchy. An advertisement in any other publication would plainly be out of the question. Then I have a brainwave. What about asking the Victoria and George Cross Association to Windsor? Surely, among their number we can find an unattached male who would not flinch from what has been described as the most gruelling job in Britain?

23 May 1976

To Scarborough, for the Inland Revenue Staff Federation Ball at the Royal Hotel. I often find it useful in countries like Britain where bribery is forbidden to cultivate the personal touch in my relationship with the Revenue Men and their amazingly tractable lady wives. Before the night is young, I have yards and yards of film, mostly of myself in various unconventional poses with a selection of unlikely companions. All the men here – and even some of the women – are in a great state of indignation about tax-dodgers. But I suspect that the real reason for so much of the unhappiness is that many Revenue staffers are dodging their marital obligations.

2 June 1976

There is a disturbing film on television called *The Naked Civil Servant* about an ageing, painfully ugly homosexualist called Quentin Crisp. At one exceptionally distressing moment, Crisp has his bottom examined by two army medical officers. Perhaps this is necessary, although we have been spared the sight of doctors examining Mrs Whitehouse's vagina in order to appreciate her point of view. I suppose it is very brave of Quentin Crisp to expose himself in this way. Or if, as he claims, he is an exhibitionist, then it must be very brave of the television people to let him expose himself. At any rate, I am sure lots of people are being very brave all over the place. I just wish they wouldn't. Perhaps it is time we had another world war and let them all work their bravery off somewhere else.

17 June 1976

I am growing rather worried about the *Beano*. For some time I have noticed how two of its main features, Dennis the Menace and the Bash Street Kids, seem to condone the sort of juvenile delinquency which has turned many of our most promising Comprehensive Schools into simmering cauldrons of violence. Another feature, about Wee Ben Nevis, has strong undertones of Scottish Nationalism in its untrue suggestion that Scotsmen possess superhuman strength despite their diminutive stature. It would not matter in the least if I did not happen to know from personal observation that the *Beano* is the main – often the only – reading of university students nowadays. These people, still at an impressionable age, are the country's leaders of the future.

16 October 1976

Just back from six days' recuperation in East Africa, I learn of the government's secret plans for bread rationing in December. Fortunately I still have 500 metric tons of wheat in my driers. It is the coming shoe shortage which will bite hardest. I suppose we will all have to get used to wearing the same pair of shoes more than once. Still, I expect it will teach the lower classes to vote Conservative next time around – if there ever is another time.

Idi Amin was the most charming and attentive of hosts. Every morning at breakfast he put out new buttonholes, sometimes a carnation, sometimes a rare orchid or a rose, and on one memorable occasion a *Magnolia grandiflora*; he had them flown in from New Guinea. Of an evening we accompanied each other on the lute and viola, and sang 'A Bird In A Gilded Cage', 'Love's Old Sweet Song', 'Wait Till The Sun Shines Nelly' and other golden oldies – he in a light tenor, I in my pleasing baritone.

The visit was only slightly spoilt by a succession of frantic telegrams from my editor in London, demanding that I ask the Field Marshal if he is really a mass murderer like Winston Churchill, Harold Wilson and so many other great leaders of the past. I refused to ask him this question, partly because I judged it a breach of the rules of hospitality.

4 January 1977

I can see a major crisis arising in this country from the toenail problem. Many of us workers are too fat nowadays to be able to cut our own toenails, and with the new spirit of militancy among womenfolk there may soon be trouble on that front. Few are in my happy position of employing three Filipino au pair girls for such duties. But an even graver emergency threatens over the problem of scissors. The only scissors available in shops are made of 'British steel' and fall to pieces when confronted by anything stronger than tissue paper. Retailers assure me there is no question of anybody in this country being able to afford foreign scissors. So it looks as if we shall just have to let our toenails grow. One thinks of Mao Tse-tung's Long March, and wonders how the British working class will fare when the time comes for them to start moving.

13 January 1977

There is a photograph in today's *Daily Express* of a plump, homely middle-aged woman in slacks and bedroom slippers sitting on a sofa. She is not topless or anything like that, but I find myself eyeing her appreciatively and wondering if we have not perhaps met somewhere before. Then I look at the caption and find myself reeling back in amazement: 'A relaxed Mr Heath at his home.'

14 January 1977

Only twenty days after Christmas and our guests are beginning to leave for their various employments. It has been an expensive and debilitating business keeping them drunk enough to lose when I play them at ping-pong. The season has been marred by ugly squabbles over the Stilton cheese – between those who prefer to scoop it out and those who say that the only sane or civilised approach is to slice it like Cheddar. I have no strong feelings on the matter, but this year I've noticed a sinister dogmatism and aggressiveness on the part of the slicers. Next year we had better order two Stiltons if we are to avoid bloodshed.

Or perhaps we shall have none. God knows what the future holds at a time when the overweening truculence of the workers is met by a middle class so hideously divided.

28 February 1977

The *Evening Standard* reveals that there are thirteen officials in Westminster Council with the duty of inspecting massage and sauna parlours in what is becoming the Massage Capital of the World. This is a job I might well apply for when *Private Eye* is closed down. Massage Inspectors have the power to enter any premises where they have reason to believe that massage may be occurring, or may have recently occurred, or be about to occur. It is important to keep standards high in this vital field. Massage and escort agencies between them now account for 27.4 per cent of all foreign earnings from tourism, according to figures released by the Central Statistics Office. The scandal is that no government assistance is available.

4 March 1977

I had hoped I would be asked to be best man at Nora Beloff's[14] wedding today, since I imagine it was I who supplied a large part of the bride's dowry. It makes me happy to think that the £3000 I gave her in libel damages a few years ago might have helped her find such a suitable husband as Clifford Makins, the well-known journalist.

Perhaps I had better explain myself. Like Nora, I had been a political correspondent for some years, when, tantalised by the unavailability of my luscious opposite number on the *Observer*, I decided to make a joke about her. At least, that was what I intended to do. As it turned out, whether from incompetence or overexcitement, I made an allegation about her personal life of such a foul and loathsome nature that even now I blush to the roots of my remaining hair when I think about it.

For fifty-six long summers, Nora has resisted the advances of the coarser sex. Nothing will ever be the same again. Even as I write, I imagine that Clifford Makins is exploring the unimaginable delights of her body, never sweeter than when first sampled. If I had been best man, I would have given Clifford the advice I always give bridegrooms on these occasions: take things gently at first; there's no rush. A new bride should be treated like a new car. Keep her steady on the straight, watch out for warning lights on the ignition and lubrication panels, and when you reckon she's run in, give her all you've got. Now I suppose I had better go and get drunk.

11 March 1977

To Oxford, on the promise of a night of passion with the enchanting President of the Union there, lovely foreign-born Ms Benazir Bhutto.[15] Unfortunately, I think she takes offence at a joke about the Queen of Sheba which I make in the course of the debate. Damn. I must be more careful in future.

6 May 1977

Good news for the religious revival. The clotted blood of St Januarius, the fourth-century martyr and patron saint of Naples, has liquefied again. Even more remarkable is a discovery by doctors at King's College, Denmark Hill, London. In a project financed by the World Health Organisation, they have found that an extract from the urine of Italian nuns, called Pergonal, allows infertile women to have babies without the risk of multiple births. For my own part, I never doubted the miraculous property of nuns' urine. Where the nun is Portuguese, her urine may be used in place of anti-freeze in motor cars. Make friends with a German nun, and she will show you unusual ways of polishing silver.

6 September 1977

The culture shock of finding oneself once again among hungry, dirty, dishonest Englishmen is immense.[16] Many of the beggars in the streets have open gangrenous wounds from the recent fighting; hospitals have been closed by their 'ancillary workers'; many newspapers are failing to appear or appear in garbled, incomprehensible form with the new pupil-orientated spelling. In Blackpool, the Trades Union Congress deliberates its next programme of theft, chaos and destruction in the name of Workers' Power.

But the Tooting grounds of Lambeth Borough Crematorium prove an island of tranquillity. Here, for the very reasonable fee of £13.50, dead or allegedly dead workers are taken, injected with formalin in case a spark of life survives, and then burned in a gas oven. Then their bones, teeth, etc., are put into a 'cremulator' or bone-crushing machine, the residue is scattered tastefully over municipal lawns and their names are recorded by hand in a Book of Remembrance. Where everything in Britain is breaking down, nobody does anything properly, this operation is marked by the efficiency and quiet enthusiasm of its staff. I think I will give up everything and come to work at Lambeth Crematorium. If they have no other job available for me, I will set myself the task of learning all the names in the Book of Remembrance by heart. In that way, at least someone will remember them.

1 October 1977

A terrible stench of rotting corpses hangs over the Labour Party Conference at Brighton as the national strike of undertakers and embalmers moves into its second week. Delegates pretend not to notice as they pick their way over dead bodies lying on the pavement and ogle each other with rheumy, yellow eyes. Sometimes, in quiet moments, I wonder what I am doing at this ghastly event. Perhaps it is penance for my agreeable life at other times of the year. Perhaps I need to be reassured that such dim, ugly, spiteful people really exist. Whatever brings me here, it certainly isn't sex.

At a party given by Mr Peter Parker, chairman of British Railways, this evening, men outnumber women by about thirty to one. It would not matter so much if the women were reasonably typical of their sex, but they are all either hunchbacked or hairy-legged or obviously lesbian. This is the miserable truth behind all the lurid stories the delegates will tell when they get home to their sniffing, squinny-eyed wives.

11 November 1977

Written during a power cut, in the dark and biting cold. Many of the children on the estate have been found frozen stiff in their beds. The old age pensioners in my attics are dying like flies, but all the hospitals in the neighbourhood are closed and there is nothing to be done. Actually that is not strictly true. We have had no power cuts at Combe Florey yet; when we do, I have two emergency generators in reserve. The local hospitals are still open, and in fact I had a general clear out of OAPs from all my attics two years ago. But it seems to me that it is the solemn duty of everybody employed in the communications industry at the present time to promote a hatred and dread of all the brutal, moronic union leaders who, in the name of the working class, are leading the country into destitution and slavery. At such moments in history, I think a little exaggeration is justified.

23 March 1978

For their cultural outing of the year, I take my family to a performance of *Ruddigore* at Taunton School. It is enthusiastically
performed, but Gilbert and Sullivan always make me sad,
expressing as they do the whole spirit and glory of England at
its most confident moment of history. The few entertainers nowadays who both tickle the fancy and catch the spirit of the times
– the Goodies, perhaps, or the Muppets – offer only a shadow
of their gaiety, self-mockery and technical accomplishment.

In the orchestra I see a beautiful girl playing the oboe – always
a cardinal element in Sullivan's orchestration, and a most
becoming instrument for young women to play. When I come
to power I shall encourage all Englishwomen to learn it by
making proficiency in the oboe an essential qualification for
female employment in the Civil Service, nationalised industries,
government contracts in the private sector, etc. Men will be
divided into trumpeters and fiddlers according to their natural
aptitudes and status in life.

4 June 1978

On the twenty-fifth anniversary of the Coronation one's thoughts
go back to that dismal occasion. I decided to boycott the whole
event, having taken offence over some real or imagined slight
and spent the day in Weston-Super-Mare with a boy called Green-
Armitage. All moral inhibitions and legal restraints were cast
aside in Weston-Super-Mare on that day. Old people in deckchairs
were throwing their false teeth around and squirting each other
with Pepsi-Cola. I was caught peeing against a wall by a policeman.

'That's against the law,' he said.

'No it isn't, Offisher,' I wittily replied. 'Itsh against the wall.'

The next Coronation will be a complete shambles, of course.
That is something we can all look forward to, at any rate.

3 August 1979

Strange as it may seem, in all the 1500 years it has been running, I have never actually heard *Desert Island Discs* so I suppose I should not write about it, but if I were cast on a desert island I think I would adopt the Ayatollah Khomeini's rule and ban all music. Music, he has explained, 'stupefies persons listening to it and makes their brains inactive and frivolous'. So much of what the Ayatollah says is obviously sensible and good that it is a crying shame that he has to shoot everybody in sight to prove his point. As it is, he reduces the whole Koranic philosophy and the ancient religion of Islam to another load of bloodthirsty rubbish, like revolutionary socialism or comprehensive education.

29 December 1979

A week after the celebrations of Joseph Stalin's centenary, and Taunton is only beginning to return to normal. Late revellers pick their way carefully around the ninety-foot statue of the Grand Old Man specially erected in Vivary Park. Discarded school uniforms and underwear are all that remain where the Somerset schools held a combined People's Opera and Theatre Workshop in thanksgiving for the Comprehensive Idea, sponsored by the Arts Council. No doubt it is all in a good cause, but excess always nauseates me. I think I will go back to London.

3 February 1980

Cruising down the Nile, past palm trees, temples and palaces in the hot bright sunshine of the Egyptian winter, I find myself wondering why anyone stays in England at this time of year. Perhaps they are mad, like St Simeon Stylites who sat on a fifty-foot-high column in the Western Desert for thirty years, preaching about the dual nature of Christ to anyone who came near him. Or perhaps they are like the desert Arabs who actually choose to live where there is no food, no water, no shade and nothing whatever to do out of some perverse, atavistic sense of propriety.

Our party is composed of such nice, sensible Englishmen and women as one only meets nowadays on a Nile cruise – a West Country baronet and his eccentric wife, two professors of medicine, a retired radiologist and some elderly managing directors. Their views about everything are eminently sound. As servants scamper around with drinks, or to beg the favour of being allowed to polish our shoes, we decide that what has gone wrong with England is the Welfare State. The modern Englishman has lost his sense of service, and the only sensible thing to do is to ignore him.

5 February 1980

There were more modern Englishmen in the bar of the Winter Palace Hotel, Luxor – bearded, foul-mouthed, dirty and drunk. I pretended to be a German professor of Egyptology. Today in Aswan, I hear of the ruined sixth-century monastery of St Simeon, less than an hour's camel ride across the desert, and wonder whether this was the spot where the saint sat on his column for thirty years. The more I see of the English working class, the more I understand his behaviour.

I find a small party to go with me, but there is no sign of a column in the ruined monastery, which has been systematically looted and desecrated by Bedouins for the past 800 years. Belatedly, I remember that St Simeon Stylites lived in Syria, near Aleppo, and not in Upper Egypt. On the return journey my camel bolts for no apparent reason and throws me off – a ridiculous and very painful incident. But I still think that St Simeon may have had the right answer to our exciting new proletarian culture. When I come to power I shall make him the Patron Saint of England in place of St George, who probably never existed.

23 April 1980

Nearly all my friends seem to be going to Moscow to sneer at the sweaty louts who claim to be representing Britain at the Olympic Games, but I have no curiosity to see that accursed country or meet its unpleasant, lying inhabitants. We can perfectly well persecute the half-witted 'British' athletes on their return; for the present we must just hope they all have heart attacks or foul themselves publicly in the stadium.

Possibly my friends hope to be seduced by beautiful KGB agents, but I could tell them that these Russian girls are hideously self-conscious in bed – no doubt because they know they are being photographed from the moment they remove their *mifjik*s. I think I will go to Yugoslavia to celebrate the death of Tito. With a bit of luck, by waving a Press Card, I will be able to get myself into the death chamber and settle for all time the mystery of whether this odious tyrant was, in fact, a woman all along. My late father claimed to have seen her once during the war breastfeeding a seal pup on the Island of Vis. 'There's nowt so queer as folk,' he remarked in his broad Lancashire accent.

11 May 1980

On the first night of my assignment in Japan as Lord Gnome's special emissary to discover whether or not the Japanese have pubic hair, I find myself in a bar with Mr Murray Sayle, the Oriental philosopher and sage. He argues that the question cannot be approached empirically but must be studied within the context of Japanese social conditions and economic history.

The best person for me to consult, he says, would be the Emperor of Japan, who has been around in Tokyo longer than anyone else and has probably seen a thing or two in his time.

There are four of us in the bar – myself, Sayle, his beautiful young English wife and their gifted son, Alexander. We have one glass of beer each – possibly, Alexander has a second – and the bill is 36,000 yen, or about £72. Luckily, Lord Gnome has guaranteed my expenses, so I pay up merrily. I think I'm really on the track of my enquiry now. What old Bandylegs does not know about the Japanese simply isn't worth knowing.

12 May 1980

A busy morning on the telephone trying to arrange my meeting with Hirohito. I tell a delightful secretary at the Imperial Palace that I wish to discuss the current Japanese situation in the context of social conditions and economic history; also that I am a noted expert on Gilbert and Sullivan and can, if His Highness wishes, whistle several arias from *The Mikado*, including 'A Wandering Minstrel I' and 'Tit Willow'. Anyone would think I was asking to marry his sister.

The bedside table of my room in the new Otani Hotel, Tokyo, is like the cockpit of a Concorde airliner with innumerable buttons, dials and flashing lights. Eventually, a flashing light on the control panel informs me of a message from the Imperial Palace, that the Emperor will be pleased to receive me to tea on Thursday afternoon. Suddenly I'm struck by an appalling thought. Perhaps any sparseness of body hair among the adult Japanese is something to do with the two atom bombs dropped on Hiroshima and Nagasaki. If so, it would be dreadfully tactless to ask the Emperor to explain the phenomenon. Tomorrow I will go to Nagasaki and make enquiries.

13 May 1980

In the Peace Park now situated at the epicentre of the atom bomb explosion in Nagasaki, there stands a forty-foot black stone column. At the bottom of it, I find an ugly, mad American woman of uncertain age sitting alone on the ground and weeping. Foolishly, I ask her why. She replies that she feels badly about the atom bomb but cannot explain this to the Japanese, being unable to talk their language. When she tries to embrace them, she says, they become embarrassed.

I explain to her the reason for this, that it is widely believed among the Japanese that all Westerners have VD. She starts weeping again, saying she does not want or expect sexual intercourse, merely to make some symbolic gesture of peace. I advise her to take a bath.

This vile rumour about Westerners is put around by Japanese men who suspect we are after their lovely almond-eyed womenfolk. In this matter, of course, they are quite right, but it does not make my enquiries any easier. Whenever I ask Japanese women the vital question they cover their faces with their hands and laugh delightfully. This may be out of embarrassment or it may be because, living on a diet of raw fish, they have a slight breath problem. All the girls in the brothels, it appears, are Irish. One has no curiosity about their secret parts. Japanese women, by contrast, are highly circumspect in their behaviour. Perhaps I will have to marry one to uncover her secret.

2 July 1980

The morning is spent sitting for my portrait by Gerald Scarfe, the cartoonist. This may seem a curious thing to do, but I am persuaded that it is one's duty to leave posterity such a memorial, showing warts and all. Scarfe's problem is one which has confronted all the caricaturists who have ever faced the task of making something ugly or grotesque out of my bland, symmetrical features:

there are simply no warts to show. Many have been driven to suicide, and Mark Boxer, sent by the small but resourceful Dame Harold Evans to mock me, had to be led away after quietly, inanely, swallowing mothballs for a week.

As I watch Scarfe wrestling with the problem of finding ugliness where there is only refinement, stupidity out of high intelligence, spite out of good humour, affectation out of manliness, a strange transformation comes over him. First, I notice a wild, frustrated look in his eyes, then his lip begins to curl like a cabbage leaf, ending up as a sort of jam-and-chocolate swiss roll; next his tongue elongates like a snake until it lies ten feet long, red and glistening, on my carpet. His eyes pop out on curious antennae and his penis . . . but then, perhaps I had better not say what happens to his penis, as this is a family magazine read by many impressionable young people.

7 September 1980

Sad to be leaving France,[17] although I noticed on this visit that people are beginning to talk about the servant problem. Soon the French will be reduced to our own pitiful condition, unable to afford cauliflower leaves and fighting for caterpillars. Everyone in Britain looks miserable, but I expect this is something to do with the food. In France, the President of the Republic takes dinner once a month with typical working families who write in and ask him. The idea is to show how unsnobbish he is and to learn what ordinary people are thinking.

It would be quite impossible in this country. Even if the food was not too disgusting to contemplate, the British lower classes seldom think of anything. They are usually too mean to invite people in for meals and in any case they don't eat dinner, only some sort of snack in front of the television set at teatime. They practically never talk except to ask someone to pass the sugar, or brown sauce, or shut his trap because they can't hear the telly. I know all this because I have studied the brutes. When

I come to power all television stations will be closed down between eight and ten thirty every evening to allow them time for a decent meal.

30 January 1981

A terrible night spent worrying about the poor and unemployed. Their position is now so desperate that the Salvation Army has set up a soup kitchen in Mexborough, Yorkshire (where over 3000 of the 17,000 population are out of work) to feed the starving. In ninety minutes they served only one person. The others, I suspect, were already too weak to make their way to the soup kitchen. Or they might have felt it was the Salvation Army's job to bring the soup round to them. What is urgently needed is a Meals On Wheels to every household in the country. If people refuse to accept the soup, or if they are out, it should be poured through their letterboxes.

6 July 1981

A weekend of violence at Combe Florey,[18] sparked off by the Church fête on Saturday in the grounds of Combe Florey House, leaves a bruised and bewildered populace wondering where we have all gone wrong. Theft and looting – mainly by crazed nonagenarian whites – left two milk bottles broken beyond hope of repair, cakes from the cake stall seriously nibbled, and one book from my own stall of review copies badly foxed. Needless to say, the police were quite unable to contain the violence, which is thought to be non-racial in origin. When I suggested to PC Barnes, our village policeman, that he use CS gas or even plastic bullets against a particularly quarrelsome group of old dears around the china stall, he revealed that he had not brought them with him.

Various conclusions can be drawn from all this. In the first place, geriatric terrorism must be recognised for what it is – the unacceptable face of the Welfare State. This may mean arming the police and reversing the government's entire economic policy. Next, the government must provide play schools for elderly folk where they can work off their aggressive instincts on each other. Massive government spending may be necessary. The overriding question must be whether we, as a nation, can afford a repetition of events at Combe Florey on Bloody Saturday.

15 May 1982

Street violence of a kind familiar to London and Liverpool has at last broken out in Combe Florey, where an old age pensioner in the village reports that her cat has been shot by an air rifle. A nice Taunton CID man who calls at the house for permission to interrogate some of my tenants admits the police are baffled. A check is being made on all registered aliens but I'm afraid we may need to look into our own hearts and into the nature of our own community for the answer to this one.

Whether do-good schoolteachers are to blame for it, as most sensible people seem to think, or unemployment, as left-wing extremists maintain, or the decline and collapse of organised religion, as Prince Philip avers, this epidemic of mindless violence has now reached a point where the traditional forces of law and order can no longer cope. With Charles Bronson's example in mind, I am organising a task force of vigilantes who will patrol the village streets from sundown to sunrise, disguised as cats, but with shotguns, crossbows and special Worlock cat-to-person missiles slung under their bellies. First we will need about 500 cat skins, but they should be easy to organise. There is a New Spirit abroad in the land, the spirit of Death Wish.[19] Let the world's Galtieris ignore it at their peril.

16 May 1982

Been laughing all morning at the news from Liverpool, where striking NUPE workers insist on inspecting all patients to decide if they are ill enough to be operated on. The thought of Liverpudlians showing their varicose veins, piles and diseased livers to the ward cleaners and dustbin executive disposal operatives for approval somehow tickles me. This is what a People's Health Service should be all about. As part of their plan to win the next general election, Labour hope to introduce the same system into the newspaper industry, so that lift boys, electricians and tea persons will have to pass anything before it is printed.

15 June 1982

To Bilbao to join the carnival atmosphere.[20] Armies of drunken red-faced Englishmen stampede up and down the esplanade blowing whistles and overturning tables. Locals run in terror as tattooed, shirtless Britons in Union Jack hats shout witty insults and throw bottles at them. I applaud politely as a Liverpool railwayman, on a flexible roster, draws a knife and starts stabbing one of his companions who is already unconscious on the ground.

Later, I point this man out to the police. They assure me he will suffer the garrotte, a peculiarly Spanish method of execution involving a metal band which tightens slowly, driving a nail into the cervical vertebrae. Normally I am opposed to capital punishment and am even prepared to be quite pompous about it but on this occasion – I don't know – I suppose it must be something to do with the holiday atmosphere.

2 July 1982

Nearly 2000 readers have written to ask my advice on whether or not Prince William of Wales should be circumcised. It is not an easy question to answer, and I have the impression that much more may hang on this little point than anyone realises. It all depends on what sort of a monarchy people want. Uncircumcised males generally tend to the sciences rather than to the Arts. Their terror at being exposed makes them cowardly and unreliable in a tight corner, but they are sometimes good at games like ping-pong and Monopoly. For all I know there may be sound reasons for leaving the little chap alone. I feel it should be made the subject of a national plebiscite, like the Common Market referendum. We have to think of something to keep us amused now the Falklands are over.

30 July 1982

Aude, France
For a week I have done no work at all, and marvel at the stamina of the English, who somehow manage to do none all their lives. After a few days, I found myself in a state of nervous exhaustion and moral collapse.

5 January 1983

Two letters in the post cause intense irritation. The first is from the Central London branch of the National Union of Journalists, announcing it has increased my subscription to £88 a year. These greedy, self-important shits know they can demand any sum they choose in blackmail, since membership of the Union is now compulsory. The second is a begging letter from Christ Church, Oxford, asking if I will contribute to a hideous new quad they are planning to build in St Aldate's so that their new Comprehensive intake and lower-class research students can be accommodated in the comfort they expect.

I expect all old Christ Church men will treat this appeal with the contempt it deserves. If I could pay them not to build the new quad – and to pull down the terrible Comprehensive Wing they built in Blue Boar Lane ten years ago – I would happily do so. One problem with the lower classes, as they emerge from centuries of richly deserved obscurity, is that they are greedy. Another problem, of course, is that they are ugly, boring, humourless and desperately conceited. Perhaps when they have built the new St Aldate's quad I'll go and set fire to it and see if I can roast a few.

16 May 1983

A peasant from the Sichuan province of China has just been imprisoned for two years for killing and eating a giant panda. It is a sad thought that I who have eaten squirrels in Somerset, crocodile meat in Cuba, dogs in the Philippines, raw horse in Japan, toads in Egypt and snakes in Northern Thailand may never eat a giant panda, unless this abominable curse of socialism can be driven from the earth.

5 September 1983

Today brings even worse news on the sexist front. A man who has spent two and a half years in jail for a rape he did not commit, after being described as a 'Beast' by a judge and being beaten up by fellow prisoners in jail, has received compensation from the Home Office. Has the country gone mad? Men are *always* guilty of rape, just as every woman is by definition a rape victim. The existence of the male sex is an act of violence against women. If any men are ever to be let out of prison, it is the women who should receive compensation.

13 October 1983

At the Young Conservatives Ball in the Winter Gardens in Blackpool I find myself unexpectedly closeted with Margaret Thatcher, whom I have not seen since she came to a *Private Eye* lunch over ten years ago. She obviously expects me to ask her to dance, but it would be as much as my reputation in Fleet Street is worth to be seen dancing with her so I make my excuses, saying I have a particularly violent attack of AIDS. Also, I was rather hoping to find someone younger and juicier, although it might be rude to say so.

9 March 1984

Dr Germaine Greer has a beautiful face, a pretty wit and a warm heart, but she will always remain a mystery to me. I doubt if I will ever get underneath the dough to the jam at the centre. When in *Sex and Destiny* (Secker & Warburg) she describes the male attitude to sex as 'squirting jam into a doughnut' she is in fact quoting some foreigner who made the observation first.

What neither of them seems to realise is that the jam is not put into doughnuts in this way. You lay your dough flat, put a teaspoon of jam in the middle then wrap it round the jam before deep frying. Germaine may be the greatest expert in the world on the politics of human fertility, but she knows nothing about making doughnuts. I wonder if this explains why she is still unmarried – and whether, in fact, she really understands about how babies are made.

15 May 1984

The moment John Betjeman died the sun went in and the heavens opened. Like so many other Englishmen at this time of desolation, nursing their private grief, I wander around my rainswept acres killing adders. I do not know whether the plague of adders which has visited Somerset has anything to do with the death of our greatest son. Perhaps we are being punished for not having cherished him enough. Swarms of holidaymakers have already died and there is a conspiracy among the local authorities to hush the matter up.

Tonight we will build a hecatomb in honour of the poet, burning the corpses of all the holidaymakers who have died. The most important thing is to avoid a panic. Nothing must stop all these dear people from the Midlands and Northern England from coming down in their caravans to avail themselves of our toilet facilities. Most of them, I fear, are too unintelligent to notice whether they are alive or dead. When a great nobleman dies we are all diminished. But with the death of Betjeman even the fields and churches of Somerset seem to have shrunk.

1 June 1985

The great joy of the London Docklands Development may be that no-one will ever see it. A stretch of the desolate East End is being given over to whatever monstrosities the archi-tects can devise – vast concrete prisons rising from a windswept cemented plain decorated with notices and litter bins. It might be specially designed as a recreation area for vandals in search of a telephone box, sex maniacs in search of a public lava-tory. But it is a part of London where I have never been and I can't honestly think of any reason why I should ever wish to go there. If architects could be persuaded to practise their filthy trade only in places like the Isle of Dogs, then there might be some hope for the bit of England that survives. Another good policy to adopt towards architects is, if you meet anyone in a pub or at a party who says he is an architect, punch him in the face.

Chapter Eight
In the Lion's Den

Every journalist who writes for more than one newspaper carries in his mind at the time of writing a certain image of the reader he is addressing. My image of the *New Statesman* reader was that of a taut, slightly embittered female schoolteacher, possibly in Coventry but certainly in one of the less well favoured areas of the country, struggling valiantly against the inherited and environmental disabilities of her charges to preserve some quasi-theoretical hope in the socialist future. She was a convinced atheist and a convinced progressive in sexual matters, although her own experiences in that field had seldom been encouraging. In foreign affairs she was endlessly progressive but in home affairs subject to strange disciplinarian urges which might suddenly demand unspeakable punishments, not only for racists, rapists and male chauvinists, but also for litter louts, cigarette smokers and males generally. She approved of homosexuality and unmarried mothers, disapproved of drink and drugs, approved of education, disapproved of anyone excelling in it, approved, rather nervously, of the working class in most of its manifestations, except football hooliganism, and represented, in fact, the only surviving bastion of middle-class values. It was to this person – no doubt a figment – that I addressed myself and carried on a relationship which lasted thirty months. Our relationship was never an easy one, and I think she suspected that my real affections lay elsewhere, but it survived for thirty months nevertheless – sometimes flirtatious and teasing, sometimes stern and admonitory, occasionally quite ugly and sarcastic. I would like to think that we both learned something by the experience.[1]

For most of his admirers, who devoured his weekly missives in conservative journals like the *Spectator*, Waugh's strange sojourn as a *New Statesman* columnist constitutes a forgotten chapter in his career. And no wonder. This Fabian periodical was an unusual forum for his anti-proletarian polemic, especially in the early seventies, when even the Tories usually sought to appease the unions, rather than daring to confront them. So when the *New Statesman*'s editor, Anthony Howard, asked him to become a columnist, Waugh accepted with some misgivings. 'Although the readership of the *New Statesman* in those days undoubtedly included all that was brightest and best in the country,' he reflected, 'it also included a solid mass of deeply serious, deeply committed Labour supporters with very little sense of humour, who might well be deeply shocked by his choice of a frivolous, deeply uncommitted columnist of pronounced anti-socialist views.'[2]

Waugh was right to be wary. 'If many were puzzled by Mr Howard's choice, a few were also enraged by it, and it says much for his determination and resolve that he continued to print these pieces,' he recalled. 'In that time, the circulation of the *New Statesman* continued its relentless decline, and it must have been unnerving, to say the least, to receive a regular crop of letters threatening to cancel long-standing subscriptions.'[3] Yet the political climate of impending doom, with its strikes, power cuts and three-day weeks, gave him a subject, and an attitude, inspiring some of his finest writing. While his left-wing colleagues cast around for earnest solutions to the nation's ills, Waugh approached the crisis with cheerful fatalism, happy in his role as the man who fiddled while Rome burned.

Yet this enjoyable interlude in the lion's den might easily have been cut short, depriving *New Statesman* readers of gems like 'Thoughts on the Libel Law and Death of a Goldfish'. 'My

New Year's Resolution is to work less hard, so I have sacked the *New Statesman*,' wrote Waugh in his *Private Eye* Diary, on New Year's Eve 1974. 'Although the official reason for this is Howard's stinginess in refusing to raise his fees after eighteen months of loyal and devoted work from me, the real reason may be that I have been paying too much income tax. This can only encourage the lower classes to batten off the productive elements still further.'[4]

Fortunately, he was persuaded to continue for another year. 'A telephone call from nice young Tony Howard of the *New Statesman*, vastly increasing his offer,' wrote Waugh, in his diary the following Sunday. 'After all, I have decided that everybody must be prepared to roll up our sleeves and work a little harder for the national emergency.'[5]

Despite the threats of its subscribers, Waugh wrote for the *New Statesman* for more than two years, first fortnightly and then weekly, turning out nearly a hundred columns in the process, and this unlikely alliance produced some of his finest (yet least familiar) writing. Most of Waugh's opinions must have been an anathema to most *New Statesman* readers[6], but writing against the grain suited him. It gave him something to tug against.

*

OF COMFORT NO MAN SPEAK
(*New Statesman*, 15 February 1974)

Walking down Greek Street last week I saw a dead rat in the gutter. It seemed a supernatural benediction on all my efforts to spread alarm and despondency over lunch, a long and prodigiously expensive affair taken up with trying to alert my companion to the gravity of the situation. I told her how workers in London and the main industrial centres would be scratching each other's eyes out in the dark over a single cauliflower leaf; how they would soon take to cannibalism. She replied with wistful, fatuous noises about the ideal socialist society. The dead rat shimmered slightly where it lay, either the result of noxious gases rising from its body or of my own senses being slightly stupefied by food and drink. It reminded me that I had forgotten another element in the scenario – the bit about untreated sewage flooding the streets of London, closely followed by the Black Death.

As a child of the war, my earliest years were haunted by an image of the good old days when sweets were unrationed and bananas freely available. Occasionally, one glimpsed advertisements in railway carriages of delights one had never known – six bottles of differently coloured cordials with stone tops struck a particular chord, I remember. But one only half believed in the existence of the good old days. Normality was a state of constant shortage, rationing and queues, with accepted areas of privation – the cold in winter, filthy food all the year round and occasional brutality both from and towards one's fellows. The experience of National Service, for most of my generation, was little more than a return to normality. Since leaving the army, life has been an incredible stroke of luck, a delirious, wickedly enjoyable skive which miraculously seems to have lasted for fifteen whole years.

Edward Gibbon,[7] choosing a period in the history of the world where the condition of the human race was most happy and prosperous, fixed it between the death of Domitian and accession of Commodus, AD 96–180. I should choose a shorter period, between the general election of 1959 and 1974 in England. One never supposed that these golden years could last. Those with a more highly developed social conscience or tidier minds than my own felt it wrong that they should last, although I could never quite see the moral force of this argument. The great election refrain of 1959 – 'You've never had it so good' – caught the national mood as a sober statement of fact rather than a sectional appeal. None of us had ever had it so good and a few of us – myself, for example – were getting it even better than others, which only increased our enjoyment by adding a sense of precariousness.

A worrying aspect of the present situation is the extent to which nobody seems aware of the privations ahead. A few have sensibly started hoarding sugar, coffee, nails, lavatory paper, cartridges, jam jars, linen sheets and olive oil, but all that anyone has been told is that Mr Heath rather doubts whether we can continue to rely on the annual increase in our living standards to which we have become accustomed. Nobody has told us that our living standards are going to sink like a stone, or that there is nothing whatever we can do about it. It may have needed some of Mr Heath's particular genius for making wrong decisions and sticking to them for Britain to confront the oil crisis with a £2500 million deficit, but it can scarcely make any difference now whether we elect a Conservative or Labour government, whether we join the revolution or combine to oppose it. Redistribution can scarcely provide the answer at a time when, tee-hee-hee, there will be nothing left to redistribute.

For myself, I have insufficient confidence in the accuracy of my own analysis of the situation to start hoarding in a big way, even if I had the spare cash. My personal experience of hoarding is that one has always consumed the hoard within days of buying it. On the other hand, I am prepared to take quite sporting bets, payable in potatoes or rolls of lavatory paper, that our parliamentary system will have collapsed by the end of the year. I don't think it can long survive the collapse of the currency, and I don't think that even by mortgaging the North Sea oil fields the new government will be able to prop it up for more than six months. Any takers?

My purpose in trying to spread as much alarm and despondency as I can is twofold. In the first place, it is a service to the cause of historical truth, in the second to the cause of entertainment. I have often been irritated by those who think they will welcome the arrival of civil breakdown and revolution, lacking the imagination to see what it will really be like. Of course it is quite possible that a few schoolchildren and bored housewives welcomed the arrival of the Black Death in 1347. My only point is that they were wrong. Nothing which can possibly be going to happen will make life any better for workers, middle class or rich, and it is as well that everybody should know it. In the second place these last few weeks before the election are in fact the last we shall see of the golden age. Although a dramatic decline in living standards is not the same thing as the end of the world, it would be a dreadful shame if this historic moment were allowed to pass without any celebration of its passing.

A former Labour minister I happened to meet on Paddington Underground station last week remarked that the present crisis was different from any crisis which had preceded it for the one reason that he could think of absolutely no solution, no advice to give anyone, no idea of what he would do himself if he were prime minister. I am less modest. Anybody with any money left should spend it quickly; the only solution for the educated man is to retire into the room where he keeps his books and cultivate his soul. If I were prime minister, or aspiring to be prime minister, I should practise my swimming against the day I was thrown into the Thames; but if I were merely the sort of person who likes to take an intelligent interest in the management of his fellow citizens I should accept that there is no solution, nothing to be done, and I had quite simply been mistaken to take such an interest in the first place.

DEATH OF A GOLDFISH
(*New Statesman*, 7 February 1975)

Last week my pet goldfish was found floating upright in her tank. Marigold had shown no sign of illness the night before and ate her chopped mosquito larvae without complaint. No noise escaped from the kitchen where she slept and no ripple was left on the surface of the water to mark any death struggle. She was a blameless fish and died as she had lived, giving a minimum of trouble.

America, I have been told by a friend, is stuffed with books called *How to Cope With Your Grief Reactions* and titles in a similar vein. The stages of grief are carefully listed, with hints about how to progress through them in an approved and healthy way: first, bereavement is met by a refusal to accept it; then by a bitter wish that it had not happened; then extravagant sorrow and self-pity, possibly touched with guilt. Finally, there comes a settled acceptance, when the bereaved person is ready to return to society free of the emotional instability which might, uncorrected, lead him to anti-social attitudes and behaviour.

I find myself stuck in the guilt stage. We discussed raising a monument over Marigold's grave, but this seemed an unworthy way of coping with our grief reactions. Can storied urn or animated bust back to its mansion call the fleeting breath? Instead we buried her with minimum fuss – no useless coffin enclosed her breast – but this, too, seemed somehow ratlike and furtive. She lay like a warrior taking her rest with her golden scales around her, but her dignity rebuked us. There was no explicit reproach in her eye as we steadfastly gazed on the face that was dead and we bitterly thought of the morrow. The guilt was in our own hearts.

For more than six years that goldfish had lived with us and shared our fortunes, ever since my wife had won her by throwing hoops at the Mop Fair in Marlborough, Wiltshire. In all that time I never introduced Marigold to another goldfish. Probably, in the course of the six and a half years she spent swimming backwards and forwards in her tank, she lost any memory that other fishes existed. It is true that she always had plenty to eat and was kept cold and wet in well-ventilated conditions. Her water was changed and her tank decorated with semi-precious stones – amethystine, quartz, fool's gold, agate and chalcedony. But she never knew the meaning of companionship, laughter and the love of friends – or, indeed, the pleasures of sex.

Sex. Beyond one cursory glance at where I imagined her private parts would be if she had any (she did not appear to) I never made any serious attempt to discover whether Marigold was a male or a female goldfish. I never spared a thought about how she coped with her libido, if she had any. Quite possibly, she never learned about such things, never associated any strange bodily urges which may have visited her with anything but indigestion. Do female goldfish have monthly troubles? Do lonely male goldfish experience nocturnal emissions and if so, how do they distinguish wet dreams from any other type of dreams in the encircling wetness?

Stricken by remorse after her death, I have taken to reading all I can find in the house on the subject of goldfish. It would have been quite easy, I learn, to decide whether she was male or female. Spawning occurs in spring and as the season approaches the female's colours grow brighter while the male may develop pinhead-sized tubercles (or shag spots) on his gills.

This only makes me feel guiltier. The thought of Marigold blushing brightly in her prettiest colours every spring (or growing fine, manly tubercles on his gills, as the case may be) strikes me as unbearably poignant in light of the fact that nobody ever noticed:

> Full many a flower is born to blush unseen
> And waste its sweetness on the desert air.[8]

I know, I know. It is all very beautiful and poetic. But I do feel we might have *looked*.

It may be possible to live a full and satisfactory life without any experience of sex. Many monks and nuns achieve it and quite a few secular priests, I dare say, but they at least have the consolation that they are storing up riches in Heaven. A hairy young monk at the establishment where I received my education (it did not prepare me to look after goldfishes properly) used to invite his Religious Instruction class to think of Heaven as a perpetual experience of sexual intercourse. Being a callow fifteen-year-old I took him at his word. Then I thought I understood why that pungent monk was so unswerving in his fidelity to the vows of poverty, chastity and obedience. It is only as I get older that I am less tempted by the thought of perpetual intercourse, more by Sydney Smith's⁹ notion of eating *pâté de foie gras* to the sound of trumpets. Perhaps this preference is something to do with the air at Combe Florey, where Sydney Smith lived 135 years before me.

But even if Combe Florey water has the same properties, there is no reason to suppose that goldfish like *pâté de foie gras* and every reason to think they detest the sound of trumpets. A thoughtless guest once put Marigold on an organ in my house and then played 'Faith of Our Fathers' simultaneously on the dulcet, diapason, sub-bass and vox humana. Her resulting agitation marked only the second dramatic event in her life, the first being when the cat decided to try his luck at gaff-hook fishing about a year before. On that occasion – how the guilty memories torment me now – I tended to take the cat's side. What cat's averse to fish, I argued, and what pleasures could possibly await Marigold in the years ahead which would compare with the cat's pleasure in eating her?

Next I begin to reflect that Marigold was almost certainly so stupid that she never even noticed when she died, like certain chickens I have seen senselessly trying to fly after their heads have been cut off. If an animal is too stupid even to notice whether it is alive or dead there can be no sense in shedding intelligent human tears for it. Why, for that matter, should one goldfish occupy so much valuable space in a serious weekly magazine when hundreds of thousands of goldfish die every week unwept, un-honoured and unsung?

But then I think of the tender sight of her little corpse. It would have been an act of unspeakable callousness to recycle that innocent thing into cat protein. Like the Tomb of the Unknown Soldier there must always be privileged exceptions from which everyone else can draw comfort and inspiration. Now I feel I have passed through all the stages of my grief reaction and am ready to return to normal society.

LADYBIRD, LADYBIRD, FLY AWAY HOME
(*New Statesman*, 12 December 1975)

Whatever else may be said about 1975, it has been a wonderful year for ladybirds. All summer, it seems to me, I have been pulling these lovely pop art creatures out of my hair, rescuing them from my drinks or organising ladybird derbies over the papers on my desk as I sit pondering the mighty issues of the moment. At other times, I can only sit and marvel at the beauty and delicacy of the little beasts. In the Middle Ages they were held sacred to the Virgin Mary. The nurse in *Romeo & Juliet* uses them obscurely but I think as a term of endearment. The nursery rhyme 'Ladybird, ladybird, fly away home, Your house is on fire, your children all gone,' was apparently sung by hop pickers in Kent when they burned the hop bines after harvest. At one time ladybirds were prescribed and eaten in large numbers as a cure for measles. There is much to be learned from ladybirds and many interesting thoughts to be had on the subject, but what I concluded from seeing about forty of them marching over the unanswered letters and unopened bills on my desk last week was that I needed a part-time secretary.

In two weeks of mild illness during which I could just finish essential work before retiring with a packet of aspirins, a glass of whisky and a loud groan to the nearest armchair, I find I have accumulated nearly half a hundredweight of unanswered letters, unopened bills, packets and parcels of books. The presence of forty odd ladybirds crawling over this pile seemed to add a note of hopelessness and decay calling for decisive action.

In my thirty-six years of not employing a secretary I have always tended to despise people with secretaries as ostentatious, self-important loafers. In protest, I have never felt any moral obligation to answer a letter if it was typed and sometimes this prejudice broke out in more dynamic form, when I burned all typed letters before opening them and vowed I would have nothing more to do with such people. But those cohorts of ladybirds, busy like mice among the ruins of Miss Havisham's wedding feast, finally persuaded me that I was being affected and silly, that this sort of attitude would eventually involve more inconvenience and impoverishment than it would avoid.

So I put two advertisements for a part-time secretary in the *West Somerset Free Press* and the *Somerset County Gazette*. Within a few hours I received thirty-three applications for the job, which is very badly paid at a pound an hour, with no allowance for petrol or time getting here, and a maximum of six hours' work a week. It soon appeared that every female in west Somerset wanted the job.

Well, nearly every female. In these last days before the Sex Discrimination Act comes into operation, two men who applied were given very short shrift. But if ever, in an idle moment, I had thought the job might appeal to some long-legged, doe-eyed school leaver of nineteen, eighteen, seventeen or even – let's be realistic – sixteen, my hopes were disappointed. The problem of unemployed school leavers is indeed a terrible one, and we must all do what we can for them, but you can only take the horse to water, you can't make it drink. All my applicants were married women with children and the average age, I should have thought, was about forty-five.

Then came the interviews. I had never interviewed anyone for a job before and had never in fact been forced to think of myself as an employer, a hiring and firing member of the boss class. Although I myself had been interviewed, hired and fired more times than I could possibly remember, this was my first excursion into the boss role and the boss mentality, with its assurance of superiority, its hunger to exploit others and its horrible flickers of the power urge.

Obviously, I would not be telling this story if I thought it reflected to my discredit or subtracted from the very high opinion in which I hope to be held. After I had seen five of the sixteen women I eventually interviewed, I found myself telling the rest that it didn't really matter what they said or how many skills they had as I was almost certainly going to draw the winner's name from a hat. Face to face with so many strange women, some of them old enough to be my mother, all desperately wanting a job which was only on offer because I had been upset by some ladybirds, I was visited by atrocious feelings of unworthiness: 'Judge not that ye be not judged.'

By no means all the applicants were pleased by my Solomon-like solution. A few made the noises one has come to expect from the wrong sort of labourer in the vineyard: in that case, they said, why did I ask them for an interview? It seemed fairer, I said vaguely, not daring to give my real, imponderably priggish reasons. Perhaps this sort of thing is what is wrong with Britain. Drawing a name out of a hat obviously isn't the most efficient way of choosing a secretary. Some would say it is not the most just, either, being unfair to whichever applicant had greatest skill or had cultivated her talents most assiduously. Others might argue that it was old-fashioned, reactionary and escapist, and it is only this grouping, I think, that I would seriously dispute.

It is true that there is an enormous and regrettable enthusiasm among educated people nowadays for making decisions and exerting power, but I do not think there is any complementary enthusiasm among the less well educated for implementing those decisions or deferring to power. This makes life pleasanter for those who have no power urge, although, as I often remark, those who do suffer from it simply can't accept that others don't. In conversation with a friend recently I happened to remark that I thought the *Sunday Times* badly needed a new literary editor and my friend immediately supposed that I was after the job. Nothing could persuade him that a man who is a writer by trade would not prefer to be an editor.

My only claim, as a man with an underdeveloped power urge, is that I am in the historical vanguard. Eventually, the most power mad of my contemporaries must accept that there is no joy in giving orders or making decisions affecting other people if the other people pay no attention to them. We have passed through the Age of Efficiency, seen its advantages and disadvantages, and come out on the other side. Before long, I hope, this pleasure in exerting power will seem as incomprehensible and as disgusting to the normal, well-adjusted citizen as the pleasure of the Roman mob in watching fellow human beings torn to pieces by lions seems now. Obviously, many of those Roman plebeians came from very poor backgrounds and didn't have our advantages in life, but they certainly used to enjoy that sort of thing. It is just a question of waiting for people to grow out of it. As a boy, I once did something so disgusting to a ladybird that I can't even bring myself to describe it now.

Chapter Nine
Another Voice

People complain that the vulgar newspapers place undue
emphasis on sex and crime, but sex and crime are pretty
well the only things which happen in urban society. I am
not even sure how much sex really occurs nowadays, which
may explain its news value.[1]

In 1975 the *Spectator* changed hands (again) and the new owner,
Henry Keswick, one of Waugh's old schoolmates, appointed
Alexander Chancellor as his new editor. Chancellor was a friend
of Waugh's sister, Margaret, but Waugh knew him only slightly.[2]
Indeed, most of Fleet Street knew him only slightly, as he'd
been working for Reuters as their correspondent in Rome. 'The
Spectator was going through a sticky patch,' wrote Waugh, justi-
fying his defection to the *New Statesman*. 'It had forgotten its
sense of humour.'[3] With Chancellor's appointment, that sense
of humour was regained. Chancellor invited Waugh to bring
his 'First Person' column to the *Spectator*. After thirty months
in the Lion's Den, Waugh was happy to accept. As he observed,
astutely, 'My hatred of socialism, like some facial wart which
can be concealed by make-up for only a time, was beginning to
show.'[4]

With its long tradition of idiosyncratic conservatism (quite
unlike the new Conservatism of Margaret Thatcher's modern,
meretricious Tory Party), the *Spectator* was Waugh's natural home.
Renamed 'Another Voice', his weekly column soon became an
institution. Evelyn Waugh had been a fairly frequent contributor

to the *Spectator* and Auberon was pleased to be following in his father's footsteps. However, there was more to it than that. 'The *Spectator* has always been an independent ragbag of more or less eccentric outlooks, bound together only by a concern for decent writing and the intelligent Englishman's refusal to be brow-beaten into anything commonplace,'⁵ he reflected. He could have been writing about himself.

*

TWO NATIONS
(*Spectator*, 17 April 1976)

Living as one does, or tends to do, in rather a large country mansion surrounded by its own meadows, lakes and wooded pleasure grounds, I sometimes find that the normal satisfaction a man might be expected to feel in the elegance and superiority of his own appointments is marred by a certain nervousness. Wherever the class war is being fought, it has not yet reached the Taunton area, but even in West Somerset we hear – or imagine we hear – the rumble of distant guns. My neighbours take refuge in bizarre, violent and sometimes unpleasant polit-ical attitudes, most of which seem to involve the killing or imprisonment of large numbers of their fellow citizens. Even the mildest of them demand the instant appointment of Enoch Powell to a position somewhere between that of wartime prime minister of England and chancellor of the German Reich in the same period.

In Liverpool, for instance, there is a substantial body of opinion which appears to regard him as a Catholic left-wing rebel from the Labour Party (but not so left wing as to be unre-spectable) whose chief concern is to ensure that the department of Liverpool Corporation responsible for mending windows and unblocking lavatories in council estates does its work promptly.

How on earth, it might be asked, do I know what people are thinking in Liverpool? It is a fair question. Nobody ever told me what a beautiful city it was – and still is, despite some of the vilest modern buildings in Europe – and in thirty-six years I had never so much as visited it before this week. It just seemed a good place to start if I was going to involve myself more thoroughly in the class struggle to which we should all be dedicating ourselves.

What had alarmed me in my view of the class war was that all the gunfire seemed to be coming from the other camp. Whether out of wetness or, as I prefer to believe, natural sanctity, the middle classes were taking all the punishment, not only in taxes but also in the war of words and ideas. The first task in my lonely but undeniably admirable campaign was to seek out and confront this class animosity at its root. It is for this reason that I have spent my time since returning from France trailing round the slums of Manchester, the twilight areas of Birkenhead and docks of Liverpool with a merry crew of assistants and researchers. My role has been to taunt the unemployed in pubs, lecture slum dwellers in their pitiful homes, insult dockers at their place of work and generally make myself useful in an understanding of this delicate problem.

My efforts have been surprisingly unsuccessful, although there was an excellent moment in a pub. An unemployed electrician, whom I had been taunting with the reminder of how much richer I was, leaned forward and said: 'What are your qualifications? I know exactly what your qualifications are. You bent over in the showers to pick up some soap at Eton and Harrow, like all the rest of them.'

But my most surprising discovery so far has been how little class animosity exists where one might expect to find it most. Certainly, it is not that people up here are especially polite. They are not at all polite in the conventional sense, and far franker than their equivalents in my part of the country. But they have an indomitable goodwill, a friendliness, a refusal to believe that anyone can dissent from their own conclusions and attitudes which I found almost impossible to overcome.

Among the dockers, it is true, this absence of class animosity may have been a temporary phenomenon. Insult and goad them as I would, I could only draw the tolerant, contented purr of cats which have suddenly found their cream ration doubled. But among the unemployed and poor the lack of class animosity was not the result, as might be supposed, of the sort of political apathy which is well known to afflict starving Africans and Indians. On the contrary, many of them were vocal and militant, but all their militancy was directed to securing better service from the Liverpool Corporation and more benefits from the Department of Social Security. Such animosity as existed – and was very strong indeed in places – was all directed against faceless bureaucrats in these two departments, who are regarded at the same time as the universal providers and class enemies of the entire human race outside.

It was only then that I saw the extent of the gulf which divides the English. No doubt people are friendlier in the North and conditions are also worse. For most of the unemployed there is not the slightest prospect of employment even if they wanted it very much indeed, which some of them do. But those who are employed have exactly the same attitude, that if a window is broken they will wait three months for the Corporation to come and mend it. In the course of time they will pester the Corporation offices with telephone calls and personal appearances, they will take days off work to organise a petition and even a demonstration, they will expend twice the money and twenty times the energy needed to mend the window themselves, but they would sooner live with a broken window for the rest of their lives than mend it themselves. If anybody doubts the truth of this, I can take him on a tour of estates in Manchester, Liverpool and Birkenhead which will prove the point.

Nearly everybody I have met up here has been extraordinarily nice, but the two most dynamic people I have met were both fully (and independently) engaged in teaching their fellow citizens to claim whichever of the forty-one state benefits were available to them. They are not idle or reluctant to help themselves; the only difference is that self-help means forcing the Council or Corporation to help you.

AGAINST CHEAPER TICKETS
(*Spectator*, 16 July 1977)

Of all the problems besetting our poor, battered country, I should have thought that one of the least urgent was the problem of moving its old people about. Anybody who travels a certain amount by train as I do will realise that old people are constantly on the move. In every compartment they can be seen flashing their false teeth from behind their Senior Citizens Railcard, exerting their special brand of dumb appeal to make one carry their suitcases and budgerigar cages for hundreds of yards to where their sullen relatives are waiting to collect them. Those with motor cars usually head for Somerset to drive in an endless convoy, very slowly in the middle of the road, round and round the country lanes as they await the awful moment of judgment when they will meet their Maker face to face.

Are these journeys really necessary? I should have thought that old people had a better chance of discovering that serenity of mind which is the hallmark of dignified old age if they tried staying in the same place. People would then visit them and listen to their wise saws and present instances, pretending not to notice the lean and slippered pantaloon or the gentle slide into second childishness and mere oblivion. Old age holds many terrors in a godless generation, but immobility is surely the least of them. As a race, we are perfectly foul to our old people, turning them away from the family, and telling them they much prefer to be independent. Perhaps there is an awareness of this in the guilty, sentimental noises we all make whenever anyone mentions old age pensions. It is an observable fact that the greediest and most ruthlessly grasping trade union leaders are always the ones who make loudest noises about the old.

Problems of old age can't be solved by putting old people

on some sort of British Rail merry-go-round and hoping that under the stimulation of constant movement they will forget their falling teeth and hair, their ungrateful children, their problems of forgetfulness and incontinence and personal hygiene. We need an entirely new policy, something to inspire hope and gladness, a sense of belonging and usefulness. It is simply not enough to shut them in a train and wave them off from the platform. Quite apart from the cruelty involved, there is the consideration that other people – wage-earners, wealth-providers or what you will – have to travel by train as well, and it is rapidly becoming impossible with all these subsidised old people being pushed around, backwards and forwards, for no reason at all. A humane transport policy would try and discourage them from travelling, adding a premium on the price of any ticket sold to a woman over sixty, a man over sixty-five. This would nominally be in recognition of the additional nuisance they are likely to cause to their fellow passengers, but in fact it would be to encourage them to stay at home and acquire a little dignity.

HATRED OF CHILDREN
(Spectator, 1 October 1977)

The English are famous throughout the entire civilised world for their hatred of children. My own guess is that we hate children even more than we hate the old. Until I have had time to start a Gerontophile Information Exchange I will be unable to test this hunch, but I am prepared to bet that public reaction will be much less extreme.

If I am right, the violence of the public reaction against paedophiles should be seen as a cover-up – not, Heaven knows, for any sexual attraction towards children on the part of the general public – but as a sign of the guilt they feel for disliking children so much. I have often observed how the English, who shut their parents aware in retirement bungalows and old people's homes as soon as the opportunity presents itself, yet feel constrained to make little mooing noises of appreciation whenever an old age pensioner is wheeled onstage during a children's pantomime or other public entertainment. So it is with children. In order to understand that present phenomenon I am afraid we will need to analyse it by social class.

Members of the upper and upper-middle classes (we, gentle readers, the Beautiful People) have always got rid of our children by sending them to boarding schools. We have usually known that a small but significant proportion of the teaching staff of these establishments is paedophile. Such stirrings of guilt as we might have felt at this inhuman treatment were subdued by the reflection that the education was better and we were making enormous financial sacrifices to send our children off in this way. Those parents who were prepared to face up to the matter – I am amazed by the number of my contemporaries who assure me that homosexuality has now disappeared from the nation's preparatory and public schools – accept that there must be some consolation in the miserable life of those who choose to look after children. Which may explain the fairly tolerant attitude towards these unfortunate people which has grown up in our bourgeois society. It does not extend to child rapists or violators of pre-pubertal girls, but if the boys end up buggered that is accepted as a small price to pay for the opportunity to develop their whole characters, etc., which separation from parents must bring.

The lower-middle classes have never been able to send their children away, of course. Their method of showing dislike for their children is to refuse to talk to them, to dress in them in hideous clothes called anoraks and romper suits, to turn them out of the house or dump them in front of the television set as soon as they come in; and, if they give the slightest trouble, to stuff their mouths with sweets until their teeth blacken and fall out to lie like rabbits' droppings all over the fitted carpet in the television lounge. If ever parents of the lower class feel the slightest guilt about this inhuman treatment of their children, they overcome it by giving them huge sums of pocket money to buy even more sweets until their bodies and legs disappear and they have to be taken to school in special aluminium wheel-barrows designed by Lord Snowdon and supplied by the Welfare. But however much one may sneer, snarl or hoot at these people one must also admit that they can't send their children away and actually have to live with them. So one can see they might feel indignant at any suggestion that their children should also be buggered.

SEX IN BRITAIN
(*Spectator*, 8 December 1979)

Some months ago, I was intrigued to read that a large firm of underwear manufacturers in this country was altering its designs to take account of the changing shape of English women: their breasts had grown smaller, their shoulders broader, and their waists thicker. At about the same time I read that there could be no question of a return to the sixties mini-skirt because English women's legs were now shorter and heavier than before. At the time I filed this information away as confirming my own observation of the matter; it offered only peripheral support to my main theory, that there is an epidemic of masculinity among young British womanhood, which can be compared, in the extent of its depredations, with the blight of the Dutch elm disease.

My main observation is that, as their bodies become less feminine and less alluring, their minds are invaded by many of the less pleasing characteristics of the criminal male psychopath: senseless aggression, perverse illogicality, power mania, and egomaniac disregard for others. Babies may be aborted, children neglected or deserted, parents consigned to oblivion, all in the pursuit of some fugitive notion of personal fulfilment.

Male reactions are the least reported aspect of the female revolution, apart from the reactions of those few quislings like Alan Brien[6] who are proud to be ridden, saddled and bridled, through the women's pages of the *Guardian* or the *Sunday Times*, to announce that they have found a new fulfilment in changing nappies, emptying potties and carrying a handbag. Others gloomily announce that they have been vasectomised, but for the most part we are the people of England that have never spoken yet.

LESSONS OF THE ROYAL WEDDING
(*Spectator*, 15 August 1981)

The most sombre lesson of the Royal Wedding[7] concerns the future, not the past. Ever since becoming a father, more than nineteen years ago, I have tried to convince my children that if they neglect their studies they will end up as road sweepers or lavatory attendants. If, on the other hand, they apply themselves diligently enough to all the absurd and humiliating subjects in the modern child's syllabus, achieving satisfactory A levels in biology, physics, 'modern' mathematics, 'Nuffield' Latin, the theory and practice of positive anti-racialism, the political, philosophical and economic framework to a non-smoking policy, creative model-ling in Plasticine, etc. – then, if they are boys, they will become rich and famous like their father and grandfather before them; if they are girls they will marry, if not the Prince of Wales, at any rate a marquis, a duke or one of the better class of earls.

Even if I could think of a single unkind thing to say about our new Princess of Wales I would refuse to say it in deference to her beauty, birth and obvious amiability of temperament, but the fact remains that she has not got a single pass at O level and on that rock the whole ship of state looks like sinking. The Prince of Wales, in choosing such a mate, makes a statement of greater importance than if he had chosen to marry a girl of average educational abilities who was either black or working class. What he is saying, in effect – and instructing all his dukes and marquises down to the meanest citizen in the land – is that education is no longer of the slightest use or interest to the modern Briton.

In a sense, of course, he is right. In a society where the long-distance lorry driver earns more than the university professor, the ancillary technician in hospital more than the consultant surgeon, who needs education? A chimpanzee can be trained to perform most of the functions of the 'worker' in a modern factory, and would probably perform them with better grace.

The error in this is to suppose that education prepares people for employment rather than unemployment. Present figures for unemployment are not the product of a temporary recession, still less of the Government's non-existent 'monetarist' policies. They are the inescapable and permanent result of technological progress. The greatest challenge facing our civilisation – as opposed to the dragooned and regulated societies of the East – is the challenge of leisure. Even the lower classes grow intolerably bored with television after a time. Music is already surging ahead and literature, I feel sure, will revive once it has been taken away from the Arts Council and learned to address itself once again to its readers. Education is the key to everything. If the Prince is too busy himself he should appoint a tutor to instruct his young bride in music, dancing, poetry and all the gentler arts. If Lord Goodman's[8] health is not up to the job, I will volunteer myself.

FATHER CHRISTMAS DAY
(*Spectator*, 12 December 1981)

One of the great consolations of life in socialist Eastern Europe at this time of year must be that under socialism there is never, *never* anything to buy in the shops. Once you have bought a few extra tins of mackerel and a couple of those interminable wooden dolls which fit inside each other you have done your Christmas shopping. All of the women of England go mad at this time of year from the pressures of it all, and I wonder if this absence of anything to buy in the shops under socialism may not explain why so many otherwise sane middle-class women are attracted to the Workers' Revolutionary Party, Socialist Workers' Party, Communist Party and all the rest of that gloomy rubbish.

The idea of Christmas as a specifically Kiddies' Festival seems to be of very recent origin. The present-giving ingredient in Christmas festivities derives from the ancient Roman feast of Saturnalia, held on 17 December and later extended for a full week when no work was done, presents were exchanged, many forms of moral laxity were permitted and slaves were allowed to be impertinent to their masters. But there was nothing much for children on these genial occasions. I suspect that children crept into the Christmas idea – perhaps it would be more accurate nowadays to talk of the Father Christmas Idea, and Father Christmas Day – with the decline of religious belief: religion was seen as a fairy story for kiddies, evoking happy, sentimental memories of one's own childhood when one believed in it all and honestly thought Father Christmas came down the chimney. So now Christmas has become quite simply an orgy of presents and sweets for kiddies, when grown-ups mince around waiting on them and trying to look sweet too.

There is little or nothing we can do about it, of course, in our own little circles of influence, but I would like to leave one thought in the minds of *Spectator* readers. Father Christmas has absolutely nothing to do with the nativity of Our Lord. He is a filthy foreign importation. The presents he gives are usually rubbish. Many, if not most, Father Christmases are male homosexualists in disguise. Sadly or not, there is a strong anti-homosexual drive among the nation's youth. Children have always enjoyed pulling Father Christmas's beard and humiliating him in other ways. If we could divert the nation's kiddies from the elderly and infirm for a moment and teach them to persecute any and every Father Christmas they see, we might eventually succeed in driving the brute from our shores. It may not be much, but it is a start.

FAT CATS
(*Spectator*, 16 February 1985)

At Champney's Health Farm, a former Rothschild mansion near Tring, cut off by a blizzard from the rest of the world, one might well expect to hear the howling of wolves from the belt of larches, pine and other specimen trees which surrounds this tasteful estate, its rolling lawns now carpeted in six inches of snow. I find myself here on a week's starvation course. Could there be anything more exquisitely ridiculous than the sight of eighty or ninety people of all ages and many nationalities cooped up together and paying huge sums of money to be starved?

Perhaps the things we do together make us even more ridiculous. My chief delight, on this occasion, is the Dance Movement class. We stand in rows on the heavily carpeted floor of the dance studio: grotesquely fat Arabs and plump young Orthodox Jewish ladies from North London, exhausted executives from the Midlands and grimly determined Americans with a sort of Boy Scout trustfulness in their eyes. The walls are made of mirrored glass so that we can see ourselves and our fellow Movers. In front of us stands a wild, pencil-thin young woman in a leotard. When the music starts she begins throwing her arms and legs around, hopping backwards and forwards and wiggling her bottom. We have to follow her movements. By any standards, it is a supremely comical sight, but in a world where it is claimed that half the human race is starving – I do not accept that estimate, and would put it at about three hundredths of one per cent – it seems to transcend the comic to make a statement about the world in which we live which borders on the sublime.

KILLING FOR COMPANY
(*Spectator*, 2 March 1985)

Somewhere along the line, Dennis Nilsen seems to have got it all wrong. His father, a Norwegian soldier stationed in Scotland,

moved off at the end of the war leaving his mother to cope
with three children, of whom Dennis was the youngest. From
his earliest years, his memories are those of a client of the
Welfare State. By the time he had moved on from two forms
of government employment – in the army and the police force
– to a third, in the Manpower Services Commission, he had
emerged as such a boring and unpleasant person that nobody
could bear to spend time in his company. He was a homosexualist, of course, but even with the opportunities available to
him for making new acquaintances of similar persuasion through
his post in the Charing Cross Road Job Centre, people found
him so stupendously boring that nobody would spend more
than an evening in his company. Like so many social and
emotional cripples, he drifted into left-wing politics and became
branch organiser of the Civil Service Union, but even there his
boring self-righteousness failed to secure the warmth and
comradeship which he sought. So, if we are to believe Brian
Masters's study, called *Killing For Company*, he was reduced to
seeking the company of corpses as being the only people who
would not walk out on him.

Other people, in the same sort of predicament, become prison
visitors, but Nilsen kept his corpses under the floorboards,
retrieving them from time to time to sit them in an armchair and
harangue them with his boring left-wing opinions, his grudges
and grievances and the catalogue of his self-pity. Then, when the
natural processes of decomposition made the corpses unacceptable company, even by his own undemanding standards, he boiled
their heads, put them down the lavatory, and started looking
around for a new companion. In this way he disposed of fifteen
young men in the course of five years, before being brought to
book as a result of blocked drains in the house where he lived.

Nilsen obviously provides an extreme example of what used
fashionably to be called urban alienation – the loneliness which
town dwellers suffer who are too boring, too unpleasant or too
unattractive in other ways to make friends. He also, perhaps,
offers a paradigm for the relationship between personal inadequacies, left-wing views and bureaucratic sadism. Although I

have no particular reason to suppose that Nilsen was such a sadist as one is liable to meet in the course of any dealings with a government ministry or local authority, a glance at his face assures me that he almost certainly belonged to that group. I have often speculated about the private lives of people behind desks who spend their working hours making things difficult for other people. It would be tempting to think they all have corpses under the floorboards and return home, of an evening, to harangue them. But Nilsen, as I say, is an extreme example. His problem was loneliness, and the traditional solution to that is within the marriage bond. No man is so boring, or so unpleasant, or so unattractive that he cannot find an equally boring, unpleasant or unattractive woman to be his life's companion if he sets his mind to it and I have no doubt that the same must be true in the homosexual world. But Nilsen's only attempt at a homosexual marriage ended in mutual disgust; obviously he is better off in prison.

THE JOYS OF BEING BURGLED
(*Spectator*, 29 August 1987)

For many years, in my capacity as president, chairman, general secretary and only member of the Dog Lovers' Party of Great Britain,[9] I felt it incumbent on me to point out the salutary effects of dog mess on the pavements of London and our other great cities. It provides a form of sustenance to urban toddlers which is free and non-fattening; although excessive ingestion of dog shit is thought to cause blindness, it is probably less dangerous than the wrapping paper, elastic bands and other substances they would otherwise be eating. More important than this, the vexation which city dwellers suffer when they step in a pile of dog mess is surely good for their souls: it teaches them humility and an awareness of the fragility of social institutions, as they try unsuccessfully to scrape the evil-smelling clay from their trendy Gucci shoes, and as they subsequently walk across the wall-to-wall carpeting of their costly little homes in lingering intestinal miasma.

I do not wish to seem pious when I say that I always rejoice when I accidentally step in a pile of dog shit in London, counting the number of days in Purgatory I am saving myself as I offer up the inconvenience to the Great Dog Lover in the Sky; but I must claim that when I came downstairs last Thursday morning to find that my home had been burgled in the night – one of the burglars had thoughtfully defecated in a courtyard before gaining entry – it was not long before I began to identify the incident as another possible source of spiritual uplift.

The objects stolen included a gold chimney pocket watch with the crest and name of Evelyn Waugh engraved on the back – I hope anyone who sees it offered for sale will lose no time in telephoning the nearest police helicopter armoured gunship service – and also a pretty seventeenth-century Dutch cow creamer, of which I was particularly fond. It is the sort of thing which would have delighted the heart of Wooster's uncle, Tom Travers, and might have inspired any number of Wodehouse fantasies.

But even as I mourned its loss, I began to appreciate the various things which the burglars had not taken. Everybody, it seems to me, should be burgled from time to time. The experience not only teaches us to value and to be grateful for what we still have; it also reminds us of the snarling underworld of people who do not possess any delightful objects at all, who regard our possession of them with malicious resentment, whose fondest wish is to take them away from us and convert them into cash to satisfy whatever gross and deformed appetites of their own. Perhaps the burglar's girlfriend is even now sunning her limbs on the Costa Brava from the proceeds of this foul crime. I cordially hope she burns herself to a frazzle, contracts dysentery and is raped by ten *Sun* readers, but the truth is that one would not enjoy one's possessions so much if one was not aware that others wanted them, too.

A RADICAL SUGGESTION ON THE FUTURE
OF WOMEN IS FIRMLY DISMISSED
(*Spectator*, 26 November 1989)

Why *should* women do the housework, iron the shirts, look after the children, bear the babies? The question is often raised in ordinary conversation, as well as in Great Family Debates. After long and careful thought, I decided that the most complete explanation for this phenomenon is probably contained in the two words: piss off. Women bear children because it is their necessary biological function if the human species is to survive. To those who next enquire why it is a good or useful thing for the human species to survive, why Planet Earth should not be left to its rain forests, seal pups, whales, etc., the best answer is surely, once again, 'Piss off.' But the question seldom takes that form. It is grudgingly acknowledged that even the human species has some sort of right to a survival urge. The question is posed more subtly. Of course it is all very well for women who *want* to have children, but why should they be *expected* to want them? Why should a socially convenient arrangement such as marriage be expected to produce further human debris in the shape of soiled 'disposable' nappies, illiterate lager louts, mewling and puking *Sunday Times* readers of the future?

Why should anyone wish to fulfil his historical or biological destiny? Why should the caterpillar wish to turn into a chrysalis, the chrysalis into a butterfly? Why should the butterfly wish to lay eggs and die? At least I think that is what butterflies do. I never studied biology, and the *Encyclopaedia Britannica* entry on the subject is incomprehensible. I *think* I have seen two butterflies on the job, but I may have been wrong. What does it matter? The most satisfactory answer to all these questions is the same: PISS OFF. The important fact is that a large and growing number of modern women do not want to have babies – or are persuaded by economic circumstances not to have them. They are not prepared to lay eggs any more than they are prepared to countenance the thought of dying. And so the delicate question of who should iron the shirts, prepare the food and wash up afterwards is bound to arise.

Historically, I suppose, women did the housework because if they didn't, their husbands, being bigger and stronger, would first beat them up and then throw them out of the house (or cave, as the case may be) in exchange for a more amenable female. This brutal aspect of the marriage bond was obscured for many people over the last few thousand years – what might come to be known as the 'civilised' era of human history – by the existence of domestic servants. Now the 'civilised' age has ended, the stark reality emerges again.

Which brings us back to the institution of marriage and survival of the species. The first may seem to be secured by the free market in housing. Until fairly recently, mortgage companies were not prepared to take a wife's earnings into account, on the grounds that women's fertility made them bad risks. Since mortgage companies have been prepared to take a wife's earnings into account, the price of *all* housing has risen to a level sustainable only by a two-income family. As a result, fertility has plummeted among the house-buying classes, and would be almost out of sight if it were not for an equally dramatic rise in illegitimate, single-parent births.

The reason for this second phenomenon is that the state bribes single women to have babies – with free housing and vastly increased DHSS[10] entitlements – in a way that it is no longer prepared to bribe married women. A naturally broody woman would do better to stay single than to marry. Where single-parent households are concerned, of course, the problem of who prepares the food, washes up, etc., does not arise. In the two-parent-but-no-children household, which seems to be the pattern for the future, the question arises with increased urgency. Why *should* a woman do the housework?

Well, a husband can still beat his wife up, of course, but he can no longer throw her out of the cave or married home to seek another, more amenable wife because she owns half of it. Nor, in the claustrophobic circumstances of modern living, would many husbands relish the sort of bonding arrangement which required him to beat up his wife every time he wanted her to boil an egg or iron his handkerchief.

So, if one studies the trends, they would appear to point to two types of household in the future: the childless, house-owning couple, who are models of sharing, meaningfulness and equality; and the impoverished single-parent family, living in council accommodation where the mother does everything. Unfortunately, the overall fertility remains dangerously low, as more and more take the first option.

It is hard to know what to suggest. There is no carrot to offer, since the economy requires an ever-increasing number of women workers to offset the effects of our declining birth rate. Where sticks are concerned, it would be abhorrent to our residual morality, and electorally unviable, to propose that all women who reach retirement age without having had at least one child should be put to death. But then, fifty years ago, it would have been equally abhorrent – and electorally unviable – to propose that any inconvenient baby should be aborted. At present, we are chiefly worried about overcrowding. In ten years' time, we may well be more worried about the geriatric explosion.

A FEW SOUR OBSERVATIONS ON BEING BLACKBALLED FROM WHITE'S CLUB
(*Spectator*, 1 April 1995)

Last week, while I was in London, a reporter from *The Times* telephoned my wife in Somerset to tell her he had just heard a rumour from someone in White's club[11] in St James's Street, that I had been blackballed. Could she confirm it? She had no knowledge that I was a candidate, and gave him rather short shrift.

On the last occasion we discussed the matter some months or years ago, she advised strongly against standing. She pointed out that its members are for the most part exactly the sort of people I spend most of my life avoiding in Somerset – noisy, insecure, big-bottomed men who think that membership of White's gives them some sort of social cachet. In any case, I was bound to be blackballed, she said. If Bernard Levin and Jeremy Paxman were blackballed from the Garrick Club, if you please, what chance did Auberon Waugh have at White's of escaping his numerous enemies, built up over sixteen years as a student of the vituperative arts on *Private Eye* and twenty-eight years of opinionated columns in the *Spectator*?

I was well aware that White's has its fair share of shits and twerps and pompous bores and that such people invariably gravitate towards the committee of any club they join, but they are a hazard of life anywhere, and I also knew a fair number of jokey, easy-going people who had joined the club over the years. It was simply a question of whether friends or enemies prevailed. If enemies were in the ascendant, it would be mad to wish to join.

However, my wife did not attach enough importance to the matter to mention it to me on my return, and when *The Times* reporter telephoned again it was the first I had heard of my blackball. No, I said, I could not confirm it because nobody had told me anything, but as rumours go, it had the ring of truth. If I had been elected, that would surely be more news-worthy. Would I telephone if I heard anything? he asked. No, I said.

Next day, there was nothing in *The Times* about this world-shaking event, but one of my sponsors telephoned in some distress. It was normal, he said, if there was opposition to a candidate, to inform the proposer so that he could persuade the candidate to withdraw. On this occasion the opposition had organised in secret, as if it wished to cause as much of a stink as possible. I comforted the sobbing lad, assuring him I did not feel humiliated at all, but rather relieved and exhilarated. I had done my duty and could put the matter out of my mind.

Next day, I was telephoned by a young woman on the *Express* which had also been tipped off by someone at White's. People were working hard to give this non-story wider circulation. She sounded quite nice and sympathetic. Yes, I could confirm I had been blackballed. No, I was not particularly upset, if anything slightly relieved – the honour of being elected would have cost some £1200, and I was by no means certain of the advantages ... Why, then, had I wanted to join?

This was not an easy question to answer. I was first proposed for White's over twenty years ago by a friendly neighbour in Wiltshire called Philip Dunn, who had known my father there and thought it was time I joined. Then Sir Philip died and I forgot about the matter until I received what struck me as rather a patronising and impertinent letter from the then secretary, saying that if I wished to join I had better find myself another proposer. I replied stiffly saying I did not mind so much either way and certainly was not going to grub around asking people to propose me.

He wrote again asking whether I wished to join and I wrote back saying 'No'. At any rate, that is my memory of the correspondence. Then about ten years later an older cousin of my wife, who was cognisant of the earlier exchange, proposed me again. Most unfortunately, before the nomination could go forward he was tragically struck down by a paralytic stroke, in which condition he was unable to write the necessary letter, and the cause was taken over by a public-spirited brother-in-law ...

So why did I wish to join? My late father retained his membership of White's (with another club, so that when Randolph[12] was at one, he could go to the other, as he ungraciously remarked) as a last tenuous link with London. It occurred to me that if ever I decided to bury myself in Somerset it might be fun to retain a meeting place with a smallish range of old friends and acquaintances whom I would otherwise never see. But the plain truth, as I now see it, is that I was brought up to think of White's as a good cause, rather like the Devon and Somerset Staghounds, although it is at least forty years since I even thought of riding with them.

When first proposed, at the age of thirty-something, I was nervous, but thought the idea of membership rather grand. At fifty-five one is frightened of nobody, which is an advantage, but one has also lost all social ambition, which is sad. Unlike the saintly Groucho, I can feel nothing but mild contempt for a club which does not wish to have me as a member. Far from being humiliated that a small handful of enemies (whose names would probably be unfamiliar to me, even if I was told them) has stolen a march on me, I feel depressed that a once genial corner of the London scene has fallen to the enemy. Is it a sign of insane conceit and solipsism to suggest that the incident shows how White's is in decline?

It used to be one of my ambitions to be nominated White's club's Shit of the Year in *Private Eye*, and now I have lost the chance. But even this accolade will lose its grandeur when people realise that shits are no longer welcome, and the twerps have taken over.

Waugh called time on his 'Another Voice' column after twenty years, in 1996. 'Last time I left the *Spectator*, in 1973, it might have been for the idealistic reason that I thought it had no business to be so boring about Europe,' he wrote. 'My only reason for leaving it now is greed for money. That is all the New Conservatism has to teach, and I have learned the lesson too well.'[13]

Chapter Ten
Country Topics

Ramblers are becoming a serious menace and a blot on the landscape of rural Britain. These people are encouraged by their association in the serious error that they own the countryside. In fact the only way to own the countryside is to work hard, save up your money and buy a bit of it. Merely rambling around in an anorak is no substitute.[1]

Like the Augustan wits he resembled, Auberon Waugh's career was a tug of war between town and country. London was where he did his work but Somerset was where he lived, and his reflections on rural life comprise some of his finest writing. He loved his home in Somerset, but he was never sentimental about it. Unlike a lot of writers, he didn't suck up to country folk or play the country squire. His attitude to the countryside was like his attitude to everything – ironic, dispassionate and full of fun. 'There are dangers to be met in the West Country as well as pleasures,' he warned. 'Poisonous bracken covers a large and increasing part of the area. Wild and possibly rabid bats pose alluringly in front of visiting Londoners and then bite on the finger anyone who tries to stroke them. Savage bulls and rams are trained to attack whoever is suspect of being a Rambler. Anybody wearing a cagoule or carrying a backpack is liable, quite simply, to be murdered by local residents.'[2]

In his 'Country Topics' column for the *Evening Standard*, and in all his other rural writing, Waugh refused to reproduce the usual whimsical fantasy of Olde England. This distinguished him from those weekend countrymen who simply use the shires as holiday homes, and his writing was far more interesting as a result:

> There is tendency to describe the countryside in terms of badgers, voles, rare and beautiful plants. Of course these things are there if one looks for them, but they play only a limited part in the life of the country. To discuss the countryside in terms of its flora and fauna is to accept it at its urban valuation as a minor amenity, rather like the zoo but without the same recreational facilities. The main problem of country life is not how to protect the badger but how to avoid boredom.[3]

Waugh was mindful of the parallels between his 'Country Topics' column in the *Evening Standard* and William Boot's 'Lush Places' column in the *Daily Beast*. However, unlike his father's fictional journalist, the unassuming hero of *Scoop*, Waugh's column wasn't just about our furry and/or feathered friends: 'It not only described how "feather-footed through the plashy fens, passes the questing vole",' he recalled, 'it also chronicled the changing social profile of village life, with fewer people being employed in agriculture, an influx of commuters and the retired pushing house prices beyond the reach of the locals.'[4] And it chronicled much more besides, as these excerpts show.

*

BE WARNED BEFORE YOU COME OUT WEST
(*Evening Standard*, 1974)

Combe Florey, Somerset
First summer sunshine has a curious effect on the West Country. The roads are suddenly alive and vibrant with motor cars hooting at each other through clouds of exhaust as they crawl bumper to bumper at ten miles an hour, always in the same direction.

Taking the children to the North Cornish seaside for the day one had the impression of joining some epic migration, like the Jewish Diaspora, the Great Trek of the Boers from Cape Province or Mao's Long March.

Of course it is really nothing more than our fellow Britishers having a good time. Every car carries a polythene bundle on its roof rack until the procession resembles an army of ants with eggs on their backs. It is a beautiful thing, of course, that people who pass their working lives earning money in the noise and hideousness of the West Midlands should choose to spend their holidays motoring very slowly in procession past my gate.

On the other hand, I am not sure that if I were a Midlands car worker I should venture into the West Country at this particular moment when meat is so expensive. All the heavily subsidised British meat which comes into the market down here is immediately snapped up by Frenchmen who take it away with many greedy noises to eat in their own country. Many West Countrymen are feeling meat deprived and there have been ugly rumours of cannibalism.

People intending to take their holiday in the West Country should be warned. Many visitors who come to us from Wolverhampton and Coventry – we try to make them welcome – seem so weighed down by all the money in their pockets that they can scarcely walk, let alone run. The best they can manage is a sedate, jingling waddle from the car to the nearest public convenience. It would be a sad and rather shocking thing if at the end of the holiday season these public conveniences were surrounded by the whitened bones of holidaymakers, picked clean by scavenging natives.

THE BALLAD OF BELLSTONE FOX
(*Evening Standard*, 1974)

Combe Florey, Somerset
The arrival of a film unit in the Somerset countryside is traditionally the signal for everyone to put on his leather apron and

stand by his garden gate, sucking cider through a straw. For a few weeks now, some Independent Artists, as they are apparently called, have been galloping up and down the Quantock Hills shouting, 'Tally ho!' at each other and pretending to be country yokels, much to the amazement of the real country yokels, who feel strangely left out of it. The film they are making is an adaptation of a novel by David Rook called *The Ballad of Bellstone Fox*. As its name suggests, it is about a fox, but the film company apparently had the same difficulty with foxes as they had with genuine Somerset yokels.

Whatever qualities the English fox may have, it is quite useless at acting the part of a fox on film, just as yokels can't be trusted to act the part of yokels. All the pubs for miles around are cackling over a story of how the Rank Organisation has been obliged to purchase a consignment of Shelties – miniature Shetland sheepdogs – clip their coats and dye them red to play the part of foxes. One of them was very nearly caught by the hounds last week, which would have been a sad episode in a film about a fox which outwits its pursuers and causes the death of the huntsman. The film is causing endless merriment down here, but one worries, slightly, whether it will be received in quite the same spirit when shown to a smart London audience. Few people in the country realise the intensity of London's opposition to hunting.

Few Somerset people go anywhere near London, of course, if they can possibly help it. Occasionally, when I have mentioned in London that I came from an area of the country where fox hunting is unquestionably the principal recreation, I have been ordered to explain why I am not prominent in the campaign against cruel sports or leave the room. Although I do not hunt myself, nor do any of my immediate family, it is useless to deny that hunting is a very large part of many people's lives down here, and if I ignore it here for very much longer I will be guilty of wilful deception. Even the dear old people who come down from Birmingham and Wolverhampton to decorate our countryside with retirement bungalows are sometimes involved, when enraged hounds invade their gardens and frighten their budgerigars or – far, far worse than this – fall on their blameless pussy cats and rend them limb from limb.

Obviously it is not enough to suggest to these bereaved old people that very little happens in their uneventful lives, that they should welcome a little real-life drama, or that the violence they have just witnessed is as nothing to the violence they consume avidly, night after night, on television. It is not enough to point out that there is nothing else to do, for many people in the countryside, except chase foxes. There is a strong feeling that the country should be made fit for retired people to live in, and these excesses are no part of most people's retirement plan.

Townspeople are trained to look at the question from the fox's point of view, and it would be futile to deny that the fox has a right to its point of view. Few people in London have probably gone into a chicken house after it has been visited by a fox. Foxes have an unpleasant habit of killing many more chickens than they can ever possibly hope to eat, usually by biting their heads off. Fox enthusiasts can reasonably point out that chickens are not particularly agreeable birds, and many of them are so stupid that they possibly don't notice whether they are alive or dead. However, non-hunters like myself who have had to clean up after these visits tend to feel noticeably less tender to foxes afterwards.

People refuse to accept as my reason for doing nothing about fox hunters that I have never particularly cared about chickens. The reason certainly isn't any desire for peace with the neighbours, since country life would be insupportably boring without the fostering of what Harold Wilson used to call creative tensions. The main reason one does nothing about hunting is quite simply that the more one thinks about life, the more difficult it is to condone anything about it. When townspeople have stopped mugging each other, robbing, ridiculing, suing, and generally trampling each other, I will start wagging my finger at the Master of the West Somerset Vale Foxhounds.

MY COUNTY, MY COUNTY
(*Tatler*, November 1979)

Somerset is the elephant's graveyard of southern England. Apart from farmers, who are immensely rich and keep themselves to themselves, and holidaymakers, who like to use our hedgerows as a combined picnic amenity area and public lavatory on their journeys to Devon and Cornwall, people only come to Somerset to die. Holidaymakers are a great curse in the summer months, and for this reason I generally spend the summer abroad. Our hedgerows are probably the best in the world for their purposes, being replete with every sort of vegetable and animal life. As holidaymakers picnic or relieve themselves on the wild violets and ragged robins, they may hear the squeaky whistle of the hedge vole struggling to get away through the undergrowth, the warble of a thrush or even the homely death rattle of a retired bank manager from Solihull come to spend his last years in the dream bungalow of his choice.

It is the retired folk who set the tone. They come from the four corners of the earth – Rhodesia, Kenya, Wolverhampton, the Far East – knowing nobody, and settle with their budgerigars into a resentful solitude, awaiting the Hour, each in his own hideous bungalow. The first thing to go wrong with them is generally their bladder or 'waterworks'. Somerset's general hospitals are filled, ward after ward, with elderly people contemplating a plastic bag. At this point they become quite garrulous, but until then they are gloomy and taciturn, and it is not always easy to distinguish which are still alive.

Somerset folk, through their lonely, contemplative existence, frequently become prey to irrational anxieties. There is scarcely a retired major within twenty miles of my home at Combe Florey who will not roundly declare that the country has been taken over, unawares, by a sinister Communist conspiracy. My own anxieties, I might as well admit, centre around old age pensioners and mental patients. Where others see a Red under the bed, I see an OAP. These geriatric invaders of Somerset often seem to possess many of the less endearing characteristics of the Huns, Ostrogoths and Visigoths who swarmed over the later Roman Empire, but I suppose I am wrong to worry about them as much as I do. Where mental patients are concerned, my anxieties are even more particular. They have taken over all the big houses in my immediate neighbourhood. Mine is the only one left in private occupation. On Sundays, they are allowed out for walks in crocodiles all over the countryside, and I see them squinting under the arch of my gatehouse, even peering over twelve-foot high walls, counting the time until they will be able to gambol and lope over my terraces and *parterres*. But I have kept them at bay so far. It looks like being a long, hard fight to remain the one sane outpost in a country overrun by lunatics. But that is what Somerset does to you.

IN THE WELFARE QUEUE
(Spectator, 26 January 1980)

There are moments in life when the miseries of the world threaten to engulf it, when the precariousness of the human condition, far from adding spice and savour to the continuing fact of our survival inside it, seems an infinite rebuke. The Finns, I believe, feel like this all winter, and many of them commit suicide. My own moment of desolation comes with my weekly visit to the Post Office to buy postage stamps. I have described before the scene in Taunton Post Office, the long queues of pensioners, mothers and other unfortunates waiting to collect their Welfare entitlements.

Over the years, I do not think I have ever seen anyone, apart from myself, actually pay money over the counter. Everybody else seems to be collecting it. Nothing has changed much – they still moan gently to each other about their feet, varicose veins, operations for gynaecological disorders, and those of their friends and relations. The miseries of old age and inflation are sometimes interspersed with bitter 'jokes' about the weather. If I arrive before the Post Office opens, there is a little group of them, waiting like junkies outside the all-night chemist for their midnight 'fix'.

The conversation, as I say, does not change much, although sometimes someone has just died of cancer, or is about to do so. The only thing which has changed is the amount of money they receive. Waiting to buy my weekly £5 worth of postage stamps, I am amazed by the huge brown bundles being handed across to those in front of me in the queue. It reminds me of nothing so much as Expenses Day on the *Mirror*. We all know pensioners are terribly underpaid, but I simply fail to understand how any government can manage to hand out these wads of £10 notes to its citizens every day and hope to survive.

CONSERVATIONIST MENACE
(*Spectator*, 13 April 1985)

Irritated as we may be by those institutions which seem immovably stuck in the sixties, like the Catholic Church, there is something distinctly endearing about people like the Prince of Wales who suddenly appear to have discovered that confusing decade a quarter of a century after everyone else. His latest outbreak is against farmers who despoil the countryside in the interests of agricultural productivity – or 'greed' as it was more fashionably called before 'greed' became a cheer-word. 'Fascinating places, wetlands, moorlands and hedgerows have been lost, often in response to greed,' he said. 'We have come to look on the land as an almost endless source of increasing income.'

Of course it is absolutely true that many farmers, left to themselves, will behave like pigs, leaving horrible plastic sacks all over the countryside and putting up hideous metal barns and grain driers as well as tearing up hedgerows and chopping down trees. Other farmers prefer not to live in a pigsty and keep their hedgerows and trees, at some cost to themselves. Until very recently, the government was paying farmers to plough up moorland and pull down hedgerows. It was called land reclamation and improvement. Now, in some cases, it pays them not to do so and leave the land untilled. That is called conservation. I do not see how any great issue of morality is involved. It rather depended on how many people were going to be fascinated by a particular piece of wetland, as against the rather larger number who might have had to pay an extra penny on their loaf of bread for allowing a sedge warbler to warble on his own patch – possibly delighting the soul of some bearded creep hiding behind the reeds, possibly not.

The Prince of Wales urged farmers to develop new skills, specifying tourism, light industry and forestry, in order to discourage them from destroying what is called 'the environment'. This would seem to confirm the countryside in the role of recreation area for townspeople – who are themselves exiled from the countryside by their own greed for money – rather than as an area dedicated to agriculture and its own pursuits. The farmer's role is to show misty-eyed townspeople his sedge warblers and possibly serve them a cream tea afterwards. It does not seem to occur to these bird fanciers and nature fanatics that they are as much a pest as the voles, rabbits and squirrels they admire, and that any farmer who took his job really seriously would poison their cream teas as surely as he pours cyanide into a wasps' nest.

HOW THE RSPB IS CONTRIVING TO DRIVE US ALL MAD
(*Spectator*, 19 May 1990)

Whatever one may have against butterflies – and I agree that in the present plague affecting the entire West Country, they can be intensely irritating – at least they make no noise. Nor, unlike Rottweilers and ladybirds, do they often attack human beings. Many have forgotten the old age pensioner who was bitten to death by ladybirds outside Minehead in the last great plague of

1976. Up to then, people had thought that ladybirds were disappearing, and a few old dears had written to the newspapers saying what a shame it was. Then they came back, like something out of Hitchcock. The rumour went round west Somerset that the corpse of the old age pensioner, when they eventually got to him, was a more horrible sight than anything seen in the Blitz. What made the man's death particularly poignant was that he was a visitor to the neighbourhood, who had come to enjoy the beauties of the countryside. We country folk are used to the hazards and know how to protect ourselves against them by various wily tricks, like never going out of doors unless we have to, or covering ourselves with sacks and binder twine when we do.

As I say, I have never yet seen butterflies attack a human being, but then we had never heard of homicidal ladybirds before 1976, and I would not be at all surprised to learn of some appalling tragedy, almost certainly in Somerset, where the whitened bones of an amateur naturalist, or ecologist, or environmental enthusiast, or whatever these people now call themselves, are found with only a pair of damp, horn-rimmed spectacles glinting optimistically over the eye sockets to serve as a clue. I have no doubt that even butterflies can be goaded beyond endurance by the yelps and coos of these people. It will be a brave butterfly fancier who ventures down to west Somerset this summer. The fields are swarming with vipers, too – another protected species – and in the present state of government cuts, it is unlikely that any anti-snakebite serum will be available.

I must admit that I am on the side of the butterflies against the butterfly fanciers, if only because butterflies make no noise. Where egg-collectors are concerned, my sympathies are different. A recent survey of noise pollution, identifying the noises which people found most troublesome, was conducted recently by BUPA. It had two significant omissions. The first was the noise of other people's television sets, which must surely be the biggest single source of annoyance for people living in towns. Dogs, pneumatic drills and burglar alarms were mentioned, even children (or 'kids', at any mention of which even the most toughened criminal is expected to burst into tears), but not television.

The other significant omission, affecting most particularly those who live in the suburbs and country places, was the racket set up every morning at this time of year by songbirds and other feathered friends, sometimes called the Dawn Chorus. Birds too, you see, are sacred. At least half of all country and suburban dwellers must suffer from this persecution, and nobody dares complain because we have all been brainwashed into thinking birdsong pretty. So it is, sometimes, when you have two or three of them on the job of an evening; six or seven hundred of them, yelling and shrieking their silly heads off at five o'clock in the morning, are more than anyone can be expected to endure. I have often observed how soon majors and other people who retire to live in Somerset tend to go mad, but I always attributed it to the influence of loneliness, and listening to BBC radio. Now I tend to think it is the result of being woken up every morning by the hideous cacophony of these warbling cretins.

SAVING THE COUNTRYSIDE
(*Daily Telegraph*, 18 May 1994)

Those of us who have the good fortune to live in the country must be very careful whom we accept as allies in the battle to prevent the face of England being taken over by theme parks, holiday villages, New Age camp sites, scramble courses, teenage raves and pop festivals. Bird lovers may seem harmless enough, as may animal sentimentalists, wild flower enthusiasts, tree experts and ramblers. It would be easy to ask ourselves what purpose there is in preserving the countryside if it is not for the benefit of people who live in towns, so that they can count the birds, stroke the animals, sniff the flowers, identify various trees.

On the other hand, if the land is no longer required for agriculture, why should anyone decide that bird watchers and wild flower enthusiasts have greater moral claim than ramblers, scramblers and teenage ravers? They make just as much nuisance of themselves to farmers and sportsmen, often more, demanding that whole tracts of land should be set aside exclusively for their own pleasure. The great error is to see the countryside as belonging to the towns, a leisure amenity to be enjoyed in whatever way they see fit. The land belongs to an enormous number of people and it does not, thank God, belong to *the* people. If the people wish to claim it they will have to start a revolution and see who wins.

If they do not own the land or live in the country it cannot really be any of their business what goes on there, at any rate until they acquire an interest. Townsfolk can always join groups which will provide resources for bird watching or private meditation, hunting or preventing other people hunting. Private property is what distinguishes the free citizen from the slave, mankind from brute creation. Until this point is better understood I think we would be well advised to oppose the building of public toilets in the countryside. Many townspeople feel strangely disorientated by their absence. If we do not supply the facilities, I feel they may easily stay at home.

Chapter Eleven
Other Places

In 1975 I attended a strange literary conference at Lahti, in northern Finland, which happened to coincide with the celebration of Midsummer Day, when all the Finns go mad and prance around in the burning sun at midnight, collapsing under trees out of drink and exhaustion. It was most unlike life in Somerset, and for the first time I began to develop a taste for the company of foreigners such as had been my poor Uncle Auberon's ruin.[1]

Waugh often used to argue that travel was a waste of time, that tourism was a destructive force which ruins what it covets, and that everyone would be far better off if they simply stayed at home:

Nearly all the historic monuments and beauty spots of England are swamped by hordes of tourists. Like starlings, they disfigure wherever they settle, destroying its peace and serenity with their noise and their mess; like locusts, they strip its vitality, leaving a wilderness of car parks and 'toilets' behind. But the phenomenon is not confined to Britain. It is a product of worldwide prosperity. People can think of nothing to do with their money except move from place to place, spending it as they go. I do not honestly think that many of them really wish to see Wells Cathedral, or the Roman Baths or the Oxford and Cambridge Colleges. They have simply been told of these places – all now ruined – as possible destinations for their journeys.[2]

Waugh's reaction to this problem was twofold. On the one hand, he did his best to dissuade Britons from travelling overseas:

The whole of abroad is strewn with dragon's teeth. In Spain, holiday makers are mugged and given poisonous cooking oil to eat. In the South of France, they are burned to death in forest fires, in Italy and Austria, poisoned by anti-freeze in the wine. They are cheated by devious foreigners who take advantage of their lack of formal education every time they change money. Even if they can escape the foreigners, they are likely to be assaulted and stabbed by their fellow countrymen who see abroad as a good place to get drunk.[3]

He also did his utmost to discourage foreign tourists from visiting Britain, especially Americans, whose absence from London in the wake of various terrorist atrocities had a highly beneficial effect, he found, on the availability of taxis, theatre tickets and tables in the best restaurants:

Americans would be mad if they left their own beautiful country, with its exciting amusement parks and catering facilities, to visit Britain. Even if they avoid being shot down by crazed Arab gunmen in the street, blown up by Irish freedom fighters or attacked by American pit bull terriers – nobody in Britain is allowed to carry a weapon in his own defence – they will almost certainly catch a cold in our climate. They will be robbed by our taxi drivers and shop assistants wherever they go. Any 'kids' they bring to Britain will almost certainly be sexually abused by the natives. Worse than any of this, the British diet is not suitable for delicately nurtured Americans. On first contact with our salmonella-infected chickens' eggs, our listeria-ridden dairy products and our beef made from mad cows, many American visitors have found that their stomachs have simply dropped out.[4]

Yet despite this rousing rhetoric, Waugh was actually a prolific traveller – almost as prolific as his father – and, like his father, he wrote many fine travel stories in the course of his career. He was so happy to avail himself of the hospitality of various airlines, tourist boards and public relations agencies that Lynn Barber once called him 'the freebie king of all time'.[5] Yet unlike a lot of journalists, there was more to his travelogues than a fondness for free trips. Wherever he ended up, he brought the same acerbic wit to bear, whether he was travelling at his own expense or someone else's. And the best thing about foreign travel was escaping from his fellow Britons, as this magnificently grumpy piece, written on his return from France, attests.

*

ON RETURNING FROM ABROAD
(*Spectator*, 30 August 1986)

The New Britons are a peculiarly odious race and it is hard to feel much patriotic involvement with them. In the past ten years I have travelled through the world, and although the Moroccans may be slightly dirtier – not much – and some Australian Aborigines may eat slightly more disgusting food, it would be hard to find a more revolting collection of human beings than I found on the five o'clock Sealink ferry from Cherbourg to Weymouth last Saturday.

There were no football fans on board – or at any rate none identified himself as such – and only a small sprinkling of drunken louts of the type we have come to accept as part of the price we must all pay for being allowed to drink at all. Children were the most obvious horror – whining, moaning, clinging to their unattractive, harassed parents and stuffing horrible food into their mouths, non-stop, throughout the four-hour crossing. Even worse, when one came to examine them, were the parents, all trying to look like teachers, and reading in special, patronising voices to their loathsome children out of whatever sanitised rubbish had been approved by the local library sub-committees on race relations, on women, on hetero-sexism and on animal welfare – not to mention the local committee of Women Against Violence Against Women, union leaders and representatives of other minority groups – as suitable for reading to British kiddies.

But if the children were terrible, and the parents were even worse, the worst of the lot were the Young People. By some extraordinarily malevolent arrangement between British Rail and the railways of Europe, our Young People are allowed to travel non-stop around the Continent for a month in exchange for a £120 InterRail ticket, and this is precisely what they do. Every train in Europe is full of them, always asleep, more often than not in the corridors. Talking to a group of them, I realised that they practically never left the trains and when they did they never left the station. One group had been to Munich, where there were cockroaches in the station waiting room, to Venice, where the coffee in the buffet was overpriced, to Zagreb station, which scored highest for hot dogs, to Vienna, Barcelona and Paris, leaving the railways stations only at Venice, to visit a pizza bar, and Toulouse, to visit a steakhouse. For the rest, they just slept, or tried to sleep, making rail travel extremely disagreeable for everyone else.

Waugh's natural flair for travel writing first revealed itself when he was only seventeen, in a letter home to his father about his gap year adventures in Italy, alongside his friend from Downside, Rob Stuart.

JOURNEY TO ROME

The journey to Rome started like an early comic film. We had been told that it was 380 kilometres, but neither of us had any idea how large a kilometre was. I had always been under the impression that if one threw a stone one would be unlucky not to get it a kilometre or so – we believed the journey to be about

60 miles. Our landlady, who has eight children, declared that we would be killed if we attempted it and it was only with the greatest difficulty that we managed to persuade her to allow us to go. Despite her eight children she is a woman with infinite resources of motherliness, and adopted us both on the first day of our arrival. We had neither of us thought to enquire the way to Rome, being under the impression that in Italy all roads lead to Rome. Three and a half hours after we had been fondly embraced by our landlady, her husband and eight children, we were still in Florence when Rob's Vespa suddenly exploded. Pieces of red hot metal scattered everywhere, and it was another hour before we left on the road to Perugia, which we believed to be in the right direction. Eight miles outside Florence my Vespa simply ceased to work, and I had to be towed by Rob all the way to Arezzo since, the day being Palm Sunday, all garages were closed.

In Arezzo there was a great Communist congress as a rival camp to the Palm Sunday festivities. There we heard Mass, received our palms, for which we had to pay, and proceeded, expecting to see Rome at the turn of every corner. At night we arrived at a charming fortress town called Castelfiorentino, where we slept. We were told that Rome was still 300 kilometres away, which was the moment of our hideous disillusionment. Next day we motored solidly through the most beautiful countryside with monasteries on every hill and great lakes at the bottom of green, terraced mountains. We lunched at Perugia, saw the charming frescos by Perugino in the Cambio, and then went on to Assisi vowing not to stop until we arrived at Rome.

At night the only traffic on the roads is enormous, double loaded lorries driven by the criminal population whom it is too dangerous to lock up. Over great mountain passes time and time again they tried to murder us, and at every all-night inn where we stopped they were boasting of the people they had murdered that day. It was a charming medieval pilgrimage, and even if there were not gallows at every crossroads, there were the hulks of crashed motor cars as an edifying admonition. At every inn we were welcomed in the most friendly way by drunken lorry drivers and regaled with their anecdotes.

We arrived in Rome at half past three in the morning. The streets were quite deserted, until we saw a night watchman's fire, where we drove to ask for an hotel. Sitting around it were all the prostitutes of the North quarter, drawn like moths to a light bulb, with the poor bewildered night watchman in the middle. It was a freezing cold night, and the scene was straight from Hogarth as all these painted hags with carefully dyed hair sat cackling over their bawdy stories around the fire.

Waugh's first journalistic foreign trip was a lot more luxurious, a grand tour of European capitals for the *Mirror* in 1967, accompanied by his wife, Teresa, who was hired to write about the female side of things. They spent a week in Lisbon, a week in Paris, a week in Bonn, a week in Rome and a week in Vienna, staying in the best hotels and writing a thousand words about each place. Nice work if you can get it. Today such journalistic largesse is virtually unknown. As you might imagine, they had a splendid time, although goodness knows what the *Mirror*'s readers made of it. Michael Frayn lampooned their efforts in the *Guardian*, which made Waugh very proud.

Later that year, Waugh was sent on a less sumptuous but even more surreal assignment, a wild-goose chase worthy of a sequel to his father's journalistic satire, *Scoop*. American *Cosmopolitan* had asked Waugh to write an article about Mandy Rice-Davies, one of the two girls in the Profumo scandal which had helped to bring down the Macmillan government four years before. Mandy was now living in Tel Aviv, married to an El Al steward. The Six Day War had just begun, and *Cosmopolitan* had heard she was working as a nurse in a front-line hospital. *Cosmo* wanted Waugh to fly out to Israel and interview her straight away. 'In wartime greater priority is sometimes given to other cargoes than women's magazine journalists: bandages, blood plasma, and that sort of thing,' recalled Waugh, laconically. 'However, by making a lot of noise and pulling every string in sight I managed to get enough bandages, blood plasma, etc., taken off a plane for me to squeeze into a flight to Tel Aviv.'[6]

When he arrived in Israel, Waugh soon tracked down Mandy,

but she was nowhere near the front line. Nor was she working as a nurse. She was managing a discothèque in Tel Aviv. Undeterred, Waugh persuaded her to pose for photos, dressed in a nurse's uniform he'd bought for her. Sadly, none of these shots ever found its way into *Cosmopolitan*. However, they did make a nice spread in the centre pages of the *Daily Mirror*.

Throughout his travels, Waugh pursued a tireless quest to eat every sort of animal, however rare. He ate snake in Thailand, dog in the Philippines and raw horsemeat in Japan (which he rated better than steak tartare). In Cuba he ate crocodile and found it rather good, like a cross between pork and lobster. He even ate a kangaroo (a lot like venison), but one creature remained elusive:[7]

> By the time you read this I should be more than halfway to Australia [he told readers of his 'Way of the World' column]. All my previous visits to that beautiful and unusual country have been connected with wine, but a second, hidden, agenda has been the hope that I might get a chance to eat koala. I have eaten most of the indigenous fauna in most countries I have visited, but Australians always throw up their arms in horror at the thought of eating their sacred koalas. Now I learn that many English zoos and game parks sell off their redundant specimens for the exotic meat market. We may soon be eating it in Somerset. Next time I visit, perhaps I shall bring some jointed koala to give my Australian friends, but that will not be quite the same thing. It would be interesting to see how a diet of eucalyptus affects the taste.[8]

LAHTI LAMENTED
(*New Statesman*, 27 June 1975)

Long ago I decide that the policy of détente with the Soviet Union needed sharpening up. Adopted without question by all our political parties, it now seems in danger of drifting into the area of unprincipled and short-sighted platitudes which encompasses so much of our political thinking. The problem facing any citizen who makes an important decision of that kind is where to start.

Two months ago I received a mysterious invitation to attend the International Writers' Reunion at Lahti, seventy miles north of Helsinki. Fares and accommodation would be provided by the Eine Leino Society, a Finnish association of writers, publishers and *litterateurs*, together with the town council of Lahti, an ugly modern city of some 100,000 inhabitants. It is not the sort of invitation I normally accept, but I couldn't help noticing that a main purpose of the conference was for writers of the Western world to meet those from the Soviet bloc. It crossed my mind that it might be subsidised by the CIA and would provide a first opportunity for me to benefit from that organisation's legendary generosity. It had long been a sore point that nobody had ever asked me to join.

In the event, it seems unlikely that the occasion was set up by the CIA, although it may have had other sponsors. The heavy contingent of Soviet writers, and delegations from East Germany, Poland, Romania, Czechoslovakia and Hungary were paying their own expenses. There were two other British novelists, Sean Hignett, whose work is apparently even better known in Finland than it is here; and V. S. Naipaul, mysteriously described as coming from Trinidad (England). The balance of about 130 writers from all over the world divided for the most part into Stalinists and anti-Soviet Communists, although I met no-one from the far Left. I was chosen to speak for England on the theme of literature and national identity.

The conference had only one major division, never mentioned in public. This was between the Stalinist or pro-Soviet element, strongly represented among the Finns, and the rest. The art of wrecking conferences lies in discovering this point and discussing it enthusiastically. To achieve maximum results, I would have to say something along the lines that although we English writers look forward keenly to the sort of advanced socialist society we see in Russia and Czechoslovakia, and although we quite accept the need to impose certain standards of social responsibility and patriotism, we are tormented to know whether it is really necessary to imprison unpatriotic writers – or those with an incorrect attitude towards their social responsibilities – in mental hospitals. Goodness knows why the CIA don't employ me.

But the Russians looked so miserable in their ridiculous baggy suits, sitting apart with their KGB escorts. I had never before heard the sort of bland whoppers they are required to mouth in public, but as I listened to them droning on and on in the hot Finnish afternoon it slowly dawned on me that I was the only person listening. Everybody else – Stalinists and utopian Communists alike – had switched off the headsets translating instantaneously into Russian, Finnish, English and French. After a time I did the same. 'Oggi boggi capitalismus smashi bishi imperialismikki . . .' they droned on, quite aware that nobody was listening. Everything was addressed in a mumbled monotone, like a priest saying Mass, to the KGB escort who sat checking delivery of the speeches against the text.

What was the point in baiting these poor, smashed-up, timid little men? I was told that if I got any of the Iron Curtain writers away from their police escorts they would break down in tears after a bottle or two of vodka and admit everything they had said at the conference about cultural imperialism and national identity was a load of rubbish. After a glance at the Soviet writers Dimitri Jeremin and Fjordor Abramov I decided that four or five bottles would probably be necessary, and without the CIA to pay for them, I doubted whether the outlay would be justified in terms of entertainment value. Eventually I decided the whole thing was simply an exercise in Finnish hospitality at the time of year when the sun never sets and the whole Finnish nation goes mad with happiness or drink or both.

My own speech came on the last day. I discussed the English national identity in terms of its literary tradition for humour and satire, from Chaucer through the Porter Scene in Macbeth to the present day. This literary tradition provided the key to our economic collapse, I argued. The supreme exponent of the English attitude that whatever others hold seriously should immediately be seen as ridiculous to the civilised man was P. G. Wodehouse, I maintained, mentioning the unfortunate consequences which followed from his applying this attitude to the last war.

Now Wodehouse is widely read in Finland, and for the first time I began to sense that the Finns were on my side. Perhaps I rather laid it on for the benefit of the Iron Curtain delegates about how Wodehouse had been hounded by unscrupulous right-wing demagogues, on a trumped-up charge of treason which carried the death penalty. But when, at the end of my speech, I called upon the conference to stand in silence for half a minute in Wodehouse's memory I found it strangely satisfying to see an Eastern European delegate who had dozed off being prodded to his feet by the political overseer in attendance. The episode was immortalised by a huge four-column photograph in the main Finnish newspaper, *Helsingin Sanomat*, next day. Apparently it was the first time one of these biennial Lahti conferences had agreed on anything. Perhaps in a few years' time all the delegates will wear baggy suits and they will all agree about absolutely everything. At any rate, I feel I have done my bit.

DAY TRIP TO NAGASAKI
(*Spectator*, 24 May 1980)

Nagasaki describes itself on its tourist brochures as the City of Romance, Naples of the Orient. The sympathetic conservative tourist in Japan finds much to delight him, but he is constantly assailed by the absence of old buildings. This is sad, because apart from their instant affinity for any technological innovation, the Japanese are the most profoundly conservative people in the world. Ninety per cent of them, we are told, think they are middle class. They all wear natty blue suits, like bank clerks of the thirties. Their exquisite politeness and courtesy seem to spring from nothing more sinister than the desire to please. Their only vices would appear to be a fondness for drink and raw fish. How can one reconcile one's perception of this enchanting, tolerant, modest people with the wartime propaganda image, churned out by Duff Cooper's lie factory, of screaming, bandy-legged sadists? The answer, I felt, might be found in Nagasaki. There, at least, it would be unreasonable to expect many old buildings. Its chief tourist attraction is undoubtedly the Peace Park laid out around the centre of the atomic bomb explosion, but few Westerners ever visit it, and I found I caused something of a sensation, being asked to pose for photographs with grinning Japanese schoolgirls around the obelisk which marks the spot where the atom bomb exploded.

From the ashes and debris of that horrible occasion has grown yet another modern Japanese city, full of smiling, giggling inhabitants who seem at the same time apologetic that they should have put us to the trouble of dropping an atom bomb and intensely proud that their city should have been chosen. In fact, Nagasaki, being built on hills, was considerably less damaged than Hiroshima, and less again than Tokyo or Osaka, which had been destroyed, night after night, by firestorms as part of the American programme of 'bombing them back to the Stone Age'. Mr Glover's mansion, of *Madam Butterfly* fame, still stands in its beautiful garden overlooking the city of Nagasaki. The garden is now equipped with two moving escalators so that travellers can appreciate its delights without the trouble of walking, and electronic birdsong trills from every bush.

The Atom Museum hires out its top floor for private parties – I believe that bar mitzvahs are a speciality – and a huge, almost unbelievably ugly Peace Statue has recently been added as a further attraction. This shows a fat Japanese wrestler, seated, pointing upwards with one arm while waving in the air with another. He is leaning backwards in a way which suggests he will soon fall over, and is quite obviously drunk. Many of the Japanese spend quite a lot of the time drunk, but nobody seems to mind.

How, then, are we to reconcile these gentle, polite creatures with the screaming fanatics of wartime propaganda? It cannot all have been lies, because physical and emotional cripples of the Burma railways survive to this day, many of them with double-barrelled names, to tell the tale. I think the answer may lie in a simple misunderstanding. Officers and men building the Bridge on the River Kwai thought they were working hard to produce the finest damn bridge the British Army had ever built, but the Japanese did not understand what they meant by hard work, and thought the British were trying to sabotage the venture by slacking. If I am right, the message is clear. It is time British managers stopped trying to invoke the Dunkirk Spirit, which always fails, but thought long and hard about the River Kwai.

CONFESSIONS OF AN ENGLISH OPIUM SMOKER
(*Business Traveller*, March 1982)

There are those who go to Chiang Mai for the climate, the temples, the flowers or the agreeable inhabitants. It also has an extraordinarily pleasant English pub, run by a Rhodesian ex-public-schoolboy called Nigel and some of the most beautiful girls in the world. But what attracted me most was the promise of finding opium dens – something which were two a penny in Vietnam, apparently, before the socialists took over, and easy enough to find in Bangkok in the old days, but now threaten to disappear from the face of the globe thanks to the officious worldwide activities of the American Drug Enforcement Agency.

I had already searched Hong Kong, Bangkok and large parts of Japan for any trace of an opium den. No doubt they exist in all these places, but my experiences led me to suppose either that they are kept from foreigners or that they are so difficult to find as to be of no interest to the business traveller on a flying visit, and in this context it would be kind to sound a note of warning. Nobody should try the opium experience who wants to do any work that day, or even who has any work next day which demands great alertness of mind. No doubt regular users come to terms with the side – and after – effects, or possibly they acquire a tolerance, or possibly they settled down in less demanding occupations, but I am not writing for those who seriously wish to become addicts so much as for those who are greedy for new experiences and feel, like me, that they should be prepared to try most things once. Visits to the Far East are excellent opportunities for satisfying many of these urges.

The best way to go to Chiang Mai from Bangkok, according to everyone who has done it, is by train, for a fuller experience of this enchanting country with its gentle Buddhist pieties, its beautiful people and their friendly, cheeky good humour. But I was a man with a mission without the time to spare and flew to Chiang Mai. They say you should check in at least an hour early, but if you do so they fall over with amazement and generally put you on an earlier flight.

The Rincome Hotel in Chiang Mai is not quite so over-whelmingly grand as Bangkok's famous Oriental, being considerably smaller in any case, but the combination of a determined effort to reach the highest European standards with the peculiar Thai genius for making a guest feel welcome and important ensures that it is a memorable experience. In November it was nearly deserted – a hot, dry season in Chiang Mai, with the magnolias in full bloom (I suppose they knew what they were doing). One was grateful for the swimming pool.

An inexperienced traveller might ask at the hotel enquiries desk for the nearest opium den, but this would be a mistake. The hotel is so respectable that it does not even have hostesses in its nightclub, with the result that when I was there the night-club was totally deserted. A young lady gyrated over the record deck, psychedelic lights flashed and a barman stood disconsolately behind the bar, but there were no guests. So I went to bed. At eleven fifty there was a scratch on the door. One of the night watchmen had noticed that my lights were still on, and was concerned to think of anyone sleeping alone. Would I like to meet a nice, clean young girl . . .?

It is an even worse mistake for the opium seeker to ask at the English pub. Although this is the friendliest place on earth, with excellent European food and good beer, it is also patronised by Americans, many of whom work for the DEA, and the expatriate community is terrified of involvement in the seamier side of life in the Golden Triangle. But this English pub, scarcely 200 yards away from the Rincome Hotel, is ideal for English travellers suffering from loneliness. About 300 yards round the corner is the New Chiang Mai Honey Club, combining night-club, coffee bar, massage parlour and general fun-lovers' social centre, which cannot be recommended too highly. Prices are moderate, the entertainment is first class and Chiang Mai's beautiful people extraordinarily friendly.

There are no opium dens in Chiang Mai itself – the American presence is too intrusive – but the hill villages around are full of them. Anybody who takes one of the highly respectable hill village tours organised from the hotel to Chiang Rai, in the centre of the Golden Triangle, will be approached in one or two of the villages by an old man offering to sell opium, but it would be madness to buy any. Opium is not something to be smoked alone – you need a professional to prepare the pipe, another to make gentle, undemanding conversation, a third to act as lookout. The penalty for possession of the stuff can rise from fifteen years in a Thai gaol – no food is provided by the Thai authorities, and there is no longer a British consulate in Chiang Mai – to death by firing squad. On top of this, the rewards for information paid by the police and the Drug Enforcement Agency are out of all proportion to the effort involved, and by no means all dope peddlers are as scrupulously honest as one might like.

A better approach may be to ask your taxi driver, but I never found a taxi driver in Chiang Mai who inspired the necessary degree of confidence. As in large parts of the Far East, any unaccompanied male passenger will be approached with various lurid offers by his driver, who starts by trying to dissuade him from his original destination, saying that it is of no interest, or closed, or that no aeroplanes are flying that day, then starts offering him a massage, a nice clean girl, a spectacle, a boy or any of the other joys of that hospitable region. Some of them would undoubtedly be prepared to take you to one of the hill villages for an opium session, and it is no offence to ask, but others almost certainly wouldn't. Taxi drivers are comparatively prosperous people, and often highly respectable. It would be a mistake to suppose anything to the contrary simply because they seem to act as prostitutes' touts. This, too, is a perfectly respectable occupation. It is only the opium business which, thanks to the officious activities of the DEA, has moved a little downmarket.

My own opportunity came when I was approached by a bicycle taxi man – rather a sorry specimen, who might have been a film extra in any Far East melodrama about baddies – whose conveyance bore the unmistakable legend 'Bron to love you'. It was repeated both inside and outside the carriage, surrounded by hearts. This mystery was never explained. My driver, who became a close friend but whose name (it was probably Bang or Fuck or Hi or any loud cry) always went in one ear and flew out the other whenever he told it me, merely giggled when I asked him what it meant.

These bicycle taxis are cheap but hideously uncomfortable. It is impossible to lean back, and you have a fine view of your chauffeur's bottom, but of little else. Don't, as I did, buy the fellow lunch. They hold their wind badly. My own man – let us call him Bang – also tired easily, and was liable to stop without warning in the middle of nowhere and suggest you continue your journey by taxi. But over lunch he agreed to take me to a hill village by motorbike. And after that, he said wistfully, I might be interested in a really exceptionally clean young girl of his acquaintance. She was not like other girls but worked in a factory, and never saw a man more than once in every twenty-four hours as a personal favour. Under the circumstances she was not cheap and might ask as much as 200 baht (£5) for all night . . .

The motorbike cost 300 baht and provided one of the most disagreeable experiences of my pampered young life. The village turned out to be less than ten miles away, but a large part of it was mountain path of abominable steepness with pitted wheel tracks a foot deep into which we kept falling. On arrival at the Meo Hill village I found a fleet of taxis drawn up – it is a well-known tourist resort – and booked one for the return journey. There was not a chance in hell that I could have stayed on the back of a motorbike for the return journey – it was difficult enough stone cold sober, and Bang did not really understand about gears or, indeed, about corners, and I walked much of the way. Any plan one makes with the Thais should make allowance for their lunatic optimism, but this time I was lucky.

Bang took me to a friend who took me to another friend who took me to one of the village houses, built on stilts in the steep sides of the mountain. No great secrecy was observed, although I noticed that one of our group seemed to act as a lookout. The inside of the hut was dark, with one corner set aside as a sort of dais on which I lay. The bamboo bed was designed for a Thai and about a foot short, but comfortable enough.

One old man squatted beside his little table with a candle, pipes, a pin and the rest of his paraphernalia. The village conversationalist came and made bright, soothing remarks about England. In two hours they claimed I had smoked twenty-five pipes and charged 700 baht (£17.50), a suggestion about which I was in no state to argue. But they were friendly souls, and expressed concern that I had enough money to get home.

The sensation lasts many hours, and it is best not to move for a long time. Staggering about afterwards, one had the feeling of being very drunk except that one's brain was remarkably clear and one felt an overwhelming benignity towards the entire human race. I simply do not know how intoxicated or absurd I appeared to the three giggling girls who shared my taxi part of the way back, or to the lady who hired me the motorbike when I went to pay her, or to the staff of the Rincome Hotel as I walked through the lobby with extraordinary care on the way to my bedroom. They were all far too polite to notice, and in any case I dare say they were used to it. A slight feeling of nausea might have been disagreeable in other circumstances, and also the illusion that flies are walking over your face, but this can presumably become an acquired taste. Pleasant sensations of detachment lasted for nearly twelve hours, with only the slightest hangover accompanied by loss of appetite and a strange reluctance to urinate. But if I were you I should leave at least twelve hours clear before making any important business or social engagements.

THE MANILA FILE
(*Business Traveller*, April 1982)

'The visitor should not go about asking people how much they earn and clicking his tongue and shaking his head when told.' This instruction, contained in some notes on etiquette in a guide to Manila, which I bought on my first day, holds the main secret of enjoying the place. For all their cheerfulness and quite extraordinary friendliness to foreign visitors, the Filipinos really are very poor. Most of them want to get out. Any Westerner looking for a small brown wife who will be an affectionate and loyal companion to him in his old age, a good mother to his children, an excellent cook and a bedmate to rekindle his jaded Western appetites, need look no further. For everyone else, Manila provides an object lesson in how to live with poverty and like it.

The grandest hotel, in the old-fashioned sense of grandeur, is undoubtedly the old Manila Hotel on Katigbak Drive, with its Champagne Room and magnificent reception area. I chose the Manila Mandarin in Makati, which is generally thought the best of the new luxury hotels, arriving hot and bothered from Thailand with a 2000-word article in illegible manuscript, which had to be telexed immediately to London. Although it was seven o'clock in the evening, they produced a girl called Alice to take it down on a typewriter within minutes of my arrival. Not only did words like 'melancholic' and '*cloisonné*' trip off this smiling girl's fingers at enormous speed and without a single mistake, but she actually fed me chocolates while I read it to her. There are restaurants in Manila where delightful young girls sit in front of you, putting the food in your mouth with their fingers. That may be too much for some tastes, or at least takes a bit of getting used to, especially as many of the girls are so painfully thin. But from the very start, I realised that Filipino women have the right idea.

An Australian drilling engineer I befriended on my first evening told me that the island on which we stood and several others in the group were sitting on a goldmine of thermal energy. They could have virtually free electric power, he said, which with a huge labour pool and a fertile soil could turn the Philippines into an incredibly prosperous country, except that foreign investment was discouraged by a 60 per cent national requirement and the Filipinos simply weren't up to it. At least 10 per cent, often 20 per cent, of any contract must be set aside for bribes, he said. He didn't really know why he bothered, except that he liked the free and easy lifestyle.

Further enquiry confirmed what I had suspected. He was thinking of the women. It was normal, he said, for the oldest girl in a poor family to go out to work to keep the rest. This normally meant that she became a bar girl or entered one of the grades of prostitution. Other girls worked their way through university in this way, while also paying for their younger brothers and sisters to be educated. 'Those are the best girls,' he said. No Filipino would marry them afterwards, which was probably for the best, as Filipinos make abominable husbands. They frequently leave their wives after the first four or five children. Then the deserted wife has to work as a *mama-san* in a bar or brothel to feed her children – at any rate until the oldest girl is old enough to earn a decent living as a prostitute. The only hope for these girls, unless they eventually find a career in America, is to marry a Westerner, when they make, as I say, the dearest little wives.

All of which sounds like a hell on earth. President Ferdinand Marcos and his formidable wife, the First Lady Imelda Marcos (who combines being Mayor of Metro Manila with her strange and immensely powerful post as head of the Human Settlements Agency), can reasonably claim to have rescued the country from near anarchy. Martial law was immensely popular throughout the length and breadth of the Philippines, whatever our Western neighbours may say. Only a few subversives in the Catholic Church and the universities even pretend to be pleased that it was lifted, under pressure from the disastrous President Jimmy Carter. But can they really be proud of a society in which the mixture of Western affluence with Oriental poverty condemns a substantial proportion of their more beautiful young women to work as prostitutes?

One would have thought not, except for the enormous gaiety which these young Filipinos bring to their work. It might not do for our own daughters, but it seems to do very well for them. This may seem cynical, even opportunistic, but I can only urge people to wander round the innumerable girlie bars of Ermita and see for themselves. There is little to choose between them, except the volume of noise and the amount of hassle. At first one is depressed by the extraordinary ineptitude of the go-go dancers, who look spare and silly. No doubt they are working out complex mathematical problems in their heads, or brooding about the relationship between gross national savings and gross national investment. Their heart is certainly not in the dancing, unlike their equivalents in Bangkok's Pat Pong Road. One can also be depressed by reflecting on their obvious availability. It is only if one buys them a drink that one discovers how witty and friendly they are, as well as beautiful, charming and reck-lessly prepared for any adventure. There is really no need to pay the bar fine (which varies between £5 and £15) and take them back to your hotel (which will charge a nominal £4 or so for double occupancy) unless you are one of those people inca-pable of sleeping alone.

Perhaps it is because they are nearly all Christians, rather than Buddhists or Hindus or – watch it – Muslims that there seems to be no racial tension between Filipinos and Westerners. Out of sight, they practise unimaginable acts of cruelty on each other, as one reads in the Manila newspapers. Family feuds, murder and revenge are all part of their way of life. But so long as the visitor is friendly and treats them as human beings, there is no culture gap – as there undoubtedly is with Thais, Japanese, Malays, Chinese and most people of the Far East. They see themselves as Westerners who just happen to be a little bit browner and smaller, and a great deal poorer than the rest of us. They do not resent our greater affluence but genuinely welcome it and even find it funny. Nor do they treat poor travellers with disdain. They are simply a very friendly, very cheerful people.

CUBAN CABARET
(*Business Traveller*, June 1982)

All that remains of sinful old Havana, with its brothels and casinos and wild nights of every imaginable dissipation, is the cabaret. Heavily subsidised (like everything else) by the state, four or five huge cabaret shows are put on every night, with anything between fifty and a hundred girls apiece performing complicated gyrations in any number of lavish costume changes. The girls are usually divided into two teams, one roughly white, the other roughly black. Their performances are straight from Hollywood of the 1950s at its spectacular best. Nothing indecorous or lewd is allowed – even their long legs are clad in tights – but there is no pretence that these girls with their dear, tight little bums and notable shortage of shelf kit are anything but sex objects. Among the many things which Cubans have been spared in twenty-three years of a rigidly controlled press is the *Guardian*'s Women's Page.

These cabarets are not only extraordinarily lavish, they are also very cheap and the visitor to Havana had better like them because they are all that is going in the way of entertainment. Most Cuban women not actually employed in cabaret – admittedly an enormous number of them are – appear to be extremely fat. This may be because of all the sugar they eat, or it may be because the regime's policy of no unemployment means that nearly everybody is seriously under-employed. Every hotel has its public relations staff, its five or six porters and an army of people to demand room cards [bona fides] from any unaccompanied female. It is quite usual to find small, fully automatic lifts manned by two enormous black women, leaving little room for anyone else. Business travellers' wives need feel no anxiety while their husbands are in Cuba. Diplomats and others posted there are warned to treat it as an Iron Curtain country, with all the possibilities of blackmail arising from any apparently casual encounter. Neither businessmen nor tourists are likely to be tempted into any indiscretion, either by the native women or by the parties of huge Eastern Europeans in ungainly costumes, moving around in groups with their socialist-approved husbands looking furtive and bashed up and generally disapproving.

For the last five years, Castro's Cuba has been making efforts to attract both businessmen and tourists. Whatever their Marxist analysis of Western economic prospects may be, the Cubans have been investing large sums in building tourist hotels and even factories in which Western businessmen are invited to take a 49 per cent share, providing them with the plant and a docile cheap labour force in exchange for Western management and marketing skills. I do not know how efficient they would prove to be as a labour force. Despite revolutionary posters everywhere exhorting them to greater efficiency, one has the impression that Cubans have never really taken Time and Motion studies to their warm revolutionary hearts.

The projected tourist boom has never really taken off, but Cuba receives about 25,000 winter visitors every year from Canada and desperately wants to expand its summer trade from Europe. The Cubans have much to learn about tourism, as might be witnessed by their choice of myself as a suitable guest for their tourist agency's promotional efforts. My Cubatur guide was convinced that I wanted to see worker housing projects, concrete factories, worker playground parks and mysterious things called day centres, which the working classes seem to find useful. At first I was rather angry about this, reckoning we never insist that visitors must inspect our concrete factories and day centres. After a time, one began to see it as part of the charm of the place that they honestly suppose we are interested in their dismal social arrangements. If they have much to learn, the Cubans are unlike most socialists in being quite ready to learn it. They are probably the friendliest people left in the Caribbean, and although the endless paperwork and unbelievably slow service make the simplest purchase a headache, they do not have Eastern Europe's joy in applying absurdly inappropriate rules. If the rule seems silly, they scrap it.

There are only three decent hotels in Havana – the Riviera, which is the best, the Havana Libre (formerly the Hilton), which looked pretty ghastly, and the Nacional, which is the oldest and might be the grandest if it did not also have to cater for dingy groups of holidaymakers from Eastern Europe. They, of course, are used to having to queue for everything, and I am afraid the hotel's standard of service reflects these modest expectations. On arrival I found that they had lost the key to my room. I would not have minded being accompanied to my room by a porter on every occasion if only there had always been a porter on duty. The air-conditioning had broken down. There was no hot water. There was no plug in the bath – no socialist anywhere in the world can be trusted with a bath plug. All these failings were later rectified, but the list was all the more impressive, I thought, by virtue of the fact that I was Cubatur's guest and they were actually trying to impress me with the efficiency of their operation. Those less favoured will find that a tumbler reversed over the bath's outlet makes a better plug than a flannel or a heel.

One evening after a day spent sailing and swimming in Santa Maria del Mar I was taken to what was described as an Afro Cuban Night in a sort of field outside. This was entirely a tourist occasion, like some of the 'voodoo' ceremonies around Port au Prince, and sponsored by Cubatur. The audience consisted for the most part of elderly, slightly drunk francophone

Canadians. The highlight of the evening was a simulated religious ceremony of the Santería, or Afro-Cuban religion. As the
bongo drums beat out what should I suppose be described as
their insistent rhythm – that is to say, they got it in time once
every four or five beats – an agitated, sweating Negro produced
a chicken tied by one leg to a string in his hand. All the Canadians
went 'ah', 'how sweet', etc., just like a pantomime audience when
the little white ponies come on stage. The Negro danced around
with the chicken, which was plainly scared out of its wits, occasionally shoving it in the face of the audience until the wretched
animal started clucking in time with the music. We all clapped
politely. Then the Negro seemed to get angry about something
and started waving the chicken around violently, occasionally
letting it escape and pulling it back by the string attached to
one leg. I noticed a few of the blue-rinsed brigade look a little
uneasy. Next he started plucking its neck. I thought, Steady on,
old chap, there is an Englishman present. The bongo drum-
mers started going out of their minds – some of them were
quite attractive mulatto girls who, I later learned, double up in
cabaret. Then the chief dancer put the chicken's neck in his
mouth and bit its head off. A few Canadian women screamed.

Oh dear. It really was rather disgusting, but I couldn't help
laughing. Then they put its neck in a glass to collect the blood,
added *agua ardiente* and offered it around. The chief dancer
pushed the severed head into faces in the audience; another
Negro put the neck of the unfortunate bird in his mouth and
started dancing with the corpse dangling in front of him. The
mulatto girls came and asked us to dance and the party livened
up. At last I thought I had glimpsed a real Cuba underneath
the socialist rubbish. It would be no good pretending that the
occasion was an unqualified success with all the tourists present,
but I could not help admiring the genius of a nation which
makes it suppose this is the sort of thing that tourists want to
see. My Cubatur guide, a conscientious young man called
Raimondo, who practically never left my side, unwound for the
first time as we drove back to Havana long past our bedtimes.

'Wo,' he said to me, 'you are going to write about Cuba.

Tomorrow, I am going to write a report on you. I shall say, "Only mulattes make Wo liff." At least I know what is in my file.

NEW HISTORY OF ZIMBABWE
(Spectator, 2 October 1982)

On the plane between Harare (formerly Salisbury) and Masvingo (as Fort Victoria was renamed on the day of my arrival, having spent an interval as Nyanda; these are great days for Zimbabwean sign writers), I sat next to a fat, middle-aged Frenchman. He said he now lived in retirement near Tours, but came to Zimbabwe every year to shoot an elephant. The Zimbabwe government sells licences for this as part of its programme of culling the 20,000 or so elephants which roam the country (somebody gave me that figure – I have not tried to count the brutes). For the price of a permit, which is enormous, you get whatever parts of the beast you want stuffed, mounted and delivered to your door with the tusks. My French friend now had an enormous collection of these things. He lives for the moment every year when he can point his gun at an elephant, shoot it, and come home again, happy as a skylark.

Later, seeing an elephant roaming around the great Wankie Reserve, I tried to imagine what he felt. I watched the elephant, from the safety of my Land Rover, and the elephant watched me, but neither of us could summon up much interest in the other. My guide told me that when they flap their ears it does not mean they are angry, as I had thought, but only that they are hot. That was quite interesting, but really the sort of thing one should have learned from Mr Attenborough's excellent television series. For the life of me, I could not imagine any possible joy in shooting it, as it stood twenty-five yards away flapping its ears. Perhaps it would look funny if it fell down very suddenly, but that was all. Far better to leave it alone to lumber around as best it knows how.

There are those who sneer at these game reserves, as if it is a cruel perversion of nature that these splendid, proud, etc., wild animals should be gaped at and photographed by tourists. But after several days of watching tourists stare at wild animals and wild animals either staring back or ignoring them I decided that these game reserves marked an important step in human evolution. Human beings are no longer hunters and at last we are coming to terms with the fact, however many fat young merchant bankers insist on blasting away at pheasants on their weekends. Wild animals are now things for humans to gape at and photograph, rather than kill for food or sport. Those who hint darkly that the Wankie National Park is aptly named have got it all wrong. Man has evolved the system of factory farming for his simple nutritional requirements. Whether the new system involves more or less suffering for animals is neither here nor there. Who cares? Lion, warthog and elephant certainly understand their new role in the scheme of things, as they pose in nonchalant attitudes before the safari buses. A new relationship has been born between human beings and wild animals.

LESSONS OF JAMAICA
(*Spectator*, 16 March 1985)

I should have been prepared for the discovery that a significant proportion of the Jamaican population is more or less permanently stoned, but I confess that it came as something of a shock to me when my first taxi driver in Kingston – Jamaica's dilapidated and violence-ridden capital – took both his hands off the wheel and started jigging to the offensively loud reggae blaring from his radio. In some ways he was a perfect taxi driver – courteous, cheerful and reasonably cheap – but he understood nothing I said to him and nothing he said made any sense.

Wherever I went (except, perhaps, in the luxurious British-run enclaves of Round Hill and Tryall, around Montego Bay) the pattern repeated itself. Continuous ingestion of the drug would appear to make people happy and amiable, at any rate in public, but terrifyingly stupid, forgetful, inefficient and more or less unemployable by Western standards. It is an observable phenomenon throughout most of the Jamaican scene that three people must be employed to perform the simplest job for one person. In my own extremely pleasant cottage in Round Hill, it took three women from six o'clock in the morning to scramble two eggs by a quarter past nine. I do not suppose for a moment that any of these women had ever so much as experimented with *ganja,* which is illegal in the country and also forbidden in Round Hill, but it seems to me that the *ganja* smokers set the pace throughout Jamaican society. It was also noticeable that if ever one asked for an egg poached, it arrived scrambled, if ever one asked for it scrambled it arrived boiled and so on, to make life a constant succession of delightful surprises.

The difference between being unemployed in Jamaica and being unemployed in Britain is that if one is unemployed in Jamaica one is quite likely to starve. In many ways, a system where three people are required to do one person's job might seem to approximate to the modern Church of England's idea of Heaven, the solution to all our problems. But Shirley Williams's victims already suffer from an entirely different set of disqualifications from most forms of employment: it is not so much that they are more ignorant, or illiterate, or even undisciplined than previous generations as that they have never been confronted with any particularly good reason for wishing to work. They are spoiled and lazy to the point of resenting any call upon their attention, let alone the manifold inconveniences of regular employment.

In the past, I have urged that the unemployed – and for that matter the whole population – should be allowed free access to such a comparatively harmless euphoriant as cannabis as the best means of keeping everybody happy and preventing them from creating that social or proletarian wealth which disfigures the landscape and spreads a cancer of uncouth noises, sights and smells all over the country. Having examined the Jamaican model, I must now conclude that I was wrong: if one added the *ganja*-inspired qualities of stupidity, forgetfulness and inefficiency to all the other factors which make such a large proportion of Young Britain unemployable, the final result would be a general squalor such as would make even the South Bank theatre and entertainment complex seem acceptable.

So I end up with no solution to the unemployment problem and a firm conviction that the general sale of cannabis should continue to be forbidden. But the fact remains that it is an extraordinarily pleasant substance, if taken infrequently and in moderation, at times when it is unlikely to interfere with one's work or one's prospects of employment. One again, Jamaica shows the way, where *ganja* smoking is an established element in Rastafarian worship. If cannabis were forbidden under the severest penalties throughout the week, and permitted only on Sundays inside Christian churches, when supervised by a Christian minister of religion, every objection to its use would be overcome and many benefits accrue. Nobody would be irritated by the fatuous or ignorant opinions expressed from the pulpit, everything would be accepted in a spirit of amazed, finger-clicking benignity; the Church would have found a role.

SOME LEISURELY MEDITATIONS ON THE SYDNEY OPERA HOUSE
(*Spectator*, 27 February 1988)

My bedroom in the Regent Hotel, Sydney, looks down from a great height on the harbour and on the Sydney Opera House nestling in a corner of it. This strange and costly building, designed by the Danish architect Jørn Utzon in 1955, was opened on its magnificent site, surrounded by water on three sides, in 1973 to cries of wonderment and disbelief from the rest of the world. Briefly, it seemed to have fanned the dying embers of the Modern Movement; it remains the focus of a certain bemused pride in Sydney and throughout the whole of Australia. On my last visit I was taken behind the stage and into its bowels, marvelling at the lack of functional justification for the design. Even judged as decoration, it ignores the first principles of artistic integrity, since in order for the huge concrete sails to be filled with air (they contain nothing else) in the manner of real sails, the wind would have to be blowing simultaneously from opposite directions.

This time I have not ventured inside. Instead, I brood over it twinkling underneath me in the morning sunlight as I eat my breakfast, glimmering in the evening light as I return to change for dinner (the Australians are very formal about dress) and glowing once again by floodlight when I eventually return to bed. From this great height it looks very small and strangely vulnerable, enshrining, as it does, a last residual hope for the future that Modern Art was a good idea. Epstein's contortions and Moore's polished lumps expressed a vision, an alternative aesthetic, a justification for modern culture. All the nicest and most intelligent people I know have convinced themselves that this is the case, just as all the nicest and most intelligent Australians have convinced themselves their Opera House is beautiful. It is not beautiful, of course. Nor is it ugly. It is merely absurd. It is a Mickey Mouse construction, straight out of Disney World. It is a harmless little joke about modern architecture rather than an example of the real thing – which would inevitably have been brutal in its desire to shock, offensive in its ugliness and sinister in its contempt for mere humanity. The Opera House is none of these things. It is purely absurd, and utterly endearing in its absurdity.

What makes it so endearing is the mystery of how a sceptical, satirically minded nation allowed it to be built – at such prodigious cost, and with such flamboyant disregard for any canon of good taste or common sense. It is a monument to a particular Australian quality, which is seldom remarked in discussion about the country but one which impresses me more with every visit. At its least interesting, it takes the form of an astounding level of tolerance. Sydney's Gay Mardi Gras, when all the homosexuals of Kings Cross cavort in the streets, is an example of this. The friendliness with which they are received would be unthinkable in Britain, even before AIDS. In Sydney, it is welcomed as another opportunity to show good humour and friendliness. More impressive than this tolerance, which might otherwise be mistaken for indifference, is a quality of fair-mindedness, of openness to other views. This may make them suckers for committed pressure groups, but it also produces such entirely pleasant absurdities as the Sydney Opera House.

IN SEARCH OF THE NOCTURNAL KAKAPO
(Spectator, 14 November 1992)

It is not easy to find a surviving, ambulatory, nocturnal kakapo parrot in New Zealand, and for a very good reason. Discovering that on those blessed islands it had nowhere in particular to go, it soon forgot how to fly. A large bird, sometimes nearly three feet high, it spends its time waddling around in the dark. When alarmed, it simply stands still in the hope that the danger will go away. This ploy may have worked with the Maoris, but it proved ineffective against the cats and dogs brought by early settlers from Britain. Now it is well and truly endangered, unlike so many of the species officiously listed by our own RSPB.

In the course of a speech at the National Press Club in Wellington I proposed that New Zealand should adopt the kakapo as its national symbol in place of the kiwi, which spends its waking hours frantically dashing around, making silly squeaks and mysteriously contriving to lay eggs that are several times bigger than itself. The kakapo, in all its vulnerability, seems to sum up a peculiarly innocent, trusting quality, which I found among our kith and kin at the bottom of the world and which makes them as different from their Australian cousins as the proverbial chalk from cheese. When this quality is added to their beautiful, hospitable manners and sunny natures, they strike me as being a species in need of protection. They believe whatever you tell them. When Americans arrive in Auckland with their outlandish clothes and farouche, boastful speech to announce they are millionaires, presidents of some important company, they are invariably believed, and many New Zealand fortunes have been lost as a result.

Perched on their green islands so many thousands of miles away from anywhere else, New Zealanders are touchingly concerned to learn what visitors think of their country, which is surely as close to heaven as any country can decently be. In accordance with the old Fleet Street convention that any hack returning from a foreign country is London's greatest expert on that country for about ten days, I will record, from my own observations, that all New Zealanders read the *Spectator*; that they are even fonder of the Queen than they are of Lady Thatcher and are seriously worried about the marriage of the Prince and Princess of Wales; that they have beautiful English silver services of 1820–40, the time when the English silversmith's art was at its height; that many of the women, as well as being healthy and exquisitely mannered, are very prettily tattooed.

There is also a tough and nasty, but mercifully very small, industrial working class, mostly composed of whingeing Poms from the Mersey and the Clyde who arrived on assisted passages after the war. When asked what I wanted to see in New Zealand, I foolishly said, 'A geyser,' imagining that every field was full of them. There is only one important site at Rotorua and it has all the horrors of any major tourist attraction, with Maori feasts and Maori maidens shouting in bogus American accents: 'Now I want everyone from Germany to lift their arms. Come on, folks, let's give a big hand to our friends from Germany. Anybody from Finland?' My quest for the kakapo was lonelier, ending up at the Wairarapa National Wildlife Park with a stuffed specimen. At least, I think it was stuffed. But my conclusion, having travelled about 17,500 miles to get there, was that I had ended up among my own people. They understood what I said when I spoke to them, and I understood what they were saying when they spoke to me.

Chapter Twelve
Other People

As soon as a man starts issuing writs for libel he immediately assumes many of the properties of an angel. His body is no longer the weak, farting, nose-picking thing we all recognise as a human body, but emerges in its glorified or resurrected state without a spot of blemish.[1]

Waugh was a ruthless portraitist, with the eye of a Hogarth or a Gillray. He could sum up someone in a single sentence – frequently unfairly, but with devastating accuracy all the same. His judgements were remarkably acute, and often ahead of the game. 'We should not look at Blair's pretty little Chihuahua face,' he warned his readers in 1997, a few months before the British electorate gave Tony Blair his first landslide victory. 'We should watch the hideous wolf's tail wagging him from behind.'[2] Yet Waugh wasn't just a caricaturist. He was also a diligent reporter. Unlike a lot of columnists, he actually took the trouble to get out and meet people, to talk to them and listen to what they had to say. He was a good interviewer, and he wrote some revealing and penetrating profiles. Here are just a few of them. At the time when they were written, a lot of them passed by unnoticed, but like great cartoons they have a staying power that more scrupulous studies rarely share.

Like all the best portraits, Waugh's profiles also reveal a good deal about the writer. His enemies tended to dismiss him as a misanthrope. Even his fans were often most enamoured by his celebrated bile and bite. However, his sketches of his friends and colleagues reveal a warmer side to his nature, even when he abhorred their politics (like Paul Foot) or was bewildered by their faith (like Graham Greene). Waugh was fiercely tribal, dividing his world into foes and allies — but although he was a ruthless adversary, for those he loved or respected, his affection and admiration knew no bounds.

*

GRAHAM GREENE
(*Sunday Telegraph*, 23 September 1982)

Even while he was writing his new novel, *Monsignor Quixote*, Graham Greene was gloomy about its reception. It would annoy Catholics and Marxists, he said, and nobody else would be remotely interested in it. When, having read the book, I told him I did not think it would annoy Catholics much – in fact, it was almost impossible to think of anything which would annoy Catholics nowadays – he looked even gloomier. 'The book starts with a joke about the Trinity. You don't feel they might think it goes too far?' he asked hopefully. To annoy his fellow Catholics might almost be an essential part of the practice of his faith, a solemn Christian duty. As he gets older, Graham Greene seems to become more and more Catholic, although he denies this hotly. 'I believe less, and accept more, through obedience. For instance,' he added wistfully, 'I could easily do without the virgin birth. But my faith tells me I am wrong.' Smugness and certainty are the greatest enemies of religion, he believes, a curious attitude for a convert to Roman Catholicism. Doubt is an essential ingredient of any faith, whether Catholic or Marxist.

When the hero of his latest novel, a Spanish parish priest travelling around with the Communist former mayor of his village, feels the first twinges of that theological despair which, with pride, is the ultimate sin in the Christian book, it is because he feels he may be losing his doubts. Any religion – or political ideology – based on certainty is repugnant to human nature, an insult to reason and a denial of free will, Mr Greene has decided. At seventy-seven, he looks extraordinarily well on this diet of doubt. There is a natural sweetness of nature, a modesty and friendliness about the man which make all who know him well fiercely proud of their friendship. In my own case his benevolence is transferred. He knew and loved my father, and will believe no ill of the son.

The friendship between Graham Greene and Evelyn Waugh was a strange and rather beautiful thing. In elevated or conceited moments I imagine I understand exactly those qualities in each which appealed to the other. Waugh was a sucker for certainties; Greene is a sucker for doubts. What they shared, I think, was a certain honesty, a recklessness, and a keen awareness of everybody else's absurdity. At any rate, it was enough to bind them together with hoops of steel. The happy result, from my own point of view, was that I inherited a hoop or two.

There is something bland and beautiful in his trust. Conversation jumps disconcertingly from whether the Pope is trying to commit suicide with his programme of world travel to the effects of opium on sexual performance, or from malicious rumours about his own sex life to the politics of South America – all discussed with total honesty and without a trace of self-consciousness. He speaks in a speculative, tentative voice. Everything is open to discussion. Nothing is likely to shock him.

He is not a remotely political person himself, despite being obsessed by political struggles. He has lived in Antibes now for sixteen years, dividing his time between a modest two-roomed flat overlooking the harbour and a more daunting one in Paris where he keeps most of his books. It is crammed from floor to ceiling with them, and although he seldom spends more than eight weeks a year in Paris, he does miss his books. At other times he goes on his travels. Until recently he went every year to Panama, whose military leader, General Omar Torrijos, was a close personal friend.³ Greene learned of his friend's death in an air crash just as he was about to leave for his annual visit, and took the news very hard.

Torrijos replaced Castro in his esteem – he has not seen Castro for nearly twenty years – and seems to have been a worthier candidate for it. Even after Torrijos's death, the South American connection is kept alive in Antibes by mysterious telephone calls asking him to mediate in the release of kidnapped bankers. Whole plots for novels come pouring over the telephone in odd Spanish accents – Mr Greene does not speak a word of Spanish and not much French, although he reads it without difficulty. But he does not use these stories, except obliquely or in minor details. Something of the discretion of the old MI6 agent still sticks to him, and I was alarmed to learn that an MI5 man who later transferred to MI6 lived downstairs. Perhaps his retirement job was to keep an eye on Greene, I thought, but said nothing. Better leave these uncertainties hanging in the air, adding a little to the atmosphere.

GRAHAM GREENE
(*Daily Telegraph*, 6 April 1991)

It was impossible for anyone to agree with everything Graham Greene said or did. His Christianity seemed to be nonsensical, owing more to Gnosticism, the mother of all heresies, than to Roman Catholicism, while his 'Communism', taking no account of class struggle, history or economic planning, would have been easy to dismiss as housewife's whimsy if events of the past two years had not proved that all other interpretations of Communism are equally futile and disastrous. But Greene was not a theologian, nor a politician philosopher. He was a novelist, concerned chiefly to tell stories showing us the world through his eyes, and in that he was triumphantly successful. There was a radiant goodness in his nature which no amount of wrong-headedness could dim; to the very end his was a gigantic presence on the world scene.

Those who were lucky enough to have been taken into the warmth of his confidence cannot help but see themselves as a race apart, however brief or infrequent those moments in the sun. Perhaps a certain spirit of competition will grow up between them, about which knew him best or understood him most. I hope not. Unlike so many great geniuses of the twentieth century, Greene explained himself perfectly well as he went along. There is no need for a babble of voices to explain him further. Let us sit down and meditate about him, gratefully, in silence.

OSWALD MOSLEY
(*Books & Bookmen*, November 1982)

Much has been written about Oswald Mosley,[4] by himself, by his widow and various others. His elder son (I wish someone would tell me what has happened to the other one) here sets out his own account of the Early Years,[5] up to the death of the author's mother and the launching of the British Union of Fascists. The value of Nicholas Mosley's first-hand testimony on this period is limited by two factors: he was ten years old at the end of it, and he saw very little of either of his parents. Like most children of the upper class he was shut away in the nursery most of the time even when his parents were at home. They were running around all over the place, trying to interest the masses in their own patent remedies for unemployment and other rubbishy schemes.

Even so, young Nicholas manages to get in a few peeps not vouchsafed to the rest of us. Looking out of the nursery window on one occasion, he saw his father walking naked in his garden as he composed a speech about the need for socialist planning of the economy or some such drivel. This is quite interesting. Many politicians, I believe, are given to nudity. Among them was Winston Churchill, who also had the unpleasant habit of receiving his subordinates while he was sitting on the lavatory – as did Lord Beaverbrook and various others. Nicholas Mosley does not tell us whether his father had this particular taste, but he reveals that on a stolen visit to his parents' bathroom he once saw an extraordinary apparatus – all tubes and bulbous rubber douches – which he later learned was an enema machine.

Students of politics will find this highly significant. The taste for colonic irrigation, as it is called, has always been a specialised one. Respectable establishments which cater for it exist to this day in places like Wigmore Street. Those, like the reviewer, who have been subjected to the discomfort and indignity of an enema in preparation for surgery find it the least comprehensible of all tastes. But there can be no doubt that a fancy exists – its members probably have their own magazine – and if only I knew more about it, I feel it might prove an important clue to the Mosley enigma.

The great tragedy of Mosley's life, as I see it, is that he never became a homosexualist. Everything about his background pointed in this direction. He had a father who was weak, negligent, usually absent and occasionally brutal; a strong mother whom he adored; he detested school. As he wrote in his autobiography, 'The dreary waste of public-school existence was only relieved by learning and homosexuality; at that time I had no capacity for the former and I never had any taste for the latter.'

Therein, I feel, lies the clue to the enigma. Mosley was always a rebel. Instead of calling his first-born son Oswald, as his father, grandfather, great-grandfather and great-great-grandfather had done, he called the lad Nicholas. Instead of retreating from the pressures of his background into homosexuality, as upper-class waifs have traditionally done, he became a compulsively promiscuous heterosexualist; far worse than this, he developed an interest in politics. These two passions destroyed him, as his son relates. If only Sir Oswald *père* had been around to recognise the first symptoms – like anorexia in a girl, political interests are easy to spot and discourage in a growing boy if one can catch them early enough. A thoroughly good dose of cod liver oil at the right moment would have spared much suffering all round, as, no doubt, it would have done in the case of Adolf Hitler, V. I. Lenin, Edward Heath and the rest of them. As it was, he was left with his enema machine, his row of girlfriends and his preposterous urge to create a Better Britain.

The body of Philip Dossé, the founder and proprietor of *Books & Bookmen*, was found in his flat in Notting Hill in 1980. He had committed suicide. Waugh was a regular contributor to *Books & Bookmen*, which had recently been forced to close. 'His life's achievement was suddenly in ruins,' wrote Waugh. 'He was left at the age of fifty-six with no savings, no personal assets and debts of over £200,000.'[6] Waugh was famous for his fierce critiques, but he wrote just as many eulogies, such as this tender requiem for his friend.

PHILIP DOSSÉ
(*Books & Bookmen*, November 1985)

I first met Philip Dossé in the summer of 1974 when he visited me in the Westminster Hospital bearing a huge basket of flowers, fruit and crystallised delicacies. We had been corresponding for about a year and a half, our letters getting more frequent, as well as odder, as the months passed. I had scarcely heard of *Books & Bookmen* when Philip first wrote to me in December 1972 asking for my opinions of the best and worst books in that year. However, I was already well disposed towards the magazine because in 1968 it had chosen my own fourth novel, called *Consider the Lilies*, as its novel of the year – the only recognition it ever received.

Philip's method of approach was to write a fan letter of such unstinting praise as might make anybody except an unrecognised novelist blush. With the praise came violent abuse of all my enemies, snippets of literary gossip and childhood reminiscences.

Within two months I had joined his list of favoured reviewers, and scarcely missed an issue from March 1973 until the magazine's temporary collapse on his death in September 1980.

It was only much later that I realised how he must have plucked up courage to appear in the summer of 1974 with his ridiculously large basket of presents. He was a shy person by nature, and intensely aware of his own oddness in almost every respect. The adulatory letters continued for the rest of his life, with only one awkward moment when he suddenly collapsed, most uncharacteristically, at the thought that a review of mine might be libellous. It was a strange reversal of his normal posture, which was to encourage any extreme of vituperation. He was delighted to receive rude letters about his contributors and encouraged them to answer back as violently as they chose. Quite suddenly, on this one occasion, he lost his nerve. It was very odd, but also, like everything about him, strangely endearing.

Despite our vast correspondence – at one time I was receiving three letters a day from him, usually answering them all with a single letter once a week – I do not suppose I met him more than four or five times. Once, at lunch with the Mosleys, he seemed at ease with himself. His letters grew more and more personal. I cannot believe that there was any aspect of his family, office or amorous life which he did not end up describing to me, sometimes in painful detail. I often wondered how many other people received the same or similar letters in his dreadful scrawl.[7] Was it his usual way of attracting contributors and varied company? Perhaps the best tribute to him, and the one which he would most appreciate, would be simply a list of people whom he persuaded, by one means or another, to write, sometimes regularly and always of their best, for his magazine, with its tiny circulation and minimal rates of pay.[8]

Eventually, after many false starts and nervous refusals, he came down to stay for a weekend in Somerset, preceded by innumerable letters giving exact instructions about how he was to be treated, what sort of food he was to be given, what sort of people he was to meet. He arrived with two huge suitcases decorated by a coronet over the letter B. He had borrowed them apparently from Lord Boothby. One was incredibly heavy. He said it contained books. He said he never drank anything but was prepared to toy with a glass of Champagne. We groaned rather at that. He disapproved of ping-pong but approved of young people, whom he photographed with almost embarrassing persistence. He went to bed early, he said. In the morning he came down carrying a heavy plastic bag, saying he wished to find the dustbins. A little investigation revealed the one secret vice which he had never dared to admit. His heavier suitcase had been entirely filled with miniature bottles of barley wine – about forty or fifty of them. When he retired to his bedroom he drank them alone.

I do not know if anybody ever met his mother, who died at an enormous age the Christmas before his own death. I lived through the drama of it, in his letters. He was mortified to discover, after her death, that his parents had never been married, and never forgave her for it. He was an extraordinarily odd man, most of whose time was spent in bizarre kindnesses. At some moment in 1973 he decided that one or other of my children must collect foreign stamps and sent packets of them every month for the next seven years. Nothing would persuade him that it had been a two-week enthusiasm of one child.

He spoke of his seven arts magazines as his children. When it became apparent that he could no longer afford even to pay his staff, let alone the printers, his world came to an end. At the time one felt bitter that the Arts Council, while subsidising so many worthless pet projects of its own, had never extended a helping hand. Others suggested that his depression might have been fatally worsened by an attack on him which appeared in the *New Statesman* the week before his death. It is true that while he thrived on other people's controversy, he had a fastidious horror of appearing in it himself. The *New Statesman* article accused him, without much justice, of having printed an anti-Semitic review.

But the great joy of Philip as a publisher was that he would print anything. He was the last publisher, in my experience, who genuinely allowed his writers freedom of expression. Perhaps the fact that his magazines never really achieved the circulation they deserved proves that the age has no time for such luxuries.

KENNETH TYNAN
(*Independent*, 26 September 1987)

Kenneth Tynan, who died in 1980, was the theatre critic who, more than any other, welcomed and ushered in the Kitchen Sink movement in the British theatre. That is his chief claim to fame in the history of our times, although he will also earn a footnote as the producer of *Oh! Calcutta!*, which might have introduced a new wave of sexually explicit nude variety shows, but does not seem to have done so. No doubt the Kitchen Sink school would have arrived and prospered without him. In 1956, when Osborne gave us *Look Back in Anger*, most English theatre concerned itself exclusively with the upper and upper-middle classes who made up the bulk of West End audiences, as they still do. But by then a shift was already apparent. Although the theatre audiences have remained the same, the working classes became 'interesting' for the first time.

Tynan was not the originator of this theatrical development, but at least he was its midwife. He was also a good journalist, with a pretty turn of phrase and an ability to produce the occasional striking, even memorable epigram ('one inalienable right binds all mankind together, the right to self-abuse'), which might easily earn him a place in the *Oxford Dictionary of Quotations* one day, along with Mandy Rice-Davies and other immortals.

A good journalist he may have been but, like so many good journalists, he has gone. Among the fatuous opinions and attitudes adopted by Tynan – hedonistic socialism, Brechtian Marxism, CND (he arrived at Aldermaston by taxi), free love, modern art – the most uniquely asinine of all was his belief, expressed on numerous occasions, that the theatre reviewer (dramatic critic, call him what you will) is writing for posterity, rather than for today's theatre-goer. His widow is pained to observe that 'Since Ken's death his literary reputation is more or less in limbo: his published collection of theatre reviews, essays and journalism is out of print. Millions of words of his writings in newspapers and periodicals are not reprinted in book form.'

I am sorry to have to inform her that it is the essence of good journalism that it should be read and thrown away. Practically nobody has time to read old theatre notices. She quotes Cyril Connolly's dictum that 'The true function of a writer is to produce a masterpiece, and that no other task is of any consequence.' By that criterion Tynan is no further along the road to immortality than Lynda Lee-Potter or Jean Rook.

In parenthesis, I might add that Tynan, ploughing a similar furrow, comes nowhere near Connolly in the same competition. Compare this 'rebuttal' quoted by Kathleen Tynan as evidence of Tynan's greater profundity, or compassion or something. Connolly: 'From now on an artist will be judged only by the resonance of his solitude or the quality of his despair.' Tynan: 'Not by me, he won't. I shall, I hope, respond to the honesty of such testimonies; but I shall be looking for something more, something harder: for evidence of the artist who concerns himself from time to time with such things as healing.'

Oh dear. The evidence to support the claim of Tynan as a great healer is even thinner on the ground than the evidence for his having written a masterpiece. But he was the first person to say 'fuck' on British television. Surely that will earn him a mention in the *Guinness Book of Records*. He might even appear in the same section as Connolly, who claims, in *Enemies of Promise*, to have reached the age of eighteen without having masturbated.

But Kathleen Tynan's biography and memoir,[9] which I found interesting, and eventually rather moving, has an entirely different function. It captures and celebrates a particular moment in Britain's history which is usually identified with the 1960s, but which in fact ran from about 1955 to 1975. It describes a particular lifestyle – hash brownies with Sharon Tate in Thurloe Square, knees-ups with Princess Margaret, Tony Richardson, Gore Vidal and Jack Nicholson in Bel Air – which may not have had anything to do with the lives of most people at the time, but which has very nearly passed into national mythology as the history of the sixties.

Above all, it charts a sexual revolution which seemed to promise great things at the time, but which has now fizzled out. We learn all we could possibly wish to know about Tynan's sex life – how he first masturbated at eleven, and achieved his first sexual connection on the night of 28/29 February 1945 in a shop doorway. Names are supplied in a way which few gossip columnists would dare supply them. Tynan's first extramarital fling, after marriage to Elaine Dundy (who emerges as a heroine and enchantress) was with the 'beautiful, dark-haired wife' of a Labour MP. Among his other lovers was Elizabeth Jane Howard, the novelist who later married Kingsley Amis. She said of him: 'It seemed he'd had an intricate idea as a child of what being grown-up would be like, and had jolly well stuck to it.'

This seems to me to sum up Tynan pretty well, in his purple suits, his white cigarette holders, his leopardskin trousers and mink ties. It sums him up as a socialist thinker and sexual performer, too. But it does not quite sum him up as a social phenomenon. Kathleen Tynan, daughter of a Canadian journalist married to a land-owning Canadian wife, is nearly as frank about her own sexual history. She had been married to her first husband for only six months before she fell for Tynan. Life with Tynan, involving nude bathing and the rest of it, was all very well, but 'all I wanted was sex' – and Tynan was not really up to it.

Even by the standards of journalists, Tynan cannot really be seen as a hero. As he lay dying from incurable emphysema, he instituted libel proceedings against a newspaper which had suggested he was in poor health: 'The damage to me professionally is incalculable – what publisher or editor would commission a work from a dying man?' Several did, nonetheless.

Tynan was not a hero, but he deserves a place in our social history. His widow does him justice.

Waugh's enduring affection for Paul Foot was one of his best advertisements, a testament to his open mind and his equable nature. Foot was a hardline socialist, the political personification of everything that Waugh despised. Yet this ideological divide didn't spoil their friendship. Indeed, in a strange way, it enhanced it. Waugh called Foot 'witty, wise and possibly the only true romantic of my acquaintance'.[10] Foot might well have said the same of Waugh. In most writers, such admiration would have resulted in an anodyne review, but when Foot published a collection of his journalism, written during the decade when Thatcher put British socialism to the sword, Waugh's astute critique demolished Foot's left-wing politics, but somehow left his friend's reputation for fearless and honourable reportage unharmed.

PAUL FOOT
(*Sunday Telegraph*, 9 December 1990)

Paul Foot learned his socialism in Glasgow where, after Ludgrove, Shrewsbury and Oxford, he went as a reporter on the *Daily Record* in 1961. Among the dockers on the Clyde he learned that society was divided into classes and that the classes were forever at war with one another. 'The result, in Glasgow at any rate, was a city of monstrosities, and an impoverishment of mind and body which was at once incredible and intolerable.'

Brooding on these monstrosities, he asked himself whether the stinking slums could be cleared or the threat of unemployment removed by Acts of Parliament, and decided otherwise. I confess I rather tend to agree with him. In his case it led him to reject the 'gradual route to socialism' offered by the Labour Party and embrace what seems to me a slightly confused programme of government by workers' councils – to be brought about by revolutionary ferment through the action of strikes, rent and poll tax revolts and the other occasional manifestations of proletarian resentment with which we are all familiar.

He is not unduly perturbed by the collapse of socialism – or what incorrectly passed for socialism – in Eastern Europe and has his answer ready for those who claim that numerous disastrous socialist experiments (in the Soviet Union, Poland, Hungary, Czechoslovakia, Romania, Bulgaria, Yugoslavia, China, Mozambique . . .) might suggest that socialism does not really work very well. There are different reasons in every case, no doubt, but the basic underlying reason is that none of these countries really understood about socialism, which is all to do with workers' councils.

As he explained in 1977 in *Why You Should Be a Socialist*, socialism is built on three principles or pillars. The first is social ownership of the means of production. This stops people getting rich through employing anyone else. The second is equality. This ensures that nobody gets rich at all. The third pillar is workers' democracy, by which workers' councils, controlled by the government, send workers' delegates to a Congress of Workers' Councils, from which the workers' executive (or government) is elected. It sounds fun.

Although one has to be a worker to qualify for all this democracy, it is also open to workers who don't happen to be working, whether disabled, nursing mothers or what you will. Workers' democracy ensures that nobody does any work, everybody lives in a state of acute poverty, shortage and general oppression. It may not do much for the monstrosities of Glasgow, but it is surely what all those sensitive middle-class souls in Islington and Highgate are yearning for.

This is the Only Alternative to the free market which, as Foot explains, is 'dragging us all to the rim of hell'. 'There is poverty, homelessness, sheer unadulterated misery of a kind which would not have been thought of, let alone tolerated, twenty or thirty years ago.' I try to believe that this is true. My own impression of the last thirty years, for what it is worth, is that there has always been a certain number of miserable people around, of whom some were undoubtedly poor, but that more than anything else the increase in homelessness is the product of the collapsing family.

Nearly everybody, in my observation, is better off than they were twenty or thirty years ago, and even the professional tramp or vagrant alcoholic is no worse off than he was. I doubt whether their condition provides sufficient reason for dismantling the entire structure of our society in favour of some untried system of workers' control. Nor am I convinced that government by the working class will provide a more agreeable life for the working class than our present liberal bourgeois democracy, let alone for the likes of you and me. But my chief anxiety concerns Paul Foot.

'I come from a West Country family of enormous repute,' he explains, quite rightly. We'm West Country volk know all about 'e. Us won't forget 'im's grandad, Isaac, nor 'im's dad, Hugh, the Lord of Trematon Castle. The most important point to make about this collection of journalism from the 1980s[11] is that despite its manifestly defective inspiration, rooted in the wrong side of the class war, he is nearly always right.

Perhaps the most entertaining entry of all is a note he wrote for the *New Statesman* in July 1979 on the death of his former housemaster at Shrewsbury, Anthony Chenevix-Trench. 'Trench made his name as a great innovator, especially in corporal punishment . . . He achieved the rare distinction of being hated and despised by every boy who came in contact with him, and was therefore the obvious choice to be the youngest ever headmaster of Bradfield, and then of Eton. At Eton he made the mistake of whipping the heirs of earls as though they were run-of-the-mill manufacturers' sons at Shrewsbury or Bradfield. One sensitive young viscount limped home and bared his tattered bum to his outraged father. Trench was sacked. He was appointed headmaster of Fettes.'

We may never know what Foot suffered at Shrewsbury to convince him that we would be better governed by a prosperous working class. Reading the *Sun* newspaper daily, as I do, it occurs to me that after a few months of working-class rule we would all be yearning for the return of Chenevix-Trench. There is a vindictive savagery – not to say sadism – in the *Sun*'s approach to most aspects of contemporary life which does not bode well for the proletarian millennium.

Foot explains the *Sun* phenomenon by pointing out that it appeals to the lowest common denominator – tits, bums, hypo-critical morality. But Foot does not tackle the corollary that this must be the winning formula in a proletarian society – above all in a prosperous, democratic, working-class culture of the sort he hopes to establish. Foot would not survive a week under such a regime, nor would any of his idealistic, working-class friends in the Socialist Workers Party.

Waugh was a long-standing admirer of Michael Wharton's writing, and eventually inherited Wharton's 'Way of the World' column in the *Daily Telegraph* (a job he'd always coveted) when Wharton transferred his timeless alter-ego, Peter Simple, to the *Sunday Telegraph*. Waugh's review of Wharton's second volume of autobiography was a fitting tribute for a writer who had probably inspired him more than any other. In his *Private Eye* Diary, Waugh created a comparable comic netherworld, and here he pays homage to his mentor in an especially penetrating yet unusually heartfelt review.

MICHAEL WHARTON
(*Sunday Telegraph*, 13 January 1991)

The first volume of Michael Wharton's autobiography[12] took us to the historic New Year's Day of 1957 when he sat down for the first time at his desk in the *Daily Telegraph*, with a most appalling hangover, to compose his first Peter Simple column[13]. The column itself had been founded little more than a year earlier by Colin Welch, who later eventually achieved the rank of deputy editor of the *Daily Telegraph*, largely responsible for such important sections as correspondence, leaders and leader-page articles, but will nevertheless chiefly be remembered in the annals of journalism, as I should guess, in the role of midwife to genius. He it was who rescued Wharton from a precarious existence on the fringes of the BBC and gave him, at the age of forty-three, his first regular job in civilian life.

During their fairly brief association on the Peter Simple column, Welch tended to write the serious, polemical 'lead' item – what more frivolous readers designated 'the boring bits' – while Wharton wrote the humorous and fantastical items which followed. When Welch decided in 1960 to seek fame and fortune as a leader writer, Wharton took over the whole operation and has kept an iron grip on it ever since. Although he moans a certain amount about how the column has been a tyrannical master, he its slave, how he has nothing to show for his four million beautifully crafted words printed in the newspaper except for some doubtful pseudonymous celebrity, one might observe that he has a second claim to fame, quite apart from the excellence of his genius, and that is as one of journalism's great survivors.

Newspapers, more than almost any other industry, are given to sudden frenzies of mindless change. Newly appointed executives feel impotent until they have altered everything in sight. Office jealousies ensure endless coups and counter-coups. At the first hint of a declining circulation, there is a danger that the whole newspaper will be turned inside out: the ecclesiastical correspondent will find himself writing about motor cars and the motoring correspondent will be appointed television critic. But Wharton defended his little patch with all the powers – natural and supernatural – at his disposal. At one point a new young deputy editor had the bright idea that Peter Simple should travel around England, writing his column from different places. The suggestion threw Wharton into dread and confusion, which lasted a weekend. Then he learned that the deputy editor concerned, a healthy forty-year-old, had suddenly died of a heart attack.

It was shortly after Wharton had taken over the column,

towards the end of 1960, that I made my first application to be taken on as his apprentice. I was a tender twenty-one-year-old at the time, having just secured a precarious foothold on the 'Peterborough' column. The editor, Sir Colin Coote, was anxious that Simple should have an assistant. Wharton received me courteously, and as courteously showed me the door. He writes of the episode: 'Young Auberon Waugh . . . would prob-ably have done very well – perhaps too well: my unconscious reason for refusing his offer . . . may well have been a fear, typical of me, that with his superior social connections and greater confidence in himself he might soon have taken over the column altogether.'

There is this constant leitmotif of Wharton's social inepti-tude, his humble origins and lowly outlook which prevented him taking his rightful place in society. These class resentments are quite unusual in our profession. Wharton is deeply suspi-cious of such of his colleagues as Sir Peregrine Worsthorne, whose social graces carry him (as Wharton imagines) into the grandest houses of Europe, and even admits to jealousy of his secretary, Claudie Worsthorne, who was forbidden to make social arrangements in his presence. Perhaps it was to mollify these anxieties that Claudie explained, of her husband: 'Poor boy, 'e 'as not a pea to his name. 'E is as poor as a church rat.' But Wharton remained unmollified. What upsets and worries him most of all is not to reflect that he was a grammar-school boy, or that his mother (whom he loved, and who lived to ninety-seven) had a strong West Riding accent, but what he calls 'the vestigal, thinned-out yet still troubling legacy of my part-Jewish paternal grandparents'. He half jokes, when his son Nicholas decides to change his surname back to Nathan, that he will cut the boy off without a penny, but the hurt is there. He would dearly love not to have to carry this burden, which he discusses with a terrifying frankness and tends to blame for all the misfor-tunes of his life.

The simple truth about Michael Wharton, and the explana-tion for all his troubled life, is that he is an artist. His entire existence since the age of forty-three has been dedicated to an art form which, if not completely ephemeral, is not calculated to win the garlands of immortality. What makes his predicament a bitter one is that he is a supreme artist: greater by far than most if not all the novelists, painters, sculptors, architects and pseudo-poets who have been strutting around the scene, acclaimed and lionised these last thirty years. In that time he has been seducing his readers with an alternative order of creation, a glimpse of the sublime once, twice, even three times a week. But in a country which is reluctant to revere any of its writers, except posthumously, there is no honour of any sort reserved for mere excellence in journalism. He has given himself to his column, in exchange for a living of sorts and a little pseudonymous fame, but not much. Many readers believed the column was written by A. P. Herbert[14] or Randolph Churchill[15] or Lady Pamela Berry[16] or all three. He was once asked to dinner by Lady Pamela, but did not distinguish himself. He exchanged a few words with the proprietor, Michael Berry, later Lord Hartwell. That was his life.

And what a dreadful life it has been, by any standards except those of the dedicated artist. If the first volume of his autobiography is interpreted as a shout in the dark to establish his identity as separate from that of his creature, Peter Simple, the second has the more terrible effect of taking us away from the background into the process of an artist's life in contemporary Britain. One glimpse of his routine will be enough. Every day he would take a bus from Battersea to Fleet Street – a long journey – jotting ideas for his column on his copy of the *Daily Telegraph*. At lunch, every day, he would repair to the King and Keys next door and eat a corned beef sandwich and sip a double brandy and ginger ale. After finishing his column, he would go back to the pub for a few more drinks, being amused by the gross behaviour of the ruffians who inhabited it, and then return by a different bus route, slightly tipsy, to Battersea, where he would note with pleasure the sign reading Col. M. B. Wharton on the hall of his block of flats, grill himself five fish fingers – never more, never fewer – and go to bed. On one occasion, more tipsy than usual, he wedged himself in his bath all night, releasing himself in the morning to report for work as usual.

Is that any sort of life to write about? Many passages were rowdier than that, but the same melancholy shabbiness colours them all. Yet the book is quite fascinating to read, even when he describes summer holidays with his family. It is partly the fascination of following a well-known and well-loved character through his vale of tears – however much he may suppose he has hidden himself behind the personality of Peter Simple, however unknown and unloved he may imagine himself to be, there can be few readers of Peter Simple who will not 'identify' with him. It is also partly the high interest of watching a giant among familiar contemporary scenes, as if Shakespeare had emerged in the garb of Mr Pooter. His life might have been otherwise. A short story appeared in the first issue of Cyril Connolly's *Horizon*. There is a novel somewhere, published by Anthony Blond. He could easily have been seduced into the polite inanities of literary life, even securing himself a mention in the *Oxford Companion to English Literature* and a CBE. Instead, thanks to the fortuitous intervention of Colin Welch, he found his true genius in a column which, he says, he could not have started himself, lacking the confidence and the social connections.

If the book stands up on its own, without the shared knowledge and joy of the Peter Simple column, this is because it has two other major themes. The first is the love affair with his second wife, Kate, the second his continuing battle against the melancholy, despair and madness which afflict so many creative geniuses, especially those required to live by their wit and humour.

The Missing Will manages to describe ten years of marriage to his first wife without introducing her to us or even giving her a name. *A Dubious Codicil* affords similar protection to his third wife, whom he married after ten years' delay in 1974. It is the second wife, Kate, who strides like a Colossus over this second volume of autobiography; it chronicles her twenty years' affair with another man, described as a well-known journalist called 'Kenneth' – 'a man I liked and admired, an honourable man ...' A moment arrives when 'Kenneth' says to Wharton: 'I will ask you a question. If you answer "yes", the affair will go no further. Do you love Kate?' After a moment's thought, Wharton answers: 'No.' That is the dramatic cornerstone of the book. It will inspire hours of meditation in every reflective mind.

The first volume also describes Wharton's first glimpse into the 'void' – of melancholy, despair and madness – prompted by Kate's announcement of her first pregnancy. In the second, we touch the depths of a serious relapse, involving electro-convulsive therapy, from which he miraculously recovers to resume his benign presence in the *Daily Telegraph*. This relapse was prompted, so far as I can judge, by his appointment as Granada's Columnist of the Year in 1963. It is about the only recognition he has ever received. Further honours may well prove fatal. But he emerges from the ordeal not just a genius – they are two a penny in book reviews – but as a hero. The combination is extraordinarily rare. Let us honour him at least in our hearts, if nowhere else.

JOHN BETJEMAN
(*Daily Telegraph*, 16 April 1994)

'Oh, I'm so happy. This is such fun. I am having such a lovely time,' John Betjeman[17] would exclaim, clapping hands, whenever party conversation looked like flagging. Such was his energy – he would have made a brilliant Redcoat at Butlins – that people responded and laughed, but there was nearly always an element of desperation in his gaiety, a feeling of melancholy being kept at bay by strenuous mental exercises. If I had to give a single reason why he remains unquestionably the best poet England has produced since the Great War – in fact, the only poet of any but academic interest – I would say that he is the only poet who wrote with genuine passion and feeling. His passions were always close to the surface, although his rage never expressed itself in vulgar bad temper, his hatreds never appeared as bad manners, his lusts never produced Disgraceful Scenes. Of the ruling passions which spill out in his poetry – terror, lust, hatred, anger, doubt – I saw only terror surface from time to time. He had a terror of hearties and drunks and beer drinkers and impertinent workmen. I remember arranging to meet him once in the Old King Lud public house in Ludgate Circus when he was living in Cloth Fair and I was working in the hideous old *Telegraph* building in Fleet Street. I found him cowering outside, white to his lips, having been frightened by a workman inside.

I met him first as part of a lucky generation of Oxford undergraduates invited to romp around with his daughter, Candida, at their old house in Wantage. He seemed to enjoy the company of the young – although he would never have let us know if he didn't – introducing his wife, who was organising pony-cart marathons, as his Haystack. It was particularly nice of him to be kind to me as my father constantly bombarded him with Catholic propaganda, which upset him, and had been instrumental in Penelope Betjeman's conversion to Rome, which upset him very much indeed.

Shortly after Oxford he wrote an immensely generous blurb for my first novel, and we became fast friends in the way that great men always feel well disposed towards those to whom they have done a favour. For a time, we shared a hobby, colouring in the coats of arms in *Burke's Peerage* every time we met the peer concerned, as a form of competition to see who could meet the most dim peers. There were those who decided, in his last years as a famous television personality, that he spent so much time entertaining society ladies who were not his moral or intellectual equals that some of it rubbed off in a new coarseness of manner. Or so they said. I saw his last years as being more tortured than ever. There was a glorious moment in a television interview when he was asked if he had any regrets in life, and he replied emphatically: 'Yes. Not enough sex.'

There was a frankness bursting to come out of him every minute of the day. Among friends, he could be as indiscreet as he liked. As a celebrity, he had to watch his words, and although the restriction never embittered him, and he threw himself into the role of everyone's pet Teddy bear with all the generosity of his nature, the battle against melancholy became fiercer. I saw him only occasionally in his last five years, and it may seem affected to talk of a sense of loss ten years later. But as the tenth anniversary of his death approaches, many people will, I suspect, feel a pang if only in memory of his own religious doubts and terror of death alone.

DIANA, PRINCESS OF WALES
(*Sunday Telegraph*, 7 September 1997)

Last week when I sat down to write my normal *Sunday Telegraph* column, Diana, Princess of Wales, was still alive.[18] She was also in a spot of trouble, although all that has been forgotten now. She was at the centre of what *The Times* chose to call a 'deepening political row' after being reported as saying that the last Tory government had been hopeless on the landmines issue. While *The Times* recorded the 'outrage' of constitutionalists and Tory MPs, the tabloid press pursued her private life with a cruelty and vulgarity which shamed us all. It has been observed elsewhere that the tabloid press's attitude towards her veered between slavish adulation and bestial cruelty. For my own part, I belonged firmly in the slavish adulation camp ever since seeing her in the flesh, but when she reacted to the double furore over politics and her love affair with the playboy [Dodi] Fayed by disappearing for another holiday in the Fayed yacht, I thought she might have gone too far. This time she had blown it. There was too much egg around. Not even she would be able to extricate herself with a smile and a wave and an extra hug for some terminally ill toddler.

Hatred of the rich is deep in the British character at nearly every level. That is why our aristocracy has always been at pains to develop an affable manner and treat everyone as equals. Add to this the secret jealousies of a sexually repressed culture and I feared we might have seen the last of her. The Diana Admiration Society would be reduced to a small group of increasingly doddery old men raising their glasses to the Princess over the water. This seemed an unlikely end to the story, but it was never easy to imagine her growing old. Some sense of foreboding must have guided my hand last week, when I wrote that, although I grew fonder and fonder of her public image as it developed, I found myself trembling for the survival of the flesh and blood human being underneath it.

By the time the column appeared the Princess was dead. It might be thought absurd and rather offensive to see her short life in terms of a classic theatrical tragedy. By now every citizen of the United Kingdom has given his or her opinion on the drama, and I find I have no room left for any opinion at all. We might feel gratitude for the life of a lovely person and sorrow that we've lost her, as the Queen put it, but that would seem to be the limit of participation available. Yet there is anger in the air. One aspect of our repressed national character, at any rate as it affects some of us, expresses itself in an inability to feel any strong emotion without wishing to punch someone – preferably someone who is suspected of disagreeing with us. Others have noted an element of mass hysteria. Somebody must suffer for this, since the chauffeur and Fayed are beyond punishment: whether the paparazzi, the media as a whole, Prince Charles, Mrs Parker Bowles, the Queen or other members of the Royal Family. Changes must be made in deference to newly awakened popular feelings. Because they are made by unintelligent people, the suggestions are mostly unintelligent. Was it kind to make the Duke of York and Prince Edward go walkabout outside St James's Palace? Is it reasonable to expect our monarchy to become a touchy-feely-huggy institution in the mould set by Diana?

The country's neurotics, of whom there must be at least a couple of million, need some other direction for their thoughts, I feel. However scornful we may be of conspiracy theories, especially when they are advanced by foreigners, there are some very mysterious elements in the account of what happened at Saturday midnight or early Sunday morning in Paris. Murder theories, which are popular in France and the Middle East, may seem implausible, but to the extent that we are all going to continue brooding about the incident, it might be healthier for our imaginations to explore dramatic possibilities rather than settle on the troubles of a shattered Royal Family.

WILLIE RUSHTON
(Daily Telegraph, 14 December 1996)

It was when William Rushton asked to be excused from the *Literary Review*'s monthly captions conference that I felt the first twinge of alarm. In anyone else, it would have been inconceivable to expect an appearance between two visits to hospital and a dash north to entertain the masses, but for ten years he had nearly always attended them. The normal form was for one of the younger members of staff to hold a picture in front of Willie's face. There followed a stream-of-consciousness session: puns, *malentendus*, twisted quotations from Shakespeare, obscenities, clever, oblique references to popular songs and famous television advertisements which were completely unknown to me. All this was delivered in his perfect enunciation, the production of a clever, well-focused mind working at full speed. From this burble of sound the perfect caption was born. I think he must have quite enjoyed these occasions, although it seemed strange for anyone to take so much trouble for a small magazine. He already illustrated the covers, never missed a deadline in ten years, and always for a pittance. You could call it professionalism, although his attendance was unpaid. In fact, he needed a serious reason to miss one. Then, just before he went into hospital, he expressed doubts about whether he would be up to illustrating today's 'Way of the World' and did an extra drawing. Otherwise, the shock was complete. It was a rascally way to go – even if, in time, his friends will learn to be grateful that he went down with all guns blazing.

Willie's professionalism came without the slightest commercial instinct, so far as I could see. I was surprised when the *Daily Telegraph*'s excellent obituary hazarded the opinion that he was shrewd about money. Perhaps he was, but I never spotted it. So far as I could see, he had a great loathing for money. Any mention of it threw him into a panic. We started working together eighteen years ago, when I was writing a 'Diary' column in *Private Eye*. For six years it had been illustrated by Nicholas Bentley. When Bentley died, in August 1978, grief at his loss combined with a natural hatred of change to make me less than gracious when Richard Ingrams proposed Rushton for the job. His drawing in those days struck me as spiky, and his stereotypes seemed dated. Little men in black overcoats with comic moustaches and bowler hats might have appealed to the Shrewsbury set,[19] but they did nothing for me. It was not until many years later that I thought I glimpsed the origins of this stereotype. In the late fifties, *The Times* ran an extraordinarily vulgar series of advertisements over the slogan 'Top People Read *The Times*'. They showed smarmy-faced young stockbrokers with rolled umbrellas, invariably wearing a bowler hat, with the implicit suggestion that these were the sort of people we should all like to be. At some point the young Rushton must have been thrown into a rage by this suggestion. To the end, he evinced a hatred for *The Times* and a recurrent urge to introduce bowler hats – long since disappeared from the City slicker scene – for the purpose of ridiculing them. There were many reasons people worked for *Private Eye*, but shrewdness about money was not one of them, at any rate in those days.

I soon discovered that Willie could draw in any style, and did so happily. His comic genius was matched by modesty and sweetness of nature. After eighteen years of partnership – in all that time we never had a single cross word – I find political and world events now register only to the extent that they might provide material for a Rushton cartoon. I do not know how the world will react to the removal of his scrutiny. Large parts,

I fear, will cease to function, or even exist. The days between a man's death and his funeral are not the moment to celebrate his life, to tell Willie stories and remember the good times. Eventually, we may be thankful that he decided to leave us at the height of his powers, with a suddenness which took everybody's breath away, but not yet. These days are a time of bitterness and loss, a time for anger, even, as we contemplate the cruelty and horror of his death.

The one comfort is to discover quite how widespread is the affection in which Willie was held. The reason he was universally loved was not because he was so funny. In fact, there is often something disconcerting about people who are as funny as that. The real reason everybody loved him was for a basic warmth of character, a total benevolence which no amount of mocking buffoonery could ever disguise.

I have described how he detested *The Times* newspaper, but there was no malice behind his hatreds, only amazement. His jokes and drawings could appear merciless. It is only when you study them at length that you realise how the driving force behind his work is simple enjoyment. He loved the human race, not despite its aesthetic, moral or social failings, but because of them. And the human race loved him back.

Chapter Thirteen
Books & Bookmen

I don't suppose there has been a moment in the world's history where more people felt themselves to be artists, or when less art was produced.[1]

Waugh's political writing attracted most attention, but he earned his bread and butter as a literary critic. In the course of his career he reviewed books for virtually every newspaper in Fleet Street, from the *Independent* to the *Daily Mail*, yet Waugh wasn't only in it for the money. He also wrote for *Books & Bookmen*, an obscure magazine with a modest circulation and correspondingly modest fees. Like his father, Waugh was a true bibliophile, and his first impressions of new books that became modern classics make fascinating reading today. Yet, at their best, the titles he reviewed were springboards for inspired polemics, much as mundane news events prompted his fantastical rants in *Private Eye*. Reviewing a book about the world's wealthiest people, he wrote:[2]

The modern world is not well organised for the very rich. Few modern luxury hotels, in my experience, are much more comfortable than my own modest home and all are much uglier; the disappearance of good servants with the whole tradition of domestic service removes a large part of the incentive to become rich, and nearly all the simpler human appetites are liable to surfeit, with the quickest satisfactions available from alcohol, drugs, good food or sex being the first to turn to ashes. Perhaps it would be agreeable to keep a small harem of polite, well-trained young women from Northern Thailand and Japan in my summer palace, to drink only the very best wines in the best company, retiring to a beautiful room hung with the finest Oriental silks for my evening pipe of opium, but such fantasies scarcely connect with the daily frustrations of finding an electrician to come and mend some piece of electrical apparatus which has been broken, or a plumber to unblock a lavatory, or someone, anyone, to clean my shoes.[3]

After an opening paragraph like that, you can't wait to read the rest – but mainly to learn more about Waugh than about the book.

Or how about this one, from a review of *Burke's Peerage*?

Throughout my childhood I scarcely remember a single meal at home without someone jumping up to fetch a reference book. Meals were less enjoyable in those days through a combination of post-war shortages and the fact that nobody had learned to cook, and I find even today that I can't open a copy of *Burke's Peerage* without being reminded of cabbage smells and overcooked meat. Perhaps the fragrance is peculiar to the British aristocracy. Anybody who has been taken to lunch in the dining room at the House of Lords will recognise the smell of nursery food – semolina and bread pudding, inedible boiled mutton with capers and cabbage piled unnecessarily high on the plate. Their Lordships seem to like it. Perhaps there is some profound explanation for this. Many of them eat quite well at home, but they associate the House of Lords in some way with the security, the rituals and curious restraints of the nursery.[4]

In passages like this, Waugh elevated the workaday book review to the status of a modest art, and his best reviews will survive long after most of the books he reviewed have been forgotten.

*

HERO WITH A HEART OF ICE
(*Evening Standard*, 20 November 1973)

The Rachel Papers by Martin Amis (Jonathan Cape, 1973)

At first glance, Mr Amis's first novel appears to be more or less a standard first novel: a series of sexual adventures leading up to a first important affair, laced with plenty of introspection and told in an extravagantly sexual language. One notices that his jokes are funnier than usual, his imagery and feeling for words slightly more vivid. The teenage hero called Charles Highway explains a fancy for his sister by saying quite simply: 'There was no reason to believe that with her clothes off she would smell of boiled eggs and dead babies.' Finding himself with an infection at just the moment that he plans to seduce the heroine called Rachel, he has to cool the passions between them: 'I made polite groans, naturally, but with the professional sincerity of the wine taster as opposed to the candid slavering of the alcoholic.'

However, one soon notices a curious, almost manic detachment in the teenager's introspection. Needless to say, Mr Amis employs all the fashionable gimmicks – he is not merely writing a novel, he is writing a novel about someone who is writing a diary about himself, annotating it from time to time: 'What do I think of Charles Highway? I think: "Charles Highway? Oh, I like him. Yes, I've got a soft spot for old Charles. He's all right is Charlie . . ."' This is exactly the sort of knockabout, bantering, whimsical figure one expects to find as hero of semi-autobiographical first novels nowadays. Ruthlessly opportunistic in sexual matters, they nevertheless have soft hearts and when Miss Right comes along they grow all tender and unselfish. The big difference is that Mr Amis's hero has no such soft heart. He is funny enough to be good company but basically he is callous, self-centred and mean.

One begins to worry for the basic good-heartedness bit around the middle of the book. He is philosophising to himself on the subject of those who have problems or a harder life than most people, and about to conclude that nobody has problems, only a capacity for feeling anxious about them: 'Was this the case with everyone – everyone, that is, who wasn't already a thalidomide baked bean, or a gangrenous imbecile, or degradingly poor, or irretrievably ugly, and would therefore have pretty obvious targets for their worries?'

At first reading, one blots out the violent image conveyed by those words 'thalidomide baked bean' as an error of judgement on Mr Amis's part. It is, of course, how unthinking teenagers might talk, but Mr Amis is quite young too, and he might not have judged correctly the impact of these words on an older readership. But then, the evidence builds up and we realise that the hero, although highly intelligent and very funny, is an emotional cripple of quite a serious sort. At the end, he gets rid of his girlfriend, who has been living with him, for no better reason than that he cannot adjust himself to living with somebody. He wants to 'read a book, pick my nose, be smelly and alone'.

She and the reader realise at about the same time that the hero is utterly cold, utterly incapable of loving. His feelings for her were no more than a possessive frenzy; his jokes about himself are all true. And the reader, at the same time, comes to see that Mr Amis, under the guise of a funny, relaxed, rather dirty first novel, has been preaching a little sermon about the emotional problems of intelligent children from insecure family backgrounds.

It is very hard with first novels to judge how much is self-revelation, how much contrivance. Graham Greene once wrote that every novelist should carry a little chip of ice in his heart which enables him to witness and record the most agonisingly poignant scenes to his own advantage. If one judges his first novel as an exercise in self-revelation, Mr Amis reveals that he has a whole bucket of ice just where it should come in handiest. But we will have to wait for his second novel to know just how much use he will make of it. If, on the other hand, one sees it is contrivance – if he actually invented the characters, or found them somewhere outside himself – then he has a formidable and exceptional talent with almost certain prospect of more to come. In either case, he has written a first novel which is highly enjoyable to read, and that is all we need worry about at this stage.

THE BEST WRITER
(*New Statesman*, 28 February 1975)

Those who have no enthusiasm for his work are often irritated by the exuberant hyperbole and even aggressiveness of Wodehouse fans, who sometimes show all the least attractive characteristics of religious zealotry.[5] I confess I find myself slightly shocked when anybody admits to not liking Wodehouse, although I can see that this is an unreasonable reaction. But I think I can be dogmatic on a few points from my own observation: that Wodehouse has been more read than any other English novelist by his fellow novelists; that nobody with any genuine feeling for the English language has failed to recognise at least an element of truth in Belloc's judgement of 1934, that Wodehouse was 'the best writer of English now alive, the head of my profession'; that the failure of academic literary criticism to take any account of Wodehouse's supreme mastery of the English language or the profound influence he has had on every worthwhile English novelist in the past fifty years demonstrates in better and more concise form than anything else how the Eng Lit industry is divorced from the subject it claims to study; finally, that the university departments of English literature are manned to a large extent by people with no particular love for or understanding of English literature beyond a few rubbishy opinions about Lawrence, Joyce and Wyndham Lewis which they push backwards and forwards at each other.

I searched for Wodehouse in Martin Seymour-Smith's 1200-page *Guide to Modern World Literature*. This is a compendium of opinions on every writer of this century whom Seymour-Smith judges worthy of his attention. It assesses innumerable authors unknown to me, with names like R. B. Cunninghame-Graham and W. H. Hudson, devoting two and a half pages each to Beckett and Wyndham Lewis, five to Belloc, sixteen to Chesterton and eight to Beerbohm. I should imagine that about two thousand modern authors, five or six thousand books are treated to Seymour-Smith's lightning assessments. The enterprise was hailed by Anthony Quinton as a 'noble achievement'. Needless to say, I could find no mention of P. G. Wodehouse in all those 750,000 words.

I mention this not to abuse Mr Seymour-Smith or Anthony Quinton, but merely to illustrate the critical establishment's profound ignorance of contemporary literature. In fact, the influence of P. G. Wodehouse can be discerned in practically every English novel published today which at any time in its course diverges from the commitment to total seriousness. To dismiss him with a sneer as a purveyor of light entertainment – on a par, perhaps, with Morecambe and Wise – is to betray a blinding ignorance of the structure, form, language and philosophy of the English novel. What Wodehouse has done is to distil for all time a form of pure comedy in more or less abstract guise: without any social application, let alone political commitment; with no bitterness, cruelty, sex, rancour or any other impure purpose which comedy may serve. Whatever uses other writers may put it to, the essence remains of what Wodehouse has distilled.

There are many people who object to the Wodehouse *mise-en-scène* on grounds of its sociological partiality and political cretinism. The fact that he concerns himself more or less exclusively with the imaginary rich may indeed be an obstacle to the enjoyment among those who disapprove of the rich. It is a question of taste. I would rebuke myself, not the author, if I failed to enjoy a comedy of working-class life because I had no experience or concern or perfect sympathy with working-class aspirations.

Those who complain that there is no account of the sources of Wooster's income, no glance at the exploited urban industrial masses who sustain life at Blandings, are registering a political objection, not a literary one. He never set himself the task of writing a realistic novel and can scarcely be blamed for having failed. Nobody ever said that Wodehouse was the greatest living novelist, only the greatest living writer, to which I would add that as a writer he has had more influence on the English novel than any other writer in history, and about twenty times as much as Lawrence, Joyce and Kafka combined.

A few years ago I was asked to contribute to a volume of acclaim. I had just spent a whole Conservative Party conference urging the conference to send a telegram to Wodehouse on his ninetieth birthday. A spot check revealed only two members of Heath's cabinet who had enjoyed him, several who had never heard of him. I concluded: 'Politicians may be prepared to countenance subversive political jokes, but the deeper subversion of totally non-political jokes is something they can neither comprehend nor forgive. It is no accident that of all twentieth-century writers Wodehouse is the one they have chosen, in their time, to persecute most bitterly.' This may explain why it took thirty-four years for a British government to make amends for the cruel injustice done to him in a moment of wartime hysteria. But it does not explain the venom with which this vendetta was launched.

Bill Connor (Cassandra of the *Daily Mirror*) made his peace with Wodehouse after the war. Before he died, Connor told me that although the form of the broadcast was cooked up by himself and Duff Cooper (the minister for information) it was Winston Churchill who originally inspired it. When the BBC was reluctant to handle their lying filth, it was the old brute himself who forced it through. This interested me because Wodehouse and Churchill were rather by way of being cronies before the war, fellow members of 'The Other' dining club. After Connor's broadcast, the *Daily Telegraph* opened a correspondence for unpleasant nitwits to vent their spleen against Wodehouse, chief among them being the unspeakable A. A. Milne.[6] I have no doubt in my own mind that the animus against Wodehouse, at any rate where the three originators – Connor, Cooper and Churchill – are concerned, came from the bitter hatred and jealousy which bad writers traditionally feel towards better ones.

Well, we all know where they are now. Connor's literary output lies mouldering on the files at Colindale. Churchill has just been reissued in an 'investment' edition; it is still possible to find advertisement copywriters who pronounce him the finest English prose writer of the century, if not of all time – but nobody else, I should imagine. While as for the fiendish Cooper, who died covered with honours in 1954 as the 1st Viscount Norwich PC GCMG, his memory is kept alive by – of all things – a literary prize.

THE PROFESSOR STRIKES GOLD
(*Evening Standard*, 11 November 1975)

The History Man by Malcolm Bradbury (Secker & Warburg, 1975)

The trouble with reviewing novels every week and always – or nearly always – finding something nice to say about them is that when something truly excellent arrives one discovers one has run out of credible adjectives. In the past I overcame this diffi-culty by awarding notional medals, of bronze, silver and gold, and I think the time has come to revive it with a Gold Medal to Malcolm Bradbury[7] for the funniest and best-written novel I have seen for a very long time.

It can be read simply as a fictionalised burlesque version of the various Black Papers on Education which are produced from time to time by worthy concerned academics, although its descriptions of life in one of our new universities – here situated at Watermouth, on the south coast – are far more alarming and more convincing than anything to be gleaned from those documents. It can also be read as a satirical portrait of that strange animal which has grown up in our midst since the war – the New University Radical.

This animal is illustrated by a husband and wife team, Howard and Barbara Kirk. He is a sociology lecturer teaching – and imposing – the radical outlook, organising student unrest and spouting the usual drivel about interpersonal relationships as his seduction patter; she busies herself with the Children's Crusade for Abortion and suchlike causes in a constant state of indignation. Their home life is not harmonious, but they are united in a common Kirkness, and by separating the various qualities which make up this horrible condition to create a new comic stereotype, Professor Bradbury may have achieved for English letters what Tom Wolfe did for the Americans in his famous essay on Radical Chic. All this part of the novel can be read as a jolly farcical romp among the concrete corridors of hideous Scandinavian design where the minds of our young people now receive their conditioning. The jokes are not all new, but they are very well condensed. It is only as the plot develops that one begins to hear a little cry of pain and anger, but Professor Bradbury has a true satirist's instinct for keeping the farce alive, and in his combination of the book's two functions – to entertain and to alarm – I think he shows a technical skill which puts him among the masters.

Two narrative threads run side by side in the plot. One of them shows Howard Kirk as a fun-loving mischief-maker – he invents a rumour that a well-known geneticist, suspected of harbouring unprogressive views on race, is to visit the university: the result of this is that the man *is* invited and student demonstrators nearly destroy the whole university. The second thread eventually shows Kirk as an evil, brutal and formidable power in the land. A dull student called George refuses to toe the Marxist line and is consequently going to fail his course, fail his degree and end his days as a lavatory attendant or novel reviewer. It is when he protests at his treatment that we see the full ruthlessness and cruelty behind Kirkism.

Central to this story is that of a young, cool, uncorrupted Scotswoman who comes to lecture in English, describing herself as an old-fashioned liberal. For a long time in the narrative, we think she will end by turning the tables on the odious Kirk, who has set himself the task of seducing her. We think she will rescue the unfortunate George from Kirk's machinations and, with the help of the few uncorrupted elements left in the university, succeed in humiliating him. That is not how it turns out. Kirk's compulsion to corrupt triumphs over the forces of decency and common sense to give us what would be a very bleak ending indeed if the writer allowed it to be. But he is too skilful to indulge himself in the bitterness and petulance which so often accompany conservative perceptions of our society, and I finished the book with that rare sensation of having been present at a major event.

ALL THE LONELY PEOPLE
(Books & Bookmen, October 1976)

Dear Marje by Marjorie Proops (Andre Deutsch, 1976)

In an engaging introduction to her account of an agony columnist's work, Marje Proops quotes from the former Archbishop of Canterbury, Dr Ramsey, who once said to her: 'Where has the Church appeared to have failed people that they need to seek help from people like you?' In twenty years on the job, Marje reckons to have answered letters from a million people. She and a handful of others in the same business discovered a vast need which was not being met by religious bodies, social services, doctors and psychiatrists. More significantly, it was not being met within the social and emotional relationships of the British family, and perhaps the most important piece of testimony in this fascinating book bears on the extent to which the collapse of the extended family, the severance of local roots, has not only put strain on the nuclear family but has also produced a race of Englishmen and Englishwomen who seem more or less unable to communicate with each other.

When I was on the *Mirror* it was an acknowledged fact that any mention of animals would double the newspaper's postbag next day. In my own department, I noticed that the mention of religion had a similar effect. It was as if one had rung an alarm bell in the corridors of every lunatic asylum and geriatric hospital in the country. Hundreds of letters would arrive in strange, coloured inks with many words written in capital letters and others underlined – sometimes as often as ten times – for no apparent reason. Nothing in my experience as a journalist leads me to suppose that people who write letters to newspapers are a representative cross-section of the population, and it would be an alarming thought that they might be. But the one thing that never fails to have an effect on Marje's postbag – often lifting it from its daily average of 50–100 letters into the thousands – is any mention of loneliness.

This seems to be the overwhelming plight of our degenerate, detribalised urban society. Of course people who aren't lonely don't write letters, on the whole, and Marje is sensible of all the shortcomings of her chosen line of enquiry, including the fact that she only ever hears one side of any case. Even so, I think a letter is probably the ideal way of approaching these things. In conversation, people are nervous and spend hours saying the same thing over and over again; they seldom take in anything said to them and feel bound to grow argumentative if they do. Nor do I think it is a very good idea to encourage people to talk about themselves, unless they are prepared to pay large sums of money for professionals to listen to their self-indulgence, as others of us might visit an ice cream parlour or massage establishment. A letter, like the confessional, imposes certain limits, and even the lady whom Marje mentions as sending 'ninety-two pages of elderly, sad, spiky writing' must be aware of the risk that little of it will be read.

Half the problems she receives relate to marriage difficulties, and a third of these are from men. It used to be the other way round, but more and more husbands are flying to Marje for protection against their wives' exorbitant sexual demands. This strikes me as rather brave of them, because although Marje is noticeably sensible on sexual matters and certainly tries to be fair, she has a built-in sympathy with the female predicament and generally urges these unfortunate men to be more imaginative, to try harder.

Nearly everything Marje says is sensible, and she is also extraordinarily informative. I never knew, for instance, that six out of ten brides are pregnant, or that one in four British marriages will now end in the divorce courts. She is seldom very specific in her published advice, although there are tantalising references to 'the Masters & Johnson squeeze technique' to delay ejaculation. Her advice to teenagers is that they should avoid sex until they are 'good and ready' for it, although she is very keen on masturbation. In the general retreat from parental responsibility, she is a surrogate mother who will generally come up with the commonsense answer to such questions as: 'My mother says I am too young to dye my hair. I am eleven. What do you think?'

She says she is never shocked by sexual deviations, only by child and wife beating, the persecution of homosexuals and transvestites, revenge, deep-seated spite and hatred. A curious list. Oddly enough, I don't find myself particularly shocked by anything on it, except possibly child beating, although there are plainly circumstances in which even wife beating is wrong. Marje is writing for a predominantly working-class readership, of course, and it would be interesting to see how a Marje would shape who wrote for *Vogue*. My own list would feature betrayals of family or friends, certain forms of hypocrisy which involved self-deception, and certain forms of stupidity which prevented a selfish man or woman from seeing that he was selfish. Even cruelty only strikes me as shocking if it is accompanied by impenetrable moral indifference, or self-righteousness. But this, at any rate, is our Marje's list and it seems to have done her very well with *Mirror* readers. It would be a mistake, I think, to see her as a robot, programmed to their tastes and moral perceptions. Although obviously not shocked by heterosexual buggery within marriage, she is very reticent about it, pointing out that it is against the law and that by the Sexual Offences Act of 1956, both offenders may face life imprisonment. I believe it is a practice much favoured by the lower orders, although I forget my authority for this belief.

Just occasionally, it is true, a little *Mirror* slop shows through: 'A big difference in age doesn't matter at all if the two people concerned are deeply in love,' says Marje. Oh, really. I should have thought that was the least important condition. Far more important, I should have thought, that at least one of them should be pretty rich, or it will almost certainly end in tears. But I will obviously have to wait until some enterprising magazine gives me my own 'Dear Auberon' column of homely advice for the middle class. Perhaps the *Sunday Times Colour Magazine* would be interested, with all its exciting new ideas.

Never mind. Marje is surely entitled to a fond illusion or two of her own. She offers two possible uses for her book – that it might be useful to those facing similar problems, or it might, at any rate, provide some interest for the mild voyeur. If I have a problem, it is that of the mild voyeur, and Marje satisfies it most admirably. She is a genuinely warm-hearted woman and caters for both categories of reader with a fine impartiality. Who could fail to be stirred by her description of the 'most pathetic letters of all' from: 'elderly women abandoned by their children, living in bedsitters simply waiting to die but clinging to life in the vain hope that one day a son or a daughter will turn up to rescue them, to love them'. Here, it seems to me, Marje comes extraordinarily close to the central contradiction of our state welfare society: many of us are going to die lonely and miserable, not for want of material comforts but because state provision has destroyed whole areas of humanity in our society. Marje doesn't worry her head about this sort of thing in the abstract. She merely remarks, in passing, that it doesn't make life any easier for advice columnists. She is the supreme pragmatist, facing each problem as she comes to it, and I find one learns more from her bright, gossipy casebook than from any amount of theorising.

IF ONLY PROUST HAD LEFT THE CAKE ALONE
(*Daily Mail*, 3 April 1981)

Remembrance of Things Past by Marcel Proust, translated by C. K. Scott-Moncreiff and T. Kilmartin (Chatto & Windus, 1981)

In January 1909, as we now know, Marcel Proust had a very important experience. He dipped a rusk into his tea and found that the taste brought back childhood memories. From that moment, it might be said, he never looked back, except that he never, in fact, did anything else but look back for the rest of his life. He had discovered his own secret of the universe, that all our past remains within us, capable of recapture.

Let us examine the moment, in the Master's own words, through the new improved translation of Mr Terence Kilmartin. Close readers will observe how the rusk has been transmuted by Proust's artistic imagination into a *'petite madeleine'*, which is a sort of individual sponge portion rather popular in France: 'I raised to my lips a spoonful of the tea in which I had soaked a morsel of the cake. No sooner had the warm liquid mixed with the crumbs touched my lips than a shudder ran through me and I stopped, intent upon the extraordinary thing that was happening to me. An exquisite pleasure had invaded my senses, something isolated, detached . . .'

Obviously, Proust quite liked his individual sponge portions. Most readers' reaction will be to notice the perfectly disgusting way he had of eating his sponge cake. Mrs Proust ought to be ashamed of herself, letting him eat like that in front of her at the age of thirty-seven. But in fact his mother had been dead for four years when the rusk episode occurred and Proust never really got over her death. It was the combination of her death and the rusk incident which decided him to go and live in a soundproof flat in Paris for the rest of his life, struggling with this wonderful idea for a novel about a chap who is eating his sponge cake dipped in tea one day when he suddenly has this strange feeling . . .

In Proust's story, the narrator goes over his life from that moment, jumping backwards and forwards in time and meditating on its significance. The narrator's general conclusion throughout most of the book – that is to say, about the first 3200 pages – is a pretty austere one: human love is seldom if ever fully reciprocated; it is no more than a projection of self-love or social ambition; humans are vain creatures, fickle, snobbish and cruel.

Then, on his way to a party at the house of his very good friend the Prince of Guermantes, he has another experience. The uneven paving stones in the Prince's courtyard remind him of a visit to Venice many years before and, suddenly, everything is all right. The exquisite pleasure starts up again and he is in business. All the narrator has to do is set down this absolutely brilliant idea he has had for a novel, about this chap who is eating his sponge cake dipped in tea one day ... These, then, are the bare bones of the 1,250,000 word yarn, hailed by its devotees ever since as one of the profoundest and most perfect achievements of the human imagination.

Proust's own story is somewhat different. Unlike the narrator, he was half Jewish and a homosexual. Although similarly self-obsessed he had a tough streak and was also a sadist, on one occasion witnessing rats being struck with hat pins and beaten to death for his sexual gratification. He was a snob who saw through the snobbery of others to such an extent that in the final stages of his super-snobbery (not believing in God) he could talk only to himself. *Remembrance of Things Past* is the monument to his self-obsession, the supreme example of one man's endlessly protracted self-gratification.

Now the small coterie of pre-war literary exquisites who went round proclaiming their joy in Proust has been joined by a grey army of post-war university lecturers and Sunday-newspaper critics, anxious not to be left behind in any promotion rat-race. Some of these sad, insecure people may even have read it all, although most, I suspect, have only read about a third, like this reviewer. But among the pages and pages and pages of self-indulgent drivel, which are the chief hallmark of Proust's masterpiece, there are several hundred pages of keen social satire and observation. I should like to think that the ghost of Marcel Proust, purged of all its snobbery, cruelty and grinding egomania, is quietly laughing at the pretensions of those who claim to see his work as the masterpiece of modern literature.

THERE'S NOTHING WORSE THAN RHYME-LESS VERSE
(*Daily Mail*, 6 August 1988)

A new life of John Betjeman,[8] the beloved poet laureate who died four years ago, has revived the terrible question of what has happened to English poetry this century. Betjeman's poems were bought by hundreds of thousands and read by millions of people, who found them a genuine source of inspiration and hope in facing the same modern world as Betjeman faced. But you will not find a single mention of Betjeman's name in *The Faber Book of Modern Verse*, the bible of the poetry establishment. It would be possible to claim that since Betjeman's death the pseuds had resumed their reign. In fact, they never left it. All that has happened is that the public has lost interest in poetry.

Who can blame them? Why should anyone waste his time trying to follow the private and incomprehensible allusions of someone he has never met who is trying to sort out his own tensions and disorders on paper? Psychoanalysts charge twenty-five guineas an hour for pretending to listen to this drivel. Why should anyone pay to do it?

Yet it is a crying shame for all that. England has the richest language on earth. Even without the mighty figure of Shakespeare, under whose gigantic shade all other poets and writers must struggle to survive, poetry is the one field in which the English have unquestionably excelled. There is scarcely an English speaker alive who has not thrilled to a particular poem at one time or another, even if it was long ago and long forgotten.

Many, if not most, people have slumbering poets inside them, waiting only for encouragement. Writing and reading poetry is a normal and natural thing for people to do who are in love or desolate or simply looking for some escape from their humdrum lives. Yet it has become the preserve of a tiny, self-appointed clique, largely subsidised by the Arts Council. Because what these people write is incomprehensible – usually lacking rhyme and metre as well as sense – ordinary folk suppose they must write in the same vein, or not at all.

The late Michael Roberts, introducing the first edition of *The Faber Book of Modern Verse* in 1936, remarked on how modern poetry was still liable to be received in a hostile spirit. People were compelled to argue that what does not rhyme, or scan, or make apparent sense, was not poetry at all. All this has changed. Modern poetry is no longer greeted with hostility, so much as with yawning indifference. The Modernists have won the battle. We are quite ready to accept the most arrant rubbish as 'poetry' if they say so, but we simply don't want to know about it. Recognising that something may have gone wrong, our poets now tend to declare themselves 'Post-Modernists', even 'traditionalists', and throw in the occasional awkward asymmetrical rhyme. There is seldom much sense there, however, and practically never any metre.

The difficulty is to persuade these people that anything which rhymes, scans or describes a recognisable human emotion is really poetry at all. 'Granny verses,' they will shout. 'Greetings card stuff.' Just as in painting anything remotely representational was liable to be dismissed as 'chocolate box' unless it actually showed a dead rat lying between a naked woman's legs with its guts spilling out, or held some other improving message of that sort. The tragedy of the present situation is not so much that practically nobody wants to read modern poetry – I honestly do not believe that much of it is worth the effort – but that it discourages other people from trying their hand at writing ordinary verse.

Two years ago I began editing a small-circulation literary magazine, the *Literary Review*. It had a noble, idealistic poetry editor who sorted through the thirty or forty 'poems' which arrived, unsolicited, every week. She was knowledgeable, highly intelligent and widely respected in the small world of modern poetry. Every month she would take enormous trouble to choose a selection of verses, but with the best will in the world I decided that I could not tell the difference between the 'good' modern poetry she chose and the 'bad' modern poetry she sent back. Since she left, we have accumulated a couple of hundredweight of the rubbish.

So I decided to try to halt the tide. Every month I set a subject – it might be 'the end of a love affair', or 'rape of the countryside' – and subscribers were invited to submit a poem on that subject for a prize of £50. The only rule was that the poem must rhyme, scan and make sense. Although the *Literary Review*'s readership was, and remains, tiny, the result was unbelievable. Soon readers were writing in offering new prizes on behalf of themselves and their firms – money, sums up to £1000, cases of wine, crates of oysters and smoked salmon, even new lavatories. The experience has shown that there is still an enormous appetite for writing and reading poetry: only the poets are killing it.

JUDGEMENT ON A MAJOR MAN OF LETTERS
(Sunday Telegraph, 27 May 1990)

Miscellaneous Verdicts: Writings on Writers 1946–1989 by Anthony Powell (Heinemann)

Anthony Powell, who was born in 1905, has justly been described as the doyen of *Daily Telegraph* reviewers. His notices in that newspaper, which form the bulk of this volume, have been appearing for over fifty years. In the last thirty of them, the fortnightly lead review by Anthony Powell has become an institution for which I can think of practically no equivalent in the whole field of British publishing, unless perhaps the excellent 'Jennifer's Diary' in *Queen*, now *Harper's & Queen* magazine. Powell himself is fairly modest about his second career as a reviewer, neglecting to mention it at all in his *Who's Who* entry, which is otherwise fairly comprehensive, listing his Order of the White Lion (Czechoslovakia) along with his T. S. Eliot Prize for Creative Literature, awarded by the Ingersoll Foundation in 1984.

Although he describes reviewing in his characteristic style as 'a craft not without intrinsic interest', he seems to feel the need to apologise for doing it, as if it was somehow an undignified, not to say indecorous, role in which to find himself: 'This does not mean that reviews *per se* are never worth a second glance. On the contrary, they can reveal all kinds of shifting in literary fashion, individual style, even proclaim the age of the reviewer.' In the volume under review, this last function is made easier by the meticulous dating of every review and article printed. Those who know Powell was born on 22 December 1905 can discover his age in almost every instance by subtracting six from the year in which it first appeared. His important review of *Burke's Peerage*, which appeared in the *Times Literary Supplement* in 1949 – 'the Labour peers and their families, by no means insignificant in number, make a decidedly interesting addition to the social order of the country' – would thus have been written when he was forty-three. Ah.

Apart from these useful clues to the reviewer's age, admirers of Powell will undoubtedly wish to reread his reviews in order to refresh themselves once again at the wonderfully recycled source of his literary style. Its main elements are the diffident double negative – 'not without all . . . interest'; 'the Labour peers . . . by no means insignificant in numbers' – and the 'elegant' or dissociative inverted comma: 'it was really Maundy Gregory's party. He certainly may be said to have "brought them in". "Orwell came back to England on leave (he had been ill) and resigned. He wanted "to write".' 'In 1936 an opportunity arose of writing some sort of "documentary" about unemployment.'

These examples, I might point out, were written when Powell

was forty-nine, sixty-six and seventy-three respectively. In the first instance, he seems to be dissociating himself from an expression which might be thought slang, or vulgar, or somehow unworthy of him; in the second, which is repeated elsewhere, he wishes to show a certain patrician scorn for anyone who wants to do anything so silly as to write; in the third, he is signalling his use of a new word and urging us not to think him common or ignorant for using it. These with the hesitant, qualified commendation ('perhaps almost one of the best parodists of his generation') and the occasional descent into the impersonal first person ('one is a trifle shocked'), make up the main elements of his reviewing style, which has stood him in such good part for the last fifty years.

I wish I could say that an analysis of the miscellaneous verdicts contained in this forty-three-year spread is equally revealing – whether about the subjects reviewed, or even about the reviewer's age at the time – but the truth is that Powell makes very few literary judgements, addressing himself by preference to the periphery. He seldom has a word to say, for example, about the novels of Graham Greene or the poems of John Betjeman. Instead he reviews, under Greene, a reissue of the magazine *Night & Day* (Greene was its film critic) and the first volume of Norman Sherry's biography, and supplies us with an only fairly successful parody he wrote for *Punch* in 1953 (aet: su 47).

On Betjeman, he reviews only Bevis Hillier's biography. On Waugh, he reviews the autobiography, a miscellany edited by David Pryce-Jones, the biography by Christopher Sykes, the *Diaries*, the *Letters*, the *Essays* and a biography by M. Stannard. Such verdicts on the writers themselves as he passes in every case are incidental, unbacked by argument or illustration, rather like a saloon-bar pundit giving his views on the political events of the day.

'An author's journalistic sundries,' he writes, 'often reveal more, anyway on the surface, about the writer than do the books.' I certainly do not wish to discuss what Powell's twelve-volume novel sequence, *A Dance to the Music of Time*, may reveal about the writer. As an early upmarket soap opera, it undoubtedly gave comfort to a number of people, becoming something of a cult during the 1970s in the London community of expatriate Australians. Perhaps it afforded them the illusion of understanding English society, even a vicarious sense of belonging to it. If so, it was one of the cruellest practical jokes ever played by a Welshman. But if we regard the enterprise as a social rather than as a literary phenomenon, then we must surely see it as beneficial, ministering to the socially and intellectually insecure and endowing them with what they most need, a sense of their own social and intellectual superiority . . .

If I decline to discuss Powell as a literary phenomenon, out of a priggish fastidiousness about his abominable English, we might at least ask what insights into the writer we are afforded by these journalistic sundries. It would be unfair to judge him by the stern standards of literary gossip writing, because in a long career he appears to have known practically no-one, apart from Osbert Lancaster and the early experimental novelist Henry Green, whom he does not mention. He was at Eton with Connolly and Orwell, without meeting them; at Oxford with Connolly, Waugh, Greene, Acton and all the rest of that crowd, without making any mark on them at all. He gives the impression of having been trapped into a literary world of which he does not approve, and about which he does not want to know.

Although one was not exactly, as it were, 'born' in 1934 at the time of Anthony Powell's marriage to the third daughter of the 5th Earl of Longford, one well remembers the sense of shock – almost amazement – which went around celestial circles at that time. 'What on earth does Lady Violet think she's *doing*?' one heard. Well, she has done rather well. From major in the Intelligence Corps to Establishment's pet novelist proved an easy step. But it is the major's sensibility which he brought to his journalistic sundries, as I maintain. His first and only meeting with Graham Greene at Balliol is soon described: 'Probably some club dinner had taken place. I addressed a remark to him at which he replied rather sharply. No doubt it was foolish or frivolous. We did not meet again until 1933 or 1934.' Of Ivy Compton-Burnett: 'We met on two or three occasions, but I never knew her well . . . In fact, both Burnetts and Comptons . . . were of the most modest origins: agricultural labourers, blacksmiths, small coal merchants.'

He met Truman Capote but once, at a party given by Lady Pamela Berry: 'I sometimes used to wonder why this dumpy figure in sun spectacles should be so photographed at so many "fabulous" millionaire parties on the strength of his literary output . . . I thought the least I could do was to make an effort to be agreeable . . . He seemed rather a dull little man.'

While complaining about Connolly's 'utter disregard of other people's well-being and convenience, and often abominable manners', he misses the entire point about Connolly, so well caught by Barbara Skelton, that he was a brilliantly successful, fully participating comic archetype. Powell also misses the point of Evelyn Waugh's remark that few of his Oxford contemporaries had any serious interest in women: 'If the last statement is admitted to be some limited extent true, [*sic*] that was surely principally because the University authorities descended like a ton of bricks on anyone seen so much as saying goodnight to a pretty waitress.'

No, Major, that was not principally the reason. In the whole book, it is a major of the Intelligence Corps speaking rather than a man of letters, let alone a novelist. Of Evelyn Waugh he writes: 'Throughout his military service . . . he kept a diary, though this was strictly forbidden by army regulations.' Of Peter Fleming, he goes further: 'One is a trifle shocked to find an officer whose job was concerned with security not only keeping a diary (strictly forbidden) but carrying it on such a jaunt.' Perhaps Powell should have stayed in the Intelligence Corps officers' mess. That, I feel, is where his heart belongs.

Waugh's review caused quite a stink. 'Like many artists, Powell did not react kindly to criticism,' he recollected, nearly ten years later, after Powell's death. 'A few years earlier he had broken off relations with an old friend, Malcolm Muggeridge, for the same reason. On this occasion, he resigned immediately from the *Telegraph*. Its deputy literary editor, Nicholas Shakespeare, held responsible for having hired me to write the piece for the *Sunday Telegraph*, was allowed to leave – a sad loss for the literary pages. More eccentrically, the newspaper decided to commission a bust of Anthony Powell by William Pye, which now adorns the main entrance to the *Telegraph* offices. History does not relate whether Powell liked the bust. People are often sensitive about these things. I should have thought it rather a risky act of contrition.'[9]

Nevertheless, Waugh maintained that his review was merely 'jokey'. 'Re-reading the piece after all these years, it still seems good-natured and friendly – even, if I dare suggest it, quite funny.'[10]

Chapter Fourteen
From the Pulpit

All my memory of church and sermons from the earliest years – in the ill-favoured small industrial town of Dursley, Gloucestershire, home of Lister diesel engines – is of demands for money from the pulpit, usually delivered straight at my unfortunate father as the only rich man in the congregation, by an Irish priest called Father Murtough.

At the end of a memorable sermon just after the war, demanding money for a new harmonium or something of the sort, Father Murtough fixed the Waugh family with a terrible stare and said that if the money was not going to come from his parishioners, he would be forced to go to the Jews for it. I suppose this was his disagreeable way of saying that he would have to ask the manager of his local Barclays Bank for a loan, but the threat created quite an impression on my young mind, unattuned, at that stage, to the horrors of racism or ethnic prejudice.[1]

For the last fifteen years of his life, after he left *Private Eye*, Waugh devoted much of his time and energy to editing the *Literary Review*. Considering the wealth of other work he could have done, this was an eccentric and endearing career choice. The *Literary Review* had been founded only a few years before, in 1979, by an Edinburgh academic called Anne Smith. Subsequently edited by Gillian Greenwood and then Emma Soames, it had become an intelligent and lively read, without attracting all that much in the way of advertising or circulation. Yet Waugh had always had an inherent sympathy for Lilliputian publications. Much of his best work had appeared in small-scale periodicals, rather than the Fleet Street papers, with their big circulations and bigger fees. Here was a replacement for the late lamented *Books & Bookmen*, the brain-child of Philip Dossé, Waugh's late lamented friend.[2]

Waugh was invited to edit the *Literary Review* by its owner, Naim Attallah, a charismatic Palestinian *émigré* who ran his own publishing company, Quartet Books, in addition to his day job as chief executive of Asprey. Waugh had met Attallah a few years earlier, while writing an article about publishers for the *Daily Telegraph*. He subsequently asked Attallah if he might be able to find a job in publishing for his eldest daughter, Sophia, who'd just come down from Durham University with a degree in English. Attallah obliged, and the two men became firm friends. When Attallah offered Waugh the editorship, Waugh said the salary was too high. He said he'd do it for less.

'So far as I have any revolutionary intention in becoming editor, it is to produce a magazine which will be enjoyed by intelligent, educated people who read books,' announced Waugh, in his first editorial, 'rather than flatter the socially and intellectually insecure by claiming some deeper meaning for whatever is obscure, muddled, incomprehensible or frankly meaningless.'[3] In his second editorial, he promised to put 'SEX' on the cover of each subsequent issue, regardless of the contents — not to attract readers, but to encourage booksellers to display the magazine more prominently. He didn't carry out this threat, but he didn't really need to. A large part of the *Literary Review*'s attraction was its discreet word-of-mouth appeal.

A lot of writers dream of becoming editors. Waugh was never one of them. Yet, to his surprise, he found he was actually rather good at it. 'If it is true, as Napoleon remarked, that every private soldier carries a field-marshal's baton in his knapsack, I suppose it must be true that every journalist carries an editor's green eyeshade somewhere among the half-eaten sandwiches and other unspeakable things in his briefcase,'[4] he observed, after a few weeks in the editor's chair. He quadrupled the circulation in his first year, and doubled it again a few years later. Since the *Literary Review* only sold about a thousand a month to start with, the magazine inevitably still lost money, but he gave it a sharper edge and a public profile quite out of keeping with its compact readership. With his wide circle of friends, he persuaded big names to write for tiny fees, much as Dossé had done on *Books & Bookmen*. He got his old *Private Eye* pal, Willie Rushton, to draw a series of exquisite cartoon covers. He instigated some clever stunts, like the Bad Sex Award, presented annually to the book that featured the most excruciating description of the sexual act (the inaugural winner was Melvyn Bragg, who sportingly turned up to accept his prize).

Under his stewardship, the *Literary Review* became required reading for bibliophiles who liked well-written books that made good sense, and poetry that rhymed and scanned.[5] It's a testament to his influence that it retains these qualities to this day, yet Waugh's ambitions remained realistic. 'Writers will have to confront the fact that nobody is much interested in them any more,' he warned his readers. 'Literature is a minority interest, like budgerigar breeding, catered for by minority magazines, kept alive by small groups of enthusiasts at ill-attended meetings in small libraries and halls. When its followers come to realise that there is no pot of gold at the end of the rainbow, they may become politer, friendlier people and lead happier lives as a result.'[6]

For the first time in his career, Waugh now spent much of his time 'soliciting copy from other people, correcting it and preparing it for press, rather than scribbling my own stuff',[7] but he was too good an editor to neglect his star columnist, himself. Each issue of the *Literary Review* opened with a signed leader, entitled 'From the Pulpit', eventually illustrated by a Rushton cartoon of Waugh in ecclesiastical garb. Much of this space was given over to parish notices (though even the most prosaic news made entertaining reading in Waugh's hands) but at its best, 'From the Pulpit' prompted some inspired sermons — ostensibly about books, but, actually, like the books he wrote about, on every subject under the sun:

> As the European and American cultures slowly drift apart into a state of mutual and impenetrable incomprehension, perhaps the English are in the best position to understand that what divides us finally is not a matter of taste – as between hamburgers and soft drinks on the other side of the herring pond, and hamburgers and soft drinks on this side – but of moral perception. We mock the idea of political correctness and point to its more extreme expressions in order to joke and laugh at them, but what we seem reluctant to accept is that the United States is evolving a system of morality which is completely alien to our own, much stricter in many respects, and uniquely attuned to the exigencies of an unequal, multi-racial society struggling to avoid anarchy, riot and terror.[8]

For Waugh, one of the main attractions of the job was the *Literary Review*'s cosy Soho office, where he spent three busy but contented days each week, in a nest of rooms above the Academy Club, which he founded for writers who were 'too poor, too mean, or too proud to join the Groucho'.[9] Poets were banned (for being boring, not paying for their drinks, and for being unfairly attractive to young women) but in virtually every other respect, it was uncommonly broad-minded.[10] Waugh called it 'a refuge or sanctuary in the West End for agreeable, well-mannered people who need a friendly, familiar place to go'.[11] Seeing him in his Beak Street den, scratching away at his desk upstairs or enjoying a glass of good wine below, you felt his life had come full circle. After all his adventures, Boz had finally come home.

*

THE ENDLESSLY FASCINATING QUESTION
OF W. B. YEATS'S LAUNDRY BILLS
(*Literary Review*, July 1987)

Librarians at the Bodleian have been trying to raise the scare of American libraries who buy up the papers of British authors, thereby denying British academics the chance of new research into the endlessly fascinating question of W. B. Yeats's laundry bills. They point out that Texas alone has already bought the major manuscripts of Evelyn Waugh, Graham Greene, Samuel Beckett and Siegfried Sassoon, not to mention the D. H. Lawrence and N. R. Foggis archives. V. S. Naipaul is next on the list, said to be offering his papers to whoever is prepared to pay around £400,000 for them. Even John Braine's papers are expected to fetch £25,000.

As one who played a minor part in selling the Evelyn Waugh papers to Texas twenty years ago, I should like to put an oar in. Authors are treated abominably in Britain, as a result of our politicians' abiding hatred of anyone who might be thought cleverer or more admirable than themselves. When an author dies, his widow and orphans are charged for estate duty as if any future, putative, income from his books represented a capital sum, despite the fact that such receipts are taxed as income, and there might easily be no savings with which to meet the estate duty bill. In other words, an author's widow has no choice but to sell her husband's manuscripts, if anybody is interested in buying them, and British universities have never shown the slightest interest.

I think they are right to be uninterested. Appreciation of a finished book is very little increased by studying the various drafts and corrections involved in writing it. Our academics in the Eng Lit departments have shown themselves marvellously resourceful in the search for things to keep themselves occupied and amused: phonetics, structuralism, Marxian analysis, *Sunday Times* style graphics, charts and doodles. Even in the sacred interests of job creation, there is no case for spending further government money on acquiring authors' manuscripts.

STOP PUBLISHING AND BE SAVED
(*Literary Review*, May 1991)

We are told there was once a time when book publishing was an efficient industry in Britain: as soon as a first printing was sold out booksellers re-ordered and subsequent impressions could be rushed through at a few days' notice; it seldom took more than six weeks to prepare a manuscript for press and print it, while allowing literary editors to receive their early editions, post them to reviewers and receive their reviews, beautifully written in copperplate, by return of post.

Perhaps these conditions applied in my grandfather's day – he spent forty-one years at Chapman & Hall, never failing to answer a letter on the day he received it. However, they have certainly never applied in my lifetime. By the time I arrived on the literary scene in 1960, publishers were amiable people who always got drunk at luncheon, never answered letters and preferred to talk of other things than books. As a profession, it attracted pleasant, idle, incompetent young men and over-educated, idealistic young women, always kept in subordinate positions because they had not been to a public school for boys and did not have the right connections.

In the publishing revolution of the seventies and eighties nearly all these pleasant, idle incompetents were pushed out; their places were taken, as we now see, by unpleasant incompetents who manage to hide their idleness in occasional bursts of officious activity. As an outsider on the publishing scene, listening occasionally to its gossip but avoiding its main celebrations, I am aware of an atmosphere which is not so different from that of a Las Vegas fruit-machine saloon, except that the players are so busy watching each others' scores that they have no time to study their own.

Perhaps the same is true of many British industries at the present time. The concentration on hitting a jackpot precludes any interest in ways of making smaller, surer sums of money. Perhaps we are becoming a nation of wide boys, spivs and quick-money merchants. The only trouble is that we don't appear to be very good at it.

THERE ONCE WAS A POET CALLED HUGHES
(*Literary Review*, June 1991)

I deliberately refrained from commenting on the poet laureate's failure to come up with a poem celebrating the Queen's sixty-fifth birthday for fear it should transpire that the laureate was suffering from some fatal illness. However, some time has now elapsed and like a dog held in rabies quarantine by the Customs, he has produced no symptoms. His silence prompted Charles Osborne, the former literature director of the Arts Council, to ask if we really need a poet laureate, arguing that it is unreasonable to expect modern 'poets' to produce verse for royal occasions.

Whether or not it is reasonable to expect such things, few enough 'poets' seem able to produce verse under any circumstances. At the time of Betjeman's death, I argued that the post should go into abeyance for a time out of respect for his memory: Larkin was not quite good enough, and nobody else was any good at all. As usual nobody paid any attention and 'Ted' Hughes got the job. Since he is not, as it would appear, terminally ill, and since he has produced no other excuse – melancholia, drunkenness, insanity, constipation or any of the thousand natural shocks that flesh is heir to – I feel a certain impatience may be justified. At a time when the air is full of horrible voices demanding a return of the death penalty, we do not wish to add our own to them and suggest that Hughes should be drowned in his butt of sack, but a ducking might be in order.

ON THE BASENESS AND INGRATITUDE OF POETS

(Literary Review, January 1994)

When the Academy was first proposed as an inexpensive club of vaguely literary associations to occupy the ground floor and basement of the *Literary Review*'s offices in Beak Street, earnest discussions followed about the sort of person we should let into it. It has been said that the purpose of forming a club is as much to exclude the Wrong Sort of Person as it is to provide a haven for Our Sort, the Right Sort. I do not think anybody involved had snobbish motives or exclusive intentions, but it is true that one or two seriously unpleasant members can ruin an entire club, and our purpose was to add to the sensual enjoyment and spiritual happiness of members, rather than create a new area of dejection. Various inappropriate suggestions were made – that we should exclude all male Americans, all lawyers, all architects, all Welshmen, all men in jeans and women in power suits with padded shoulders. All of these exclusions seemed objectionable. Exceptions could be found in every case. When it fell to me to draw up a draft Constitution and set of rules only one exclusion remained, but that was absolute: under no circumstances would any poet be considered for membership, nor would members be permitted to bring poets on the premises as their guests. In the country which produced William Shakespeare, such a prohibition may seem incomprehensible. John Betjeman, too, was a lovely man: funny, wise, affectionate, kind and infinitely poignant. The trouble with Shakespeare and Betjeman is that they are both dead, as are all the other poets we can think of.

But that is not really the point. Just as the nature of what is called poetry has changed, so a different sort of person has stepped forward to satisfy the demand. It was – and remains – my experience of life that anybody who describes his vocation as a poet, purveying the modern style of formless verse, is invariably among the meanest and most despicable in the land:

vain, empty, conceited, dishonest, dirty, often flea-ridden and infected by venereal disease, greedy, parasitical, drunken, untruthful, arrogant ... all these repulsive qualities, and also irresistibly attractive to women. We certainly did not want them in the Academy.

FIVE YEARS AFTER RUSHDIE'S REPRIEVE
(Literary Review, March 1994)

It was on St Valentine's Day 1989 that the former Ayatollah Khomeini chose to publish his *fatwah* on the English novelist Salman Rushdie, and so it was accordingly last month that the literary world chose to celebrate (if that is the right word) its fifth anniversary. The Ayatollah's announcement had been uncompromising enough: 'I inform the proud Muslim people of the world that the author of the *Satanic Verses* book, which is against Islam, the Prophet and the Koran, and all those involved in its publication who were aware of its content, are sentenced to death.' An Iranian charity immediately offered $1 million to any non-Iranian who would carry out the sentence, and this sum was increased three and a half years later, to keep up with inflation. But nobody has yet taken it up, and Rushdie is now to be seen at many of the less good literary parties in London.

In an important sense, we are all under sentence of death, as Khomeini may have reflected as he himself expired less than four months later. His obsequies were attended by such exhibitions of bizarre behaviour as might well have given the rest of the world pause in its glib acceptance of the modern doctrine that all religions are equally to be held in respect by those who do not belong to them. When the adoring multitude had succeeded in tearing off his shroud and exposing his corpse, his remains had to be put back in a helicopter and taken away before they could be buried.

Rushdie, meanwhile, went about his business in London,

announcing his return to Islam a few years later, only to have this gesture rejected by London's Islamic community on 2 May 1991. At the time, this struck me as rather tough. Islamic fundamentalists argue that apostasy from Islam is a capital offence, demanding instant execution. Under those circumstances, penitence and a return to Islam might cancel the sentence even for blasphemy. Apparently not. But I have often wondered why, if this is really what Muslims believe, their religion is permitted at all in any secular or non-Islamic country. Certainly no other society or religious group would be allowed which threatened to kill any member who left it.

St Valentine, by contrast, on whose feast day Rushdie was sentenced, after being ordered to renounce his faith by the former Roman consul Furius Placidus, was beaten with clubs and beheaded when he refused. Rushdie is still, mercifully, with us. The explanation for all this may be found in an anniversary which occurs this month. On 16 March 1989, a month after the promulgation of Khomeini's *fatwah*, the Islamic Conference Organisation, meeting in Riyadh, decided not to support the Iranian *fatwah*. Thereafter, the whole drama illustrated little more than the unhealthy state of Iran, which had fallen into the hands of fanatics. The Muslim religion is exceptionally tolerant of its fanatics. They are permitted to present themselves as spokesmen for their religion. Few dare contradict them. But Muslims are not, by and large, fanatics. That is the fact that we might celebrate on 16 March with a little tea party.

The only effect of the Rushdie episode on the world of English letters over this past five years has been to give novelists a sense of importance which they have done nothing whatever to deserve. Any idea that Iranian mullahs could tell us what we might put in our novels was always preposterous. The shame is that we have not used our freedom from this or any other form of supervision to greater effect.

WHEN PUBLIC FUNDING CAN BECOME
THE KISS OF DEATH
(*Literary Review*, January 1996)

It is often said that Christopher Wren's designs for St Paul's Cathedral, when first presented, were considered highly controversial, if not actually outrageous. We have been told this so often that a new platitude has been born out of the paradox that by no means all artists achieve recognition in their own lifetime: no truly great work of art is ever identified as such, we are told, except by a highly trained, super-sensitive élite, until many years after its first appearance. The vulgar taste in aesthetics always takes years to catch up. This rhetoric, or a variation on it, has justified the greater part of the government's subsidies to contemporary art, as well as the horrible buildings which philistine departments, local councils and commercial firms have been happy to accept since the war.

In fact, it is all based on a fallacy. Wren may not have become as obscenely wealthy as the leading architects of our own time, but he lived with great dignity in elegant quarters in Hampton Court Palace, acquired a tidy fortune and was universally respected. The noises of outrage which greeted his model for St Paul's came from a tiny handful of Protestant fanatics, Europhobes and reactionary boobies whose influence and intellectual standing may, perhaps, be measured beside the small groups which demonstrated outside Westminster Cathedral when the Queen went to vespers there.

With the outbreak of democracy in the last century, public debate on aesthetics became intense. People argued in the streets over the rival designs for the Palace of Westminster. It was only after the Modern Movement became established that public interest receded, an élite of sorts was reinstated, and the masses became as ignorant and resentful as ever. The more amenable of the lumpen proletariat may still be prepared to accept Teacher's word for it that even the Lloyd's building, for instance, is somehow progressive, a blow in the class war against bourgeois assumptions of prettiness, a preparation for the glorious ugliness of the workers' paradise. Most timidly accept that they might appreciate it in thirty years, if they are still alive, and it is still standing. Alternatively, they revert to the feudal peasant mode, and humbly conclude that they are too ignorant to pass judgement on such matters.

All of which must be highly agreeable for the artistic élite, as they dispense public patronage to their friends and those whom they choose to patronise. Just occasionally, however, they go too far and there is a blip. The Turner Prize award of £20,000 to Damien Hirst for his mutilated corpses of a cow and a calf suddenly caught the apathetic multitude on the raw. Every other cab driver in London was fulminating against it, women were distressed at the spectacle of a dead calf being exploited so shamelessly. Suddenly, the arty-tarty élite were more unpopular than the bourgeois society they hoped to mock. The *Daily Telegraph* described this Turner Prize as 'an odious and disgusting scandal', and there were few dissenting voices.

By coincidence, I went to two exhibitions on the night of the Turner award. One was in the St Leger Gallery, Old Bond Street, where Julian Barrow was showing his latest collection of reasonably priced oils of domestic and foreign scenes. A friendly gathering of polite, prosperous people bought these agreeable, undemanding pictures entirely for their own pleasure. My second call that evening was at the Dulwich Picture Gallery for the Van Dyck exhibition. Anybody who has made the journey down to Dulwich will know that the Picture Gallery is one of the greatest delights in London, housing the wonderful collection of 650 oil paintings formed for the last King of Poland in Regency times and never delivered. What both these exhibitions have in common is that neither has received a penny from public funds.

Neither, of course, has the *Literary Review*. Barrow survives commercially by selling his wares, which is surely the best way to survive. The Dulwich Picture Gallery, which has been taken under the wing of Lord Sainsbury, survives by voluntary charitable donations. We keep going with help from a few friends. Although their motives in helping us can only be charitable, we are not allowed to be treated as a charity, following a decision by the Charity Commissioners.

In paranoid moments, one might see this decision as a last throw by the adherents of the Modern Movement, who control nearly all access to public funding in the arts. Never mind. Time and again it has been proved that public funding is the kiss of death. We have our moments. History is surely on our side. Damien Hirst's mutilated cow and calf represent an extreme of the wrongheadedness that has ruled the arts Establishment for fifty years. Their literary equivalents range from monosyllabic obscenities posing as poetry to the gentler quasi-bucolic silliness of our nice poet laureate, Mr Hughes. What a wonderful thing it would be if the Turner Prize taught them all that the party is over.

Chapter Fifteen

Rage

In my old age I shall probably spend most of my time denying that I have said, written or done anything attributed to me. One can well understand the temptation. It is a good way for old people to keep the young on their toes.[1]

Waugh's departure from *Private Eye*, in 1986, to edit the *Literary Review*, was marked with a lunch at the Escargot restaurant in Soho, on Friday, 14 March. He was given a silver-plated wine funnel ('Presented to Auberon Waugh by Lord Gnome in recognition of 16 years' devoted service to his organ,' read the inscription) but Richard Ingrams 'rather stole the show'[2] with his surprise announcement that he would be departing too, leaving the magazine he'd edited for more than twenty years in the hands of his youthful protégé, Ian Hislop. Waugh pleaded with his old friend to stay, even offering to ditch the *Literary Review* if he'd change his mind, but Ingrams was adamant. Hislop would be taking over as the *Eye*'s new editor in September.

Waugh was full of praise for Ingrams ('Of all my contemporaries, he is undoubtedly the one who has made the greatest mark on his times')[3] but he was gloomy about the *Eye*'s prospects: 'It may just be a healthy middle-aged man's hatred of the young which makes me suppose that *Private Eye* will now either degenerate into a teenage comic or disintegrate under the pressure of innumerable libel suits.'[4] Yet once the dust had settled, he admitted he'd been wrong. 'At the time I thought the change was unnecessary and a great shame, and I thought the magazine would collapse without Ingrams, but in fact it jolly well hasn't, as anybody can see.'[5]

In 1992, Ingrams launched the *Oldie*, and recruited Waugh as a columnist.[6] 'If it had been anyone else,' reflected Waugh, 'I might have thought he was drunk.'[7] This was just a joke. In fact, Waugh had long believed that modern advertisers were mad to court the youth market, when older readers had far more spare cash to spend. 'How long will it take these advertising experts to grasp the simple message of our time?' he railed. 'Old age is good. Youth is bad. To be old is to be wise and rich and right. To be young is to be foolish and disgusting and wrong. The young are dirty. Many young people smell. Above all, the young have no money, and never will have until they are fifty years old.'[8] Ingrams's new magazine would test his theory in the market. Waugh was happy to champion this noble cause.

Waugh's hunch was right, and so was Ingrams's. Even the title was inspired. 'At the time of its launch, people said nobody would buy a magazine called *Oldie*,' gloated Waugh, a year later. 'Those who had the misfortune to be over fifty did not wish to be reminded of the fact, while those of even more mature years might be prepared to consider a magazine called *Afternoon Sunshine*, or *Golden Age*, but would certainly not identify with anything called *Oldie*. However, people underestimated the great hatred for young people, which is such a refreshing development on the modern scene.'[9]

Waugh's column was called 'Rage', after Dylan Thomas, but the title was a bit misleading. The *Oldie* was a lot gentler than the *Eye*, and Waugh's *Oldie* column, though irascible, was warmer and more amiable than many of his previous incarnations. 'This section of the magazine will expose the young in all their indiscipline and illiteracy, attacking employers who prefer them to the experienced middle-aged,' he wrote of his new column. 'It will expose the National Health Service, take the advertising profession by the throat and shake it. But its chief function will be to restore pride of antiquity.'[10] His writing was just as enjoyable, but Waugh had less fire in his belly. Like one of the fine wines in his cellar, he was mellowing with age.

*

GOOD LORD DELIVER US FROM *THE SUNDAY TIMES*
(*Oldie*, 5 March 1993)

Good Lord deliver us from: toothlessness in old age; hairlessness; swollen prostate glands; blindness; deafness; unsightly afflictions of the skin; forgetfulness, infantilism, Alzheimer's disease and other forms of senile dementia; from boring others and being bored; from poverty, the inability to taste or smell, from bad breath and other senile odours, from depression, bereavement, helplessness, immobility, loneliness . . .

The litany of horrors is familiar enough. Many of us face the prospect of a vegetative comatose existence at the end of our lives, possibly lasting for three, five or even six years, recognising no-one, taking nothing in, stacked in rows of bunk beds being turned twice a day to prevent bed sores . . . Perhaps, in time, this treatment will be mechanised, as the *remuage* process in the production of champagne has been mechanised, and there will be no need for nurses in attendance: our last vegetable years will be spent untouched by human hand, as so many frozen peas and Brussels sprouts can proudly claim to be untouched by human hand even now . . .

The best cure for any tendency to reflect bitterly on the terrors and inconveniences of old age, in my experience, is to contemplate the horror of being young. At least I find it comforting. It is possible to find oldies who are so obdurate in their bitterness that they swear the young have a wonderful time. We who grew up in shoeboxes or paper bags, with nothing to eat except shoe polish, and even that was rationed . . . It is true that the young nowadays are better surrounded by creature comforts than we, the over-fifty-year-olds, ever were. Children of the chronically unemployed in 1993 have colour television, hot water, electric light, plenty of food and, usually, heat . . . When I think of the extreme cold of the houses I grew up in, the genuine shortage of food and clothing (and mine was a rich and privileged background), I can see that those who affect to be indignant about the plight of the poor in England are concerned only to find something they can be indignant about to demonstrate their own moral superiority.

All that remains of genuine social indignation is to be found in the hatred of the new class for the relics of the old: royalty, the aristocracy, anybody with an upper-class accent or the faintest hint (whether real or imagined) of superiority in his manner. This hatred has always existed in journalism, but it was often kept in place by upper-class proprietors and the deferential trickle down from them. Now it is elevated to a major virtue, until such once-serious newspapers as the *Sunday Times* may be seen as little more than temples of the Avenging Guttersnipe Tendency. Perhaps some of the venom with which these people attack surviving relics of the old order springs from an awareness that the new order – proletarian or 'classless' as you prefer – has nothing to offer. It is composed of plastic objects, nasty food, boring television programmes, ugly buildings, fatuous jobs and rootless, socially crippled young people who have lost the ability to relate to each other or to anyone else.

WHY ESTUARY ENGLISH REPRESENTS AN IMPROVEMENT – OF A SORT
(*Oldie*, 2 April 1993)

Nobody I know speaks in the accent called Estuary English which is now being promoted by Andrew Neil's *Sunday Times* as 'the classless dialect sweeping southern Britain'. The *Sunday Times* assures us that it 'has taken such a hold on the way millions speak that it could become the standard spoken English of the future'. The newspaper plainly sees the promotion of this 'new' accent as a sort of crusade. We read under colour photographs of such modern heroes as Norman Tebbit, Ken Livingstone, Jonathan Ross and Ben Elton of this 'new accent for a class-less society'.

A few pointers are given in the trailer. Estuary folk have this 'distinctive vocabulary' which requires them to say 'cheers' rather than 'thank you', we are told. Oddly enough, I once met someone, about twenty-five years ago, in Newbury, who used 'cheers' in this way. He was a young man to whom I had given a lift. I was already irritated by his silence, and by a strange smell which emanated from him, and rather bawled him out. 'You don't say "cheers" when I've just driven you for thirty miles, young man, you say "thank you very much",' I shouted. Would I bawl at such a young man today? After I had done so, I felt guilty that perhaps the poor youth was mentally ill and under treatment, perhaps on day-leave from a mental hospital. Nowadays, quite a large proportion of young people seems mentally afflicted in one way or another, but since the closure of the mental hospitals they now lope around unattended, saying 'cheers' to everyone they meet.

I think we are right to bawl at them. Nobody else – neither parents, policemen nor teachers, let alone counsellors or analysts or the *Sunday Times* – will ever teach them about manners. Many Britons grow up without the faintest idea that they exist. One of the surest ways of discovering this is if you accidentally kick one of these New Britons as you go past him in the train. It is my normal practice to apologise under those circumstances, but to apologise to a New Brit is to add insult to injury. But bawling at them seems to work rather well.

Other characteristic usages by which the New Briton gives himself away are less worrying. He will frequently use words like 'basically' and 'guesstimate', but I do not see why we should be worried by that. Fifteen years ago he often used words like 'hopefully' or phrases like 'no way'. Many were indignant about it at the time, and urged us to kick people talking in that way, but I do not see that they are particularly wicked. Those with nothing original to say have always been anxious to find the most fashionable cliché or current piece of jargon in which to say it. Although I often urge readers of the *Daily Telegraph* to go out and cut the throat of anyone they find carrying a copy of the *Sunday Times* or the *Sun*, and burn down any house with a BSkyB dish, I do not think we would be justified in slitting the throat or burning down the house of anyone just because he says 'yes' before anything else on the telephone, or describes himself as 'in a meeting' when he is seeing someone, or exclaims after being given luncheon: 'What an absolu'ely deligh'fuw meaw, cheers.' The simple truth is that the New London Voice, Estuary English, call it what you will, represents an improvement on the way the same people would have been talking thirty years ago. Give them another thirty years, and they may be talking like the rest of us.

IN PRAISE OF JUDAS ISCARIOT – AND PONTIUS PILATE
(*Oldie*, 30 April 1993)

Over the years I have meditated quite a bit about the Passion and Resurrection, and doubt whether there are new discoveries to be made. According to a Gallup poll published by the *Sunday Telegraph*, 31 per cent of the population (that is very nearly one in three) have no idea what Easter is about. One addresses oneself, of course, to the remaining 69 per cent, leaving the first lot to watch Sky TV and read the *Sun*, but let it be said that I have never been happy with history's treatment of Judas. He was given a rotten part to play in the drama, but it was an essential one. No betrayal, no crucifixion, no redemption. How can one talk of Judas's free will in the face of such overwhelming historical imperatives? It would make as much sense to talk of Judas as a saviour, since he undoubtedly played a vital part in our salvation.

Similarly, but not identically, with Pontius Pilate. If Pilate had had his way – he was a thoroughly civilised man, just like you, me or Roy Jenkins – there would have been no crucifixion, no resurrection, no redemption. Under these circumstances, we would have no excuse to let the song of praise be sung, or let shouts of joy and praise outburst. Yet Pilate is blamed for his pusillanimity. He is cast as one of history's greatest villains, a sort of chinless ditherer. If Pilate had stuck to his guns and been a hero there would be no Christian religion and Jesus's trip to earth would, by any reckoning, have been a bit of a waste of time.

Four out of five people in Britain, according to the *Sunday Telegraph*, actually and consciously disbelieve the Gospel story. Is there any useful purpose in persuading them to the contrary? The *Sunday Telegraph*, as might be expected, ascribes many of the evils of modern society to this lack of religious faith – the glorification of selfishness as self-fulfilment, the exaggerated sentimentality about animals – 'more greed, more crime, more family breakdown, more violence, and an extreme restlessness . . .' All these things get worse and worse the more one worries about them. My chief doubt is whether the Bible story is capable, any more, of inspiring whatever degree of unselfishness is necessary to rescue the situation, especially among people who have more or less made up their minds that they disbelieve it.

If one examines the narrative of the New Testament one sees that it was not really Judas or Pontius Pilate who forced the crucifixion to happen. It was the multitude, the voice of the people. In former times, Christians were taught that it was most specifically the Jews who shouted, 'Crucify Him,' to the dithering Pilate, and there was particular mention in the Good Friday liturgy that the guilt of Christ's blood was on the Jews of that and every succeeding generation. Hence the long years of Jewish persecution, culminating in the worst atrocity of human history. Since the Holocaust, it has become more apparent to Christians that the bloodthirsty crowd did not represent the Jews so much as the voice of democracy. Pilate was a weedy public-school liberal judge, the crowd were *Sun* readers telephoning in (as they so often do) to demand the death penalty and express their opinion that hanging would be too good for Him.

THE BENEFITS OF MONARCHY
(*Oldie*, 11 June 1993)

Most of us will have decided that the Ozone Layer is just another of those Big Lies, like AIDS, Acid Rain, Passive Smoking, etc., put around by scientists after government funds, but there is indeed and always has been measurable damage to the ozone layer in the south of the southern hemisphere. This is the result of volcanic activity in those regions, not of male homosexuals in Sydney spraying themselves with underarm deodorant. My point is that it undoubtedly causes mental impairment. Europeans who have lived there only for 200 years are now beginning the drift downwards into Aboriginal savagery, as shown by their desire to abolish the monarchy. For a clear idea of the sun's dangers one has to study the Aborigines themselves, who lived as hunters and fishermen for 20,000 years in the great Australian continent without once developing the simplest form of agriculture, let alone inventing the wheel, learning to read or write or appointing a king or queen from their own number.

It would be insulting to the intelligence of *Oldie* readers to discuss once again those benefits we derive from our monarchy. I imagine most of us carry them in our heads and rehearse them daily: historical continuity; urban architecture and town planning; national unity and *concordia ordinum*; discipline; humility; loyalty; pride in our singularity . . . there is one further blessing which is not so often listed. Possession of a genuinely hereditary monarchy does wonders for any nation's sense of absurdity, its satirical perception and its appetite for scandalous gossip.

It is this sense of absurdity which the Australians seem to have lost when they propose an Australian president. In 927 years of a national monarchy, we have never once had an Englishman on the throne. The present Queen has scarcely a drop of English blood in her veins, and her children have even less. The whole idea of the monarchy is to prevent Englishmen and Englishwomen from growing too conceited and pleased with ourselves. By performing elaborate acts of self-abasement before these strange, humourless foreigners in our midst, we all learn to laugh at our ourselves as well as at each other and at our institutions. How are the Australians going to preserve the slightest element of self-mockery when they start deferring to one of their own number, chosen on merit?

There are those who do maintain that whatever reservations they may have about junior members of the Royal Family they still retain a lively respect and admiration for the Queen, to such an extent that she might as well have been chosen on merit. That seems an admirable sentiment, but it is not remotely necessary. Belief in the monarchy implies no affection for the monarch, beyond, of course, a readiness to die for her at a moment's notice. It might sound tendentious if I were to say that this serious, conscientious German housewife, with her relentless common sense, her Danish-German husband, with his relentlessly banal opinions on every subject, and their curious brood are the only thing keeping us sane in our national decline.

A YELLOW HELICOPTER IN THE BLACK MOUNTAINS
(*Oldie*, 25 June 1993)

On a warm Sunday earlier this month I joined a party of friends for a picnic lunch in the Black Mountains of Powys, one of the most desolate and beautiful areas of southern Britain. It was after the annual literary festival at Hay-on-Wye, and various others had had the same idea. The area of these mountains – not black, but green in early June, shared only with some splendidly ungregarious sheep, is so vast that there was no need for picnic parties to settle closer than a couple of hundred yards from each other. For a brief, rare moment on our hopelessly overcrowded island it was possible to entertain the illusion of space in a context of unspoiled natural beauty. The picnic, too, was utterly delicious, but I shall not upset people by describing the food and drink.

This idyllic scene was somewhat spoiled when a huge yellow helicopter came skimming over the mountain top, and passed a hundred feet or so over our heads. There is always something self-important and bossy about a helicopter's clatter. Five minutes later, it passed over again, in the reverse direction. Five minutes later, it passed over again, perhaps even lower and more menacing – and so it continued for the best part of half an hour. To say it destroyed the illusion of privacy would be an understatement. It was an aggressive reminder of government power posing, as usual, as concern for our welfare. The rescue helicopter, designed to pick up holidaymakers who, in their anxiety to have a good time, injure themselves abominably in inaccessible places, had no-one in particular to rescue, so it was just cruising around beauty spots on the off-chance that someone had fallen over. Or perhaps it was looking for moribund sheep or bunny rabbits in distress. Anyone who has ever had to hire a helicopter will know they cost £1500 an hour. As it was also Sunday afternoon, they were almost certainly paying the pilot and attendants overtime.

There is nowhere we can escape from the government's passionate anxiety for our health and safety. If ever you let a local Building Inspector into your house, he may order you to put fire doors and smoke detectors in every room, enlarge windows, take out any additions or improvements which have been installed without permission and effectively rebuild your house from the ground. An Environmental Health Officer may order you to re-plumb your house and, in certain circumstances (if, for instance, you produce food for Women's Institute or church functions), to refurbish your kitchen at a cost of many thousand pounds. The people with these enormous powers to order around any private citizen in the land are as often as not beardless youths of twenty.

What a wonderfully caring society we are, perhaps. But of course it has nothing to do with caring. These odious young men and women with little cars empowering them to harness all the legal services of local government to crush any private citizen who defies them are not moved by anxiety about house safety. The number of people burned to death in their homes every year is minuscule compared to the cost of enforcing these regulations (which can hope to reduce the figure only by a small percentage) on every home in the land. What fuels the endless growth of regulatory bureaucracies to recruit more and more employees is partly the appetite for personal power which seems to be one of the dominant forces in our 'classless' revolution.

When I suggested that the yellow helicopter might as well have been looking for a moribund sheep or a bunny rabbit in distress, I hope people did not think I was being entirely facetious. The gigantic armies of the health and safety bureaucracies would be just as happy applying their unwanted services to a rabbit, or a bat, or a caterpillar. A recent film of Sylvester Stallone called *Cliffhanger* had to be withdrawn for an immensely expensive re-run when preview audiences were outraged by a scene showing a rabbit being shot to pieces by a sniper. In the film, Stallone used the rabbit as a decoy to draw fire but audiences booed and howled when the rabbit was shot, despite the fact that many humans meet horrible deaths in the course of the film. Nobody complained about them. So the film was re-made with the rabbit escaping. Everybody cheers when it escapes, and the film has been a No. 1 hit in America ever since.

American society is frightening because this illness affects both its top and its bottom. American academics, who accept all the drivel of anti-racist new wave feminism, form a ghastly sort of complement with the yob culture of Hollywood sentimentality and violence. In Britain, we have so far escaped, in large measure, either of these afflictions. Instead we have the threat of a take-over from the forces of Health and Safety. Parliament might be able to protect us, if its members were not

such popinjays and idlers. Is it likely that any member of either
House will ask what a yellow helicopter was doing flying backwards and forwards across the Black Mountains of Powys on
the afternoon of Sunday, 6 June 1993?

THE BEST NEIGHBOUR IS THE NEIGH-
BOUR WHO LEAVES YOU ALONE
(*Oldie*, 7 January 1994)

Christmas decorations were hanging around the one-bedroom
flat of John Sheppard, sixty-eight, in Harlesden when police
helped plumbers break in to repair a water leak which had been
reported by neighbours. The last date crossed off his calendar
hanging on the wall was 22 December – but the year on the
calendar was 1989, and the skeleton of John Sheppard lay on
the floor of the kitchen where it had been lying undisturbed
for very nearly four years. Nobody had noticed his absence,
although he was being sued by his local council for non-payment
of rent. Later, Brent Council agreed that it had been seeking
to evict Mr Sheppard, believing him to be a pensioner of
seventy-two, although obviously in a dilatory and ineffectual
way.

Nobody was prepared to accept the blame for Mr
Sheppard's lonely death or for the fact that he had lain undis-
covered for four years, but Detective Inspector David Brown,
of Brent Police, said: 'It is extremely sad to think that an
elderly man lay dead in his home for over three years without
being discovered. It is an indictment of modern society.' One
does not like to disagree with a policeman, but I think it is
greatly to modern society's credit that he lay undisturbed by
the local welfare busybodies for all that time, or even by
convivial neighbours. Through three Christmas seasons, while
the police were out trying to terrorise motorists, and the
nation's 5.2 million public employees were otherwise occupied, his corpse quietly recycled itself with the kitchen

linoleum. He was doing nobody any harm, and nobody did him any harm as he lay there. Those who continue to live on the Stonebridge Park Estate in Harlesden would probably be embarrassed to receive *Oldie* Certificates of Good Neighbourliness, signed by the Editor, and if I turned up to pin gold medals on their chests, they would suspect I was mocking them. The best neighbour is the neighbour who leaves you alone unless asked for help, not the neighbour who is forever ringing the doorbell to ask if you are all right, and the council tenants of Stonebridge Park Estate are a shining example to us all.

There was a time when an accumulation of milk bottles would have 'alerted the neighbours' as they used to say. Nowadays when milk is not always delivered – any more than newspapers are, in the general spirit of idleness among the young – it would be nice to think that every tower block of council flats contained a sarcophagus or two where a former old age pensioner lay quietly mouldering, pension uncollected, rent unpaid, harming no-one, their privacy respected for as long as the building is allowed to stand. It would encourage us to treat these repulsive buildings with a little respect, even awe, as we motored past them on our way to happier surroundings.

The other great lesson to be learned from John Sheppard's experience – or lack of experience, as one might say – is to confirm what I have always said about not answering business letters. The great rule about any letter you receive on any subject is that, when in doubt about what to answer, don't answer it. Never answer a business letter unless there is an obvious and immediate advantage to be derived from it, and never answer a letter from the local Council under any circumstances, even when it seems to promise some advantage. Nothing the Council has to offer is worth having. It is always being hedged around with conditions and visits from half a dozen council officials, all paid through the nose for patronising you and supervising whatever tiny benefit is on offer, all required to make life as difficult and humiliating as possible. Most communications from the Council offer no benefit whatever, of course, being demands for rent or council tax, or Mrs Thatcher's disastrous poll tax, which they will still be trying to collect in ten years' time.

Most people lose their nerve after the tenth reminder in red, demanding immediate payment on pain of instant eviction and seizure of all possessions. Mr Sheppard's experience – or lack of it – proves that they are quite happy to go on sending these reminders for ever – or at any rate for four years. Occasionally we read of councils sending in the bailiffs, but their victims are the people who were foolish enough to answer the letters, to make excuses, propose ways of paying, plead for mercy or more time. So long as you never answer, as Mr Sheppard never answered (being in no position to do so, of course), they will simply go on bombarding you with warning letters in red until even that stops, and they will leave you to sleep in the bosom of your ancestors.

The poignancy of the Sheppard story has nothing to do with his death, which worked out beautifully, so far as anyone's death can be discussed in these terms. It is in the glimpse afforded of his life and last years on earth. Apparently he had two visitors, one an elderly female neighbour, the other a younger man, presumed to be his son. Both must have grown discouraged after a time when he failed to answer the door, and gone away, resolved to forget about him. Or perhaps the elderly female neighbour is herself quietly mouldering in another part of the estate. Traditional wisdom has it that the very old should be constantly visited, and it is touching how pleased many people are to be visited in the loneliness of widowhood or solitary old age. But by no means everybody wants to be visited, and in extreme old age, when most or all of the faculties have gone, I have a feeling that many people would prefer to be left to die alone, just as cats will walk away and seek solitude when they feel death coming upon them. One cannot be sure about this, of course, but Mr Sheppard is no longer around to be consulted, and it seems a reasonable guess.

THE REVOLUTION OF OUR LIFETIME HAS BEEN THE AVAILABILITY OF DISPOSABLE NAPPIES
(*Oldie*, 15 April 1994)

One of the alarming things about these New Britons is that they seem to need nappies until they are nearly four years old. Nappies are not attractive garments. I should have thought they were as destructive of self-respect in a three-year-old as they are of dignity and beauty. Perhaps they are the best training for a life of unemployment and state dependency, but is that what young parents have in mind for their young when they decide to start a family nowadays? Brooding about this in the small hours, I wondered why it should be the case. Does breastfeeding, now almost universal, weaken the sphincter muscles of babies and inhibit potty training? Are young mothers simply too idle to face the boredom of potty training, and leave their babies to train themselves? I think this is closest to the true explanation. The revolution which has occurred in our lifetime has been the introduction and general availability of disposable nappies. If these young mothers had to wash the nappies themselves, as our generation did, they would be much more concerned to see their babies potty trained by their second birthday, as used to be normal.

These paper disposable nappies have always struck me as abject, vulgar and almost certainly insanitary things. We read that the million odd nappies disposed of every day cannot be burned and threaten to smother all life under an evil-smelling mountain of paper. I will believe this alarmist talk when I see the first sign of it, but during my occasional walks in the countryside, and fairly frequent train journeys around England, I have never yet seen the smallest hillock of disposable nappies, and must suppose that it is all another pack of 'scientific' lies, along with global warming, the dangers of passive smoking, etc., etc.

The good thing about disposable nappies is surely that, by using a million of them every day in Britain alone, we are at least doing our bit to clear the world of these tropical rain forests. People may see it as affected to espouse a great hatred of rain forests. It is true, they have done me no harm. What annoys me about them is the way they have been used by the new puritans to bully two generations of Englishmen and Englishwomen, making them feel guilty and inadequate, just as previous generations were made to feel guilty about masturbation. I am not responsible for cutting down any rain forests and I refuse to take the blame or interest myself in their preservation. On balance, I think we would be well rid of them. But that is not the attitude taken by our children's generation. They have a certain positive value, these rain forests, in demonstrating the hypocrisy of young people for whom the preservation of rain forests is about the only absolute moral good, but who are nevertheless prepared to see a sturdy hardwood in Ecuador chopped down rather than wash a nappy every time their whingeing offspring perform.

My chief complaint about the young, however, is not on the grounds of their hypocrisy so much as of their intellectual vacuity. They have accepted all this drivel, which my generation thought up, about rain forests, global warming and sexual equality as if it were Holy Writ, and now serve it back to us in tendentious voices as if they had thought of it themselves – as if these were brave new ideas, which an older generation might be expected to resist. They have added nothing, amended nothing, accepted nothing. But I see one ray of hope. When my own generation stands at the bar of judgment, it must be condemned not for all the fatuous opinions it held and silly things it did – our belief in the redemptive power of soft drugs, in dropping out as a viable option, or the atrocious perversion of human nature contained within the gender revolution – but for the previous errors we failed to expose or ridicule.

My generation, coming to intellectual and aesthetic awareness in the 1950s, accepted most of the transparent rubbish which remains the foundation of socialism, adopted many of the affectations and dishonesties necessary to support a left-wing or 'radical' view of the world, and continued to bolster its sense of moral and intellectual superiority by reading the miserable old *Guardian*. But its worst sin of omission was its failure to challenge the tenets of the Modern Movement in painting, music, poetry, architecture, sculpture, drama and the rest.

By the mid-fifties, the Modern Movement, which had occupied centre stage for thirty-five years, had not only demonstrated its own limitations in every field but had also run out of all creative vitality. It could still shock a few boobies, but mostly it bored everybody. It was already the new orthodoxy in 1955, supported by the entrenched artistic establishment of mediocrities, teachers and Arts Council bureaucrats. Yet my generation never challenged their supremacy, never questioned the rubbish they talked or the junk they produced. It was as if to be 'modern' in art was the same as being 'left wing' in politics and therefore on the side of the angels.

On this one point, it seems to me, the new generation of eighteen- to thirty-year-old rainforest fanciers may be going to bring the country to its senses. A few, of course, have joined the racket, and are still turning out modern pictures for the shrinking market of American trusts and individual American boobies, but by and large there is a great impatience with it all. A gang of young musicians, calling themselves the Hecklers, and recruiting through classified advertisements in the *Spectator*, is dedicated to waging war on the general acceptance of the ugly, tuneless music of Birtwhistle, Tippett and Glass, which still receives the highest rates of government subsidy. I wish them luck. It is something we should have done thirty-five years ago. The young are not irredeemably lost.

UNLIKE LEECHES, DOCTORS DO NOT
DROP OFF THEIR VICTIMS WHEN THEY
ARE SATED
(*Oldie*, 29 April 1994)

My great-grandfather, Dr Alexander Waugh (1840–1906) was a GP in the Somerset mining village of Midsomer Norton. He was a popular, respected man in the neighbourhood, despite revolting and sadistic habits which only his family knew about. It was his practice to charge the poor in pennies, the lower-middle class in shillings and toffs in guineas. His system seemed to work well enough, although I imagine that all but one or two of his patients must be dead by now, as they would have been in any case. In those days, medicine was probably simpler. You gave them a bottle of The Mixture if there was nothing wrong with them, took blood from them if they were obstreperous, gave them laudanum if they looked badly ill and were obviously suffering from diarrhoea, and a whiff of chloroform if it became necessary to cut off a leg. But for most sickies, the choice was between aspirins and Syrup of Figs. No doubt my great-grandfather generally got it right because, as I say, he was widely respected in the Midsomer Norton, Stratton-on-the-Fosse and Chilcompton areas of north Somerset.

It was only when the Americans started inventing strange and terrible new illnesses, as well as preposterously expensive treatment for them, that the new health obsession took off. In America, doctors are now the least popular of the professions, hated even more than journalists, lawyers and politicians are in this country. If ever you get to one of the country clubs outside every moderate-sized town in the United States, you will see all the town's doctors eating at one table. They are loathed because they play on their country's neuroses about health to suck the economy dry, just as leeches used to suck patients in the good old days. The cost of health insurance to American employers is astronomical, and those employees not covered by a company scheme may find themselves spending up to a third of their earnings on health insurance. The doctors get fatter and fatter, as leeches do, but unlike leeches they do not drop off their victims when they are sated, only when the victims are dead.

One may say that it serves the Americans right, and if they were not so neurotic about their health they would not have to spend all their money on fattening up these loathsome and conceited doctors, who now deal with their patients chiefly by computer. That is not the point. It is that health is seen as something sacred, religious. Americans do not resent giving vast amounts of money to this good cause, any more than Indians resented laying costly gifts in front of their heathen idols. What they resent is seeing the doctors get richer and richer as a result of their own neurotic observances. Health is sacred; profit is something one concerns oneself with outside church. It offends American womanhood's deepest feelings of morality that doctors continue to claw dollars from inside the very Holy of Holies, her own body. The same is not true of psychotherapy. Most Americans accept that they are very boring people indeed, and it is perfectly reasonable to pay large sums of money to anyone prepared to listen to them talking about themselves. Only the body is sacred.

In Britain, we have no such illusions. The promise of a free National Health Service could carry conviction only in a country which was indifferent to its health. In fact, anybody with the slightest intelligence could see that the promise was fraudulent, even without the ruinously expensive new treatments being developed every week. If the free Health Service had confined itself to aspirins and Syrup of Figs, demand would have outstripped supply eventually. As things are, we spend £31.7 billion on a National Health Service which employs over a million people, and we still have the worst health care in Europe.

The great difference between our situation and that of the Americans is that whereas in the United States doctors are loathed, rather as drunken or corrupt parish priests may have been thought unworthy of their calling in the Middle Ages, in Britain the doctors have assumed Godlike identities. Since there can never be enough resources to satisfy a demand which is bottomless, doctors have been in a position to decide who shall receive expensive treatment and who shall not, who shall live and who shall die. That is what they have been doing, discreetly and tactfully, for the last forty-five years. In all those years, if you fancied a bit of expensive surgery, the great thing was to cultivate a friendly relationship with your GP, and choose a GP who had a good relationship with the local hospital.

All this changed with the influx of 120,000 health administrators. On top of counting their salary cheques, they wanted
something to do, so they decided that managers, not doctors,
should decide who should receive expensive treatment and who
should not. No sooner does anyone draw up a secret list of
rules than it becomes public property and all hell breaks loose.
In fact, more than three-quarters of the resources of the health
service are already diverted to keeping the over-sixties going.
The spectacle of rows of vegetative oldies, kept on a drip and
turned twice a day until they die of bedsores, is a greater scandal
than the occasional eighty-year-old who is refused a triple bypass
operation because of his age.

Some of us do very well on the system, as it is, and feel
intensely grateful for it. Nothing should disguise the fact that
a better service could almost certainly be provided by half
the number of employees, but that is incidental to the real
problem. Any service supplied by the state will always be
murderously inefficient, and at the mercy of its employees.
The particular problem with the health service will always be
that the demand for free health is bottomless. Perhaps the
fairest thing would be to share out the operations and other
treatments by ballot.

WHY THE ADVANTAGES OF WEALTH ARE
EXAGGERATED IN THE POPULAR MIND
(*Oldie*, May 1995)

Tim O'Brien thought he had won £2 million on the National
Lottery, because the numbers on his ticket all came up. His
brother, James O'Brien, said it was impossible to imagine what
Tim must have felt when he discovered that his ticket had
expired. I do not think it at all hard to imagine what Tim felt
on realising that he had failed to renew his ticket. Chagrin, rage,
mortification, a burning sense of injustice, which might descend
slowly into the general Liverpool melancholia or state of being

'browned off'. In a very important sense Tim O'Brien's débâcle illustrates the whole history of Liverpool since the last war, a city which is forever missing the boat. If only it could persuade itself to make a little more effort to get out of bed a few minutes earlier . . . but to argue that the boat should leave later is plainly wrong. Liverpool would simply miss it again. In the same way, to argue, as the Liverpool coroner, Mr Roy Barker, argued, that it would be better to have a larger number of smaller prizes misses the entire point of the National Lottery. In countries which have capped their jackpots in this way, turnover has fallen immediately by up to 40 per cent.

O'Brien's death led to widespread calls from the public, from Tory MPs and from Church leaders for a smaller jackpot, or so we read in the *Sunday Telegraph*. The Right Reverend Nigel McCulloch, Bishop of Wakefield, was especially outspoken. He said that jackpot prizes of millions of pounds were unnecessary: 'When there is a prize pool of £3 million, it is absolutely ludicrous. More money should go to charity and a smaller amount should go to prizes. Direct giving to charity has definitely fallen since the lottery began, and with this poor man appearing to commit suicide, I think that makes it even clearer why the main prize should not be so large.'

It must be the worst reason ever advanced for reducing a lottery jackpot that someone in Liverpool committed suicide when he failed to win it, but the fact that so many people advance this reason tells us much about the English attitude to wealth. Many people find it slightly disturbing. They are the better ones. Others find it disgraceful, disgusting, obscene, on the grounds that the money should be given to the poor. They are pretty bad. Some are made extremely angry by any evidence of wealth, happiness or good luck in others. They are the people to avoid at all costs.

There is a hatred of the rich that goes deep into the British psyche. Time and again, people who have won the National Lottery, and been discovered, have had to go into hiding – to escape from their former friends and neighbours, as much as from envious strangers. Lottery millionaire Alwin Holness of

Tipton, West Midlands, spoke of his £2.78 million win to the *Sun* from a secret address: 'We were happy in the house where we were. We may move but we hope people in the town accept us for the same people we were before the win. But I am afraid some people might want to give us a bit of trouble because of it . . .' What Alwin may not have realised is that as soon as you become rich you have joined the enemy.

None of which adds to the case for reducing the National Lottery prizes. In fact, it seems to me that the National Lottery may succeed where thirty-five years of punitive taxation failed – in purging the terrible envy of the British towards those who are luckier and better off. In former times, people were rich either because they had inherited their money, which was peculiarly detestable within a class system because it made them feel superior, or because by hard work and intelligence they had earned it, which was even worse. Nothing is so disagreeable as a meritocracy for those without particular merit. But there is no merit in winning the National Lottery. If it can destroy the nonsensical idea that attaches to wealth, it will have made Britain a much happier country.

Perhaps the advantages of wealth are exaggerated in the popular mind. You can eat only so many ice creams or whatever. The joys of a big car, a big house, endless holidays will pall soon enough. Possessions bring with them the near certainty of burglary. Even the possession of investments seems to achieve nothing but twenty incomprehensible letters in the post every day, informing you (at enormous cost) of the footling transactions which seem to lose money every time. Perhaps the only real advantage in having lots of money is that you don't have to worry about it.

The National Lottery is the best idea Mr Major's government ever had. If only Labour would follow the Bishop of Wakefield, and demand a reduction in the jackpot, it might yet save the Conservatives. For my own part, I shall continue to invest in it week after week, in the confident expectation of winning at least £10 million eventually. When I do win, I shall simply laugh and laugh. Although I have no particular need or use for it, I shall be happy enough to have kept the money away from everyone else.

WHY YOUNG PEOPLE WISH TO MURDER US
(*Oldie*, September 1995)

As a few older readers may remember, there were two original inspirations for this column. The first, which afflicted all my generation simultaneously, was a realisation that the prime minister was younger than we were. It went without saying that he was an incompetent, a nonentity, a pipsqueak. The point was we had been passed over, we were on the shelf, we were no longer teetering elegantly on the brink of middle age: we were old. The second inspiration, taken from Dylan Thomas's famous line, 'Do not go gentle into that good night,' was an acceptance that rage is a more attractive posture in old age than its alternative, smugness. Benevolence was out of the question. We can either be furious at the way things are going or smug that our own circumstances are noticeably better than most other people's – our houses and garden are nicer, our food and wine are superior, the company we keep is preferable . . .

I had other intimations that old age was not far away. Not only did policemen start looking absurdly young, but a High Court judge presiding at a libel trial I decided to attend seemed scarcely out of his teens. On one occasion I sat next to a young man at a dinner who told me he was in the army. 'Well done,' I said. 'What a sensible career choice! How are you getting on? Would you be a captain yet?' I did not actually pinch his bottom but my manner was distinctly avuncular. 'No, actually, sir, I am a major general,' he replied. Such episodes are enough to throw the most equable of temperaments into a rage, and I have been raging ever since at the incompetence and inadequacy of people younger than I am who are inexplicably put into positions of great authority.

Suddenly something rather unpleasant has happened. Rage has become the dominant emotion in Britain – not just from oldies, as we watch our country disintegrate into a sort of kindergarten run by vapid young women with Midlands accents. Teenagers and small children are in a rage as they realise they will never be employed, their only escape from a life on the Welfare is in stealing cars and burgling houses; horrible young men with beer bellies from Essex are in a rage when they find other motorists on the motorway unprepared to make way for them; New Britons who have been conned into shopping by their lazy wives fall into a trolley rage and batter their fellow shoppers . . .

All these rages are undignified and vile, a product of the bad manners which convince the New Britons they have a right to shout, 'No way!', insult and assault each other at will. Stupidity and bad manners are the chief characteristics of the new Britain; they are what makes me yearn for Direct Rule from the Élysée Palace. The current rage as I write is against murderers of children. At the moment the *Sun* is shouting its head off that these murderers should be hanged or at very least be kept in prison for life in specially disagreeable circumstance. I think this rage is a bogus one. The English are not, by nature, sentimental about children. In fact we much prefer dogs, and tend to dislike other people's children – usually with good reason. Other people's children tend to be noisy, unattractive and bad-mannered. This is no excuse for murdering them, of course.

This bogus rage against the murderers of other people's unknown children comes from the simple desire of the nation's punishment freaks to have someone on whom they can focus their sadistic fantasies and appetite for judicial execution. There are many people of our age who are very keen indeed on capital punishment, and I do not wish to say anything to upset them, but I would urge that they are backing a loser if they think that indignation on behalf of children (many of whom are teenagers) will carry the day. Do they not realise that three out of four burglaries and muggings are done by teenagers?

I feel that punishment freaks and fanciers of the death penalty should concentrate on the murderers of oldies. In many ways, it is much worse to murder an oldie. Today's children have for the most part a dreadful life ahead of them, sponging off an ever stingier Welfare State, terrified of sex for fear of AIDS, of food, drink and cigarettes for fear of ill health. We old people have lived through the troubles and are now taking our reward. Our children are grown-up, our houses and gardens are arranged to our liking, we have money to indulge ourselves. I understand why young people should wish to murder us, but I feel they should be heavily discouraged.

Chapter Sixteen
Waviana

I do not think my father was famous in the sense that people are famous nowadays. It was not as if he were a television personality, and none of my schoolmates had ever heard of Evelyn Waugh. To begin with, his celebrity affected me very little, but as I grew up and started to be a writer then obviously it did have an effect. People inevitably compared me with my father, since even if they had only read three books in their lives, one of those was probably an Evelyn Waugh. Journalism is a jealous profession, and anyone thought to be getting in by the back door, starting a few steps up the ladder, comes in for backbiting. In the long run, even so, I feel that having a well-known father has been more of an advantage than a disadvantage. People are interested to meet you when they would not be interested otherwise, and when they do meet you they already know something about you, so you don't have to start from nothing in creating your own image. On balance, a lot of sons of famous fathers seem to be upset by the circumstance, even destroyed by it, but I don't think they need be. It entirely depends on the personality, and if you are someone who enjoys showing off, then you profit from it.[1]

'It may seem trivial but one of the major considerations which decided me against writing the biography of my father was a ghastly uncertainty about what to call him,' revealed Auberon

Waugh. "'Waugh" seemed to invite the earth to open and swallow me up; "Evelyn" would certainly have provoked a thunderbolt from heaven if it was in his power to arrange it; "Mr Waugh" was an absurdity and "My Father" or "Papa" unacceptably coy, particularly when discussing events which occurred years before my birth.'[2] Nevertheless, Auberon wrote about Evelyn frequently, if fleetingly, in the course of his journalism, and these snippets add up to a remarkably rounded portrait – less comprehensive than a conventional biography, but ultimately more revealing:

> The strangest effect of my father's aura in his lifetime was the way it impelled people into a strong, irrational desire to please him. Comparisons with Henry VIII or Stalin are particularly odious because he never sought or exercised any temporal power whatever, even over his children to whom he was an amazingly *laissez-faire* parent, so long as they kept out of his way. What made strong men tremble at his frown, and weak men cower, was something which emanated from his presence and which cannot be defined except by experience of it . . . No innuendo of conversation or infelicity of grammar or vocabulary escaped him, and his articulacy was total. Whenever he spoke, it was in perfectly constructed sentences – not through any contrivance, but because that was how his mind arranged itself.[3]

Waugh was particularly contemptuous of academic dissections of his father's writing. Previewing a new biography by one such boffin in the *Literary Review*, he wrote:

> The author seems obsessed by a Nabokovian hatred for his subject, ascribing extraordinarily low motives to nearly everything he said or did. We would not, normally, notice such a book, if it were not for the accident that the unfortunate subject is my own father. Other literary magazines would be much less boring, in my view, if they also ignored

the outpourings of the Eng Lit departments – apart from anything else, there are too many of them – and declined to employ provincial academics as reviewers. With startlingly few exceptions, they write badly, have little concern for the English language and very few ideas of interest. No doubt there are university presses prepared to print this rubbish, and university magazines prepared to review them. If not, dons can always emigrate to America, proclaiming themselves part of some mystical brain drain.[4]

One suspects Waugh's ire was provoked by the knowledge that he could do so much better. When he wrote about his father, his observations were always surprising and insightful, conjuring up a vivid picture of a complex and contradictory personality, far removed from the usual Blimpish stereotype:

He was always slightly ashamed of having once stuck pins in Cecil Beaton's bottom at his prep school, although I am sure that most of us would have done the same. When depressed or bored (the two emotions were more or less indistinguishable in him) he could be extraordinarily brutal but I think these outrages can be at any rate partly excused on the grounds of diminished responsibility. He was frequently violent and aggressive even when in boisterous mood, it is true, but many cases of alleged cruelty which have been reported to me seem no more than a pathetic attempt to create humour and spread a little sunshine into the lives of vain, conceited and humourless men by inviting them to laugh at themselves and prove they are not quite as dreadful as they seem.[5]

Some of Evelyn Waugh's behaviour may seem bizarre by today's standards (after Auberon's machine gun accident, Evelyn was slow to visit him – or even write to him – even though it looked quite likely that he might die), but on the whole, the picture that emerges is of a reserved yet loving man – remote and rather diffident yet mindful of his parental duties, and a supportive advocate of his son's literary career. Many of his smaller shortcomings can be attributed to a dry sense of humour and a distaste for lavish affection, very much the norm for a man of his social standing in those days. In Evelyn's case this standoffishness was also a reaction to his own father, Arthur, a sentimental man whose preferment of his eldest son, Alec, left Evelyn with a deep suspicion of extravagant display.[6] For a man of his generation, when fathers had a lot less to do with sons than they tend to nowadays, Evelyn was a dependable and caring parent. His eldest son returned the compliment, defending his posthumous reputation, but he also wrote movingly and eloquently about the other members of his family, as these articles confirm.

*

MY UNCLE AUBERON
(*New Statesman*, 2 August 1974)

An hour after the family had arrived in the Languedoc, a neighbouring landowner called with the long face and polite demeanour which French aristocrats still reserve for such occasions. He had just received a telephone call from a lady in Touraine whom he had known many years ago to say that Auberon Herbert had been found dead over his Sunday newspaper that morning in Somerset. Although he had never personally had the pleasure of meeting the dead man there were members of his family who spoke highly of his many admirable qualities . . .

My Uncle Auberon's fame took unexpected forms, and he will be bitterly mourned in more outlandish parts than these, but it was not of the sort which lends itself to public notice. His death, although a shock, could scarcely be described as a surprise. In recent years it had become apparent that even his gigantic frame could not much longer support the enormous quantities of food and drink recklessly ingested mealtime after mealtime and often far into the night for fifty-two years. I had seen him only a few days before leaving England, his alert mind as quick as ever to cap a reference or a joke with some memorable and unexpected turn of phrase. But even apart from bulk, it was a question of shape. Always larger than life, his increasingly curious shape was not one which could have fitted much longer into the modern world of trade union power and growing proletarian antagonism.

Auberon Mark Yvo Henry Molyneux Herbert – as children we poor relations would chant these sonorous titles as a talisman to help us through the hard times which lay in store for all but the eldest sons of the rich – was born into a rich, elegant and highly cultivated world. His father, Aubrey Herbert, was a romantic figure, almost certainly (although the title is disputed) the model for Sandy in John Buchan's *Greenmantle*. A brother of the Lord Carnarvon of Tutankhamun fame, his early death was taken as confirmation of the legendary curse. This seems unlikely because there was no such admonition inscribed above Tutankhamun's tomb. But certainly one might see my uncle's subsequent career as being plagued by an avenging fury.

Auberon Herbert was saved from the poverty traditionally reserved for junior sprigs of the nobility by several accidents. His father married an Irish heiress, the only child of a Lord de Vesci who owned large parts of Dublin. His grandmother, a Howard of Greystoke, married Lord Carnarvon as his second wife and exerted herself to secure a share of the loot for her own offspring. Finally, the name Molyneux was hastily added to secure a property in Derbyshire, which was later found to be built on coal. On approaching manhood, he could look forward to enjoying his 4000-acre Somerset estate at Pixton, the magnificent villa built by his grandfather at Portofino, including several farms and a large stretch of mountainous Ligurian coastline, and a substantial town house in Bruton Street. But already the avenging fates had taken their first peck. Turned down by the British Army on account of a mastoid operation, he joined the Polish Army as a private on the outbreak of war.

The choice appears to have been entirely random. He had no previous connection with Poland, and at that stage Polish was only one of nine languages he spoke effortlessly. His war effort included one episode where he was beaten up by the Canadians as a suspected German spy. This gave him an abiding hatred of Canadians, but in fairness to them one must admit it would never have been easy to guess his country of origin. A more formative influence in these early years was Yalta, where he saw Poland established in permanent serfdom by the politicians of Britain and America. This event coloured his later life with a lonely hatred of Churchill and a single-minded dedication to the Cold War in which Ukrainians gradually took the place of Poles on account of their even greater hatred of the Russians.

After the war Pixton filled up with dispossessed Poles, some gloomy and despondent, others more cheerful. For several years the front door sported an arrow at eye-level, shot by one Pole at another when they decided to play William Tell after Christmas dinner. After a time it was decided he should enter Parliament – his father had represented a Somerset constituency between expeditions to Turkey and Albania, and it seemed the obvious thing for a young man with nothing else to do. First, he fought Port Talbot in the Conservative interest, cunningly describing himself among among other things as National Labour and delivering impassioned speeches about Eastern Europe in fluent Welsh to the gaping steel workers there. But it didn't work. Nor could he talk the Sunderland miners out of their allegiance to Labour. The unkindest cut was when Taunton Conservatives preferred a London businessman, at which point he gave up the unequal struggle.

The Poles lost some of their appeal when he discovered that one of his old comrades in arms had forged cheques in his name to the tune of £68,000. At the trial, it was interesting to watch reactions as the chief prosecution witness explained how he had failed to notice this large discrepancy in his current account over several years. 'A somewhat unworldly man,' commented the judge. This was not entirely true. Although he was endlessly ready to help needy Poles, Ukrainians or poor relations, this help often took the form of advising them to contact someone with an unpronounceable name in a foreign capital thousands of miles away.

It is no easy thing even for the very rich to maintain a grand style nowadays, and Auberon, who never enjoyed a very large income, combined grandeur of style with a keen instinct for survival. In his last year he was extremely busily spending £150,000, which had suddenly landed in his lap from the West Somerset Water Board in exchange for an unfarmable valley. As others dropped out of the race, life at Pixton went from strength to strength. Like many bachelors in middle age he was haunted by the fear of loneliness and filled the house with attractive-looking young people who bounced their cheques off his infinitely kind Polish manservant and guzzled his delicious food. Although loud in his appreciation of anything he served, Auberon could scarcely have enjoyed it much himself through having no sense of taste. In a life apparently dedicated to enjoyment, it was never very clear how much he had enjoyed. Endlessly convivial, his apparent purpose in life was simply to spread a little sunshine wherever he went. Perhaps he was also an agent of the Secret Intelligence Service, as he sometimes hinted. This would explain his apparently pointless trips up and down the Iron Curtain, generally coinciding with some political upheaval. But I rather doubt it. It seems more likely that his exceptional talent for languages and unmistakably brilliant mind were never put to any more constructive use than delighting his innumerable friends. How lucky for them that Taunton Conservative Association chose Mr Edward du Cann.

MY UNCLE ALEC
(*Spectator*, 12 September 1981)

A few years ago I came across a slim volume of poems by Alec Waugh[7] published in 1918, when he was in a prisoner-of-war camp. Some of these lines written in the trenches struck me as really very good indeed, and as part of a conscious and sustained policy of cheering him up about his writing I told him so. He received my congratulations with his usual urbanity, although I never really knew how successful my policy was proving – on another occasion I was able to tell him that a young nanny we employed preferred his books to those of Evelyn Waugh; on yet another occasion that his book about Bangkok was still remembered there by some of the older residents. But I suppose it was some sixty years since he had written the war poems, and he might have preferred to be reminded of some more recent achievement. Among the poems (dedicated to Barbara Jacobs, later to become Alec's first wife) is a juvenile piece, 'The Exile', written as a sixteen-year-old at Sherborne:

> When they bring back the thing that once was me
> And lay it in some quiet grave to rest,
> Say that a weary river, long distrest
> With aimless wanderings winds at length to sea.

In the context of his death last week at the age of eighty-three, I suppose that this is what we should say: that a weary river has wound at length to sea. But his teenage poem also contains the injunction: 'Weep not that I am gone' – and I must admit that I find myself overwhelmed by a great, engulfing sadness. Alec Waugh may not have been a great writer but he was a great survivor. From his survival as a professional writer, year after year for over sixty-five years, we could all take comfort – not just his family and friends, but every aspiring writer in the country.

Because of the last war, which he spent for the most part in the Middle East, he did not enter our lives until quite late on, and he was then introduced more than anything else as a biological curiosity. When my father, whose affection for his older brother never wavered, announced that we had a hairless uncle who would shortly be coming to stay, my younger sister Hattie asked in some alarm whether he also had the normal number of fingers and legs. We must have seen other bald men – Alec lost his hair gallantly in the service of this country during the Great War – but for some reason this remained his chief identifying characteristic until we were older, when we were let into the secret of his voracious sexual appetite.

This aspect of his personality got off to a bad start. Asked to leave Sherborne for what is nowadays called 'the usual thing' but was then unmentionable, he went to Sandhurst where he quickly acquired a reputation for sexual prowess. But when he came to marry Miss Jacobs, amid embarrassingly sentimental scenes from my grandfather, who was an old friend of the bride's parents, he met a problem. As he delicately describes in one of his many autobiographies, he couldn't get into her, achieve penetration or whatever: 'I who was called Tank at Sandhurst could not make my wife a woman.'

Many would have been discouraged by this, but Alec applied himself with renewed vigour to the rest of the female sex, achieving, by his own account, some considerable success. 'Venus has been kind to me,' he observed in his old age. On meeting my wife for the first time, he introduced himself: 'I am Alec Waugh, sixty-five, and still interested in women.' At the age of seventy he wrote his first pornography, or 'erotic comedy', called *Spy in the Family*, about a lesbian seduction. I thought it a very sporting effort. He still grins at me from the back of its cover – bald, slightly simian and lecherous as ever, in an open striped blazer with a silk scarf tied nonchalantly around his wrinkled neck.

I saw more of him later when I was stuck in hospital for nine months after a machine gun accident in the army. My father, who was not really at his best in the role of hospital visitor, seemed to resent his brother getting in on the act. 'The man who calls on you purporting to be my brother Alec is plainly an impostor [wrote Evelyn, in a letter to Auberon]. Did your visitor offer any identification apart from baldness – not an uncommon phenomenon? Did he wear a silk scarf around his neck? Was he tipsy? These are the tests.'

The last question reflects my father's opinion that after the great success of *Island in the Sun* (1956) Alec never drew another sober breath. Alas, like many of my father's decisions about the human race, it was based more on an artist's vision than on any first-hand perception of the world around him. One of my sisters, who visited Alec in some Midwestern university where he was Creative Writer in Residence a few years later, described him as living in a sort of cubby-hole above the students' canteen, from where meals were sent up to him on a plastic tray, which he warmed on a radiator. But he always cut a dash on his visits to London, appearing in suits which grew nattier and nattier as the years rolled on, entertaining large parties of friends to lavish meals at his various clubs.

Despite his enormous generosity as a host and kindness as a friend, I don't believe he ever paid a school fee and certainly made no very conspicuous contribution towards the support of his widowed mother. Of course he simply did not have the money, but above all, he was a free spirit. In old age, he resembled nothing so much as a tortoise – toothless, slow-moving, unaggressive, benign, with a little piping voice so soft as to be almost indistinguishable. Like a tortoise, his natural equipment was designed more for survival than for battle and conquest. But he was a Waugh, and I find myself inexpressibly bereaved.

My last glimpse of him was outside the Athenaeum, where I delivered him after a convivial evening at one or other of his curious, elderly dining clubs. He was too old for the outing and I was sickening from some illness; both of us were rather drunk. In the taxi he started singing hymns, and I left him weaving between the Corinthian columns, a tiny, upright, strangely digni-fied figure, singing his little bald head off: 'All people that on earth do dwell, Sing to the Lord with cheerful voice.' I shall miss him terribly, but I suppose, as he put it himself, the weary river winds at length to the sea, so there it is.

SCOOP
(*Folio*, Summer 1982)

Whatever may be said against Corker, Shumble, Whelper, Pigge, Wenlock Jakes and Sir Jocelyn Hitchcock, the nightmarish collection of foreign correspondents who assembled in Jacksonburg to cover the civil war in Ishmaelia, neither they nor their descendants ever bore any malice for the libellous caricature of themselves and their exalted profession which appeared in *Scoop*. Mr William Deedes, the distinguished editor of the *Daily Telegraph* was among those who found themselves in Addis Ababa at the same time as Evelyn Waugh's visit, which inspired not only the Jacksonburg of *Scoop* but also the Debra Dowa of *Black Mischief*. He has written warmly and at length of his memories of Evelyn Waugh, foreign correspondent. When I first took up what is nowadays called serious journalism, as a young man of twenty-one, I was happy to find myself sharing an office in the *Daily Telegraph* with Bill Deedes – then deputy editor of the 'Peterborough London Day By Day' column, soon to be briefly and dizzyingly promoted to cabinet minister in Harold Macmillan's fading administration. Only those who had read their *Scoop* would be able to take this heady translation in their stride. But Bill's memories of his days as a cub reporter in Abyssinia were so mixed up with his joyful identification of characters in *Scoop* that it was hard to be certain which of his reminiscences derived from one and which from the other.

The same difficulty seems to bedevil many who earn their bread as foreign correspondents. Evelyn Waugh took it better than many parents might have done when his eldest son and heir became a journalist. He was particularly happy that I should find myself working in the same office as young Deedes, his colleague of twenty-five years earlier. I pressed him to identify Deedes as Corker, or Whelper, or Pigge, but he refused. But on my occasional excursions into the field of foreign reporting, I find colleagues who seem consciously to be acting out the parts of these immortal archetypes, whether the stories told in

Scoop were always part of the foreign correspondent's repertoire of funny stories, or whether they have since passed into the tradition. I recall one occasion when I found myself stuck in Tel Aviv for the duration of the Six Day War in 1967. The scene was exactly as described in *Scoop*, and I remember one evening, rather late, being told an anecdote by a distinguished foreign correspondent about one of his colleagues which seemed vaguely familiar. Halfway through I recognised it as Corker's story about Wenlock Jakes – how, journeying to report a revolution, he had overslept in the train, woken up in the wrong country, filed a story about barricades, dead children lying like broken dolls in the roadway, and caused a revolution as a result.

I feel that Christopher Sykes, Evelyn Waugh's biographer, is a little wide of the mark when he writes of the author's loathing for these journalistic monstrosities. Into Corker, the 'quint-essential vulturous foreign correspondent,' writes Sykes, 'he poured all the dislike he had felt for most of his colleagues in the Italo-Abyssinian War'. This opinion is echoed in all the critical studies I have read, but it is not the impression I receive from reading the book or from talking to those who were with him. Nor, if his feelings for journalists were characterised by this loathing, would he have been quite so happy to see his son become a journalist. The book would not be nearly so funny if there were real hatred of the characters behind it, rather than a robust enjoyment of their absurdity.

That, at any rate, is the spirit in which most journalists have taken it. Perhaps they should be more sensitive. I do not know. But it is my experience that a journalist who has not enjoyed *Scoop* is usually a pretty rotten journalist. It is true that serious efforts have been made – chiefly by the terrible, chippy, inse-cure crowd who use the *Sunday Times* as their breeding ground – to transform the image of the journalist from the jolly knock-about figure we know to something between a High Court judge, an elder statesman and a peculiarly dedicated welfare worker. I was delighted to learn in an interview with Bruce Page (formerly of the *Sunday Times* Insight team) on his appointment as editor of the *New Statesman* that Evelyn Waugh was his least favourite author. But the old tradition survives; to its eternal credit it has absorbed *Scoop* and made a mockery of itself.

MY SISTER MARGARET
(Spectator, 15 February 1986)

Others have lost sisters before. Every day people lose husbands, wives, parents, children and friends they have loved, whose loss reduces every perspective to dullness, misery and pain. In many cases they carry the pain around with them for the rest of their lives. At moments like this, one realises that under the surface of polite society there is a great well of sadness and bereavement, an aspect of the human condition which is as inescapable as it is seldom remarked, yet looming larger in many people's lives than any of the things they pretend to think important. The only excuse for allowing my own howl of anguish to be heard is to give those as yet unbereaved a glimpse into the hellish blackness lying under the surface of their lives before they sensibly turn away and think of something else.

My sister Margaret was crossing the street in North London with some friends on the night of Tuesday, 28 January, when she was struck by two cars and killed instantly, as we now learn. Her death removed a sister from her five siblings, a wife from her husband, a mother from her five children, a cousin, niece, sister-in-law, daughter-in-law, aunt, close friend or merely admired acquaintance from the limited circle of those who were lucky enough to know her. None of these people, I imagine, has the slightest curiosity about the identity of the unfortunate drivers, nor any particular anxiety to know how the disaster occurred or how it could have been prevented. The removal of her strong personality from our midst will mean something different to all these people, even if they share the same numbing sense of sadness. All I can do is to set down what it means to me.

'As a result of these accidents,' wrote Margaret, in a post-script to Christopher Sykes's biography of Evelyn Waugh, 'I became his official favourite, a position neither resented nor sought by my siblings and one which carried with it the risks of disproportionate disfavour as well as the advantages of privilege.'

The accidents to which she refers were her removal from the nursery at an early age to escape from a cruel nanny and her removal from a first convent school where she was unhappy. But they do not explain her position in the family as official favourite to my father and unofficial heroine, eventual favourite, to the rest of us. She was the only person who could humour him when he was disgruntled, cheer him when he was melancholy, amuse him when he was bored. Her weapons were the usual charms of a pretty girl with a warm and affectionate nature, to which were added an original wit and complete fearlessness.

After leaving school Margaret went to work for the Jesuit Fathers in Farm Street.[8] Her social life centred around a group of young men whom my father insisted on identifying as her 'low friends', although they are all now pillars of society. All of them remained her friends for life. They were all to be seen, twenty-five years later, among the 200 or so people who braved the sleet and rain to travel down to Somerset and stand on an icy, windswept hillside at Combe Florey last week.

It was from the fringes of this group that she chose her husband, Giles Fitzherbert, a dashing Irishman who abandoned his promising career in business to join the diplomatic service. Although they were never rich, there was always a crazy grandeur about her lifestyle. At an age when her more successful contemporaries might have been thinking about buying a Volvo or a country cottage, she bought a huge mansion in Devon to which she would drive down, with her husband, five children and elderly Irish nanny all packed into a tiny Renault 4.

Eventually, finding diplomatic life irksome, she spent more time in London and Devon, to the great delight of her friends. No doubt she would have written other books – including, I would like to think, a memoir of her father which would have been coveted by bibliophiles for as long as anyone can read.

But there is something strangely suitable about the one memorial she left, a life of her grandfather, Aubrey Herbert, the aristocratic model for Buchan's *Greenmantle*. In her fearlessness, warmth and generosity of spirit, her total absence of vulgarity or affectation or any form of self-consciousness, she belonged more to his world than to our own.

BEACON OF HOPE
(Daily Telegraph, 16 October 1993)

Last week I went to North London to unveil an English Heritage blue plaque to the novelist Evelyn Waugh (1903–66) in the house called Underhill, 145 North End Road, built by my grandfather, Arthur Waugh (1866–1943), the publisher and book critic of the *Daily Telegraph*, in 1907. The house is now divided into three flats, and the garden where Waugh filmed *The Scarlet Woman?* has been reduced to a quarter of its size.

Underhill had a profound effect on the novelist in his twenties, chiefly in the desire to get away from it into the elegant salons of *Brideshead*. Ancient libels recycled occasionally by the journalist Alan Brien insist that Waugh was born in a flat over a dairy in Finchley Road, and that he used to walk half a mile from his home to post a letter so that it had a Hampstead postmark rather than one from Golders Green. I was happy to learn that this second story is also untrue. A kind lady who lives in one of the flats told me that North End Road used to be in Hampstead, and was officiously moved to Golders Green after the Waughs had left.

In later life, my father had warm memories of a childhood spent in rural Hampstead, with milk collected in a churn from the local farm, amid bucolic scenes of ploughmen homeward plodding their weary way, lowing herds winding slowly o'er the lea. Perhaps this recollection was no more accurate than Brien's. There can be no doubt that Waugh was born in humbler circumstances than he later attained. I would like to think that the plaque will act as a beacon of hope to the people of Golders Green, assuring them that with honest effort and application they too can end their days in a West Country manor house.

REJOICE IN THE PLAGUE OF LITERARY BIOGRAPHIES
(*Oldie*, May 1996)

In the last days of the *Literary Review*'s residence in Beak Street, we were visited by a young man called Nick Foulkes, who has set himself the task of writing a biography of Alec Waugh. Perhaps not many readers under the age of fifty will be familiar with the works of Alec Waugh, who died in 1981 at the age of eighty-three. He enjoyed an early success with *Loom of Youth* (1917), a novel of school life at Sherborne, and then, after half a century, enjoyed another great success with *Island in the Sun*, made into a film starring Harry Belafonte. The idea of anyone writing a biography of him struck me as rather quaint, although he had an interesting enough life, serving in two world wars and taken prisoner in the first, travelling extensively in the pursuit of a voracious sexual appetite, surviving in some style on the sort of income which would make members of the opposition front bench weep. But is one right to encourage this new plague of literary biographies? Alec Waugh left three orphans, even if the youngest is now nearer sixty than fifty years old. Should his memory not be left in peace?

There, it might be said, is the rub. One can scarcely talk of a memory being left in peace if the person concerned has been completely forgotten. Practically nobody in England now remembers Alec Waugh. I should have thought it the kindest thing to do to anyone's memory to revive it, even if the portrait reveals a wart or two. When Evelyn Waugh died, the *Observer* serialised his unpublished diaries. Under family pressure I wrote a fine, pompous letter to the editor of the *Observer*, David Astor, saying how shocked we all were that a respectable newspaper like the *Observer* should publish such filth. Astor replied that he was puzzled by our reaction, since we had sold him all the material. So, indeed, we had. I was too busy to read it in advance, and my mother couldn't be bothered.

This may explain the libertarian attitude adopted ever since. I happily handed bundles of Alec Waugh's letters to Mr Foulkes without having the faintest idea what they contained. Three biographies of Evelyn Waugh have appeared since his death in 1966; all received as much co-operation as was requested. Was I wrong to hand all those bundles of Alec Waugh's letters to the unknown Mr Foulkes? I do not think so. Nobody can hope to control what is written or said about them after they are dead. Far better that people should at least be writing or saying *something*. Nobody writes without hoping to be read.

Chapter Seventeen
'Way of the World'

Just occasionally, as a journalist, one is visited by the illusion that one has an important message for the world,
seeing human civilisation as we know it shuffle towards
the cliff edge of destruction. In fact, I doubt whether the
world has ever been a pleasanter place.[1]

Waugh had always coveted the *Daily Telegraph*'s 'Way of the
World' column. As a cub reporter on the *Telegraph* in his early
twenties, way back in the early sixties, he asked Michael Wharton,
creator of the column's mythical author, Peter Simple, if he
could become his assistant. 'Michael Wharton heard me out
with the exquisite politeness of an older generation, and, with
the same politeness, showed me the door,'[2] recalled Waugh.

Waugh finally acquired this column nearly thirty years later.
He wrote 'Way of the World' from May 1990 until a few weeks
before his death, in January 2001. As he readily admitted, it was
rather more restrained than 'Auberon Waugh's Diary' (mainly,
he believed, because every word was read for libel), but for
Telegraph readers, it was still strong stuff. His targets ranged from
old adversaries such as Cyril Connolly and Shirley Williams to
new recruits like Will Self and Greg Dyke, from traditional
targets (ramblers, modern architects, health campaigners) to
apparently blameless public bodies such as the RSPCA and the
RSPB.[3] He advocated a new civil war, between the House of
York (led by Prince Andrew) and the House of Cornwall (led
by Prince Charles). He even castigated chimpanzees and bats.

'I see my role as that of a comic, raising morale by making merry jokes as the country goes to the dogs,' he wrote. 'It is not the most important role, nor the most admirable one, but I cannot see that it does any harm.'[4]

*

HAPPY DAYS
(*Daily Telegraph*, 21 May 1990)

The news that the deputy head teacher of a comprehensive school in Sheffield has left to take a cleaning job in a local hotel has been greeted by the Assistant Masters and Mistresses Association with the comment that many senior staff are leaving because of the strain of the new national curriculum. This seems a perfectly good reason for leaving.

The simple truth is that with our shrinking school population we have no shortage of teachers, whereas the shortage of good domestic servants is becoming a grave embarrassment. By no means all British children are educable in any meaningful sense, after so many years of breastfeeding and other ordeals. It may seem foolish to devote too many resources to such a lost cause. By the same token, not all redundant teachers will be sufficiently intelligent, industrious or well-mannered to be acceptable as domestic servants in any but the vilest homes. But it is good to learn that for once history is moving in the right direction.

SPORTING NEWS
(*Daily Telegraph*, 26 May 1990)

An advertisement for British Gas, which showed a baby swimming underwater, has come in for heavy criticism from the

Royal Society for the Prevention of Accidents, on the grounds that many mothers will now attempt to teach their babies underwater swimming at a time when insufficient research has been done on the effect of water pressure on babies. So it looks as if we will have to cancel the babies' underwater swimming race at Combe Florey's⁵ Church Fête this year.

Even the tortoise race has had to be cancelled at the Combe Florey Church Fête as a result of this government's insanely bossy ban on importing tortoises. Secret plans are being made for a Crawling Babies Race. The babies, when let out of their traps, will be invited to chase after a Pekinese puppy. Now we must expect objections from the new pressure group, Parents for Safe Food. I can only say that during the war, when coal was rationed, we British babies ate odder things than the occasional Pekinese puppy – and, at the end of the day, succeeded in giving Herr Hitler a thrashing from which he never quite recovered.

BLACK JUSTICE
(*Daily Telegraph*, 27 June 1990)

The Lord Chancellor's Department is to examine the composition of juries in criminal trials to see whether or not they reflect the racial make-up of society. There is concern that the right of black defendants to trial by a jury of their peers may need safeguarding. The alternative is for everyone to face a jury of the same composition as the defendant. This would mean that if ever they catch me frightening a bat, or planting the wrong sort of potato, I would face a jury composed exclusively of middle-class, middle-aged, public-school-educated white Catholic journalists of conservative temperament. It may sound a good idea, but on balance I feel I might do better with a jury of blacks. Would it solve the problem if all juries were composed exclusively of Britons of West Indian extraction?

THE BEAUTIFUL GAME
(*Daily Telegraph*, 7 July 1990)

In all my West African travels, I never had occasion to visit Cameroon, where French and English are spoken interchangeably in the elegant cafés and beer gardens of Yaoundé among the streams and shaded avenues for which the country's capital is famous. Why, then, did I find myself burning with sudden Cameroonian patriotism on Sunday?[6] Why did I cheer every forward movement of their brave footballers, shining black against the Italian turf in the World Cup quarter finals, why did I groan every time they were beaten back?

Odder still, large parts of Somerset seemed to be infected with the same enthusiasm for Cameroon, even among people who had never heard of the united republic before – or, if they had, tended to confuse it with macaroon, the delicious almond-flavoured biscuit. In London literary and artistic circles, I found that support for Cameroon was more or less solid, with one or two licensed eccentrics, as was only to be expected, supporting the other side, apparently called 'England'.

The reason, I suspect, was resentment at the idea that these sweaty, incompetent louts and their grotesque supporters could possibly represent the country we know and love and call our own, the country of Shakespeare and Hardy, of Johnson, Wordsworth and Chesterton, Barchester, Grantchester, Wimbledon and the *Daily Telegraph*. The football fans of England were certainly around in Shakespeare's time. It was our responsibility to keep them whining and snarling, in their place, and we have failed. How pathetic to hope that eleven young Africans, however agile and shiny-faced, could do the job for us.

GLORIOUS THIRTEENTH
(Daily Telegraph, 13 August 1990)

Today the grouse-shooting season opens, a day late owing to
the Glorious Twelfth having coincided with the tenth Sunday
after Pentecost, or ninth after Trinity, according to taste.
Normally this column would be devoted to a round-up of
prospects on the various moors where Japanese and Arab
sportsmen will be blazing away, with carefully veiled racist hints
about the superiority of Japanese marksmen over their Arab
colleagues. But the noble sport is under attack from two directions. The Royal Society for the Protection of Birds accuses
sportsmen and gamekeepers of mistaking hen harriers for
grouse. Hen harriers are common and voracious birds of prey
which eat grouse eggs in preference to any other sort of food,
and are savagely protected by the bird fanatics, despite having
quintupled their numbers in the last five years. They are easily
mistaken for grouse, especially after lunch, but do not taste so
good.

The second attack comes from firebrands in the Ramblers
Association, who are demanding the right to ramble over all
the country's grouse moors, thereby disturbing the grouse and
destroying the sport. It is almost as illegal to shoot Ramblers
as it is to shoot hen harriers, although Ramblers do not have
the gigantic resources of the RSPB, with its electronic surveil-
lance systems, to protect them. But I am not suggesting that
Ramblers should be shot at. They are clumsy, slow-moving creatures, and there would be no sport in it. The best thing to do
with Ramblers is to arrest them on suspicion of worrying hen
harriers in the course of their rambling and hand them over to
the RSPB, who will know what to do.

FASTER, FASTER
(Daily Telegraph, 1 December 1990)

The latest issue of *Police* magazine has a story in it which will touch a chord among many motorists. It appears that last September PC Michael Batey stopped a driver on the M25 who seemed to be driving too slowly. The driver asked him if he was near Durham. PC Batey replied no, Durham was about 300 miles away. The driver was visibly shaken. It appeared that he had left his home, near Rochester, Kent, ten hours earlier, to drive to Durham, and had been driving round and round the M25 ever since. When stopped, he was twenty miles away from his home, but thought he must be near his journey's end.

It is not just all motorways which look alike in modern Britain. Even destinations tend to be indistinguishable, unless you happen to catch a glimpse of some surviving landmark, like the cathedral or castle in Durham, or the old Player's cigarette factory in Nottingham. Perhaps one day it will occur to all these people scurrying around that there is very little point, nowadays, in going anywhere. With all these wonderful new machines, we can communicate instantly with anyone, anywhere. Even this seems a questionable activity, when few of us have anything of interest or importance to communicate.

CUT ABOVE THE REST
(Daily Telegraph, 16 January, 1991)

The Israeli government has set aside £2 million for circumcising as many of the expected million immigrants from the Soviet Union as apply for this service. Soviet Jews, it appears, are seldom circumcised for fear of provoking anti-Semitic persecution. There was always a certain amount of friction between circumcised and uncircumcised boys at my prep school, but not on anti-Semitic grounds, since we were all Catholics. It seemed to resolve into another aspect of the class struggle, with circumcised boys, mysteriously called Roundheads, fancying themselves more upper class than the uncircumcised, called Cavaliers.

There was a ferocious debate in California, which I followed closely a few years ago, on whether the Princess of Wales had had her two sons circumcised, but the class aspect was not mentioned. Californians are interested only in matters of health. What should be our attitude to this matter in John Major's[7] new classless society? What does the prime minister advise? I feel he should give us a lead, one way or another.

THE DELIGHTS OF HORSEMEAT
(*Daily Telegraph*, 18 March 1990)

Last week's newspapers all carried gigantic photographs of a horse having its throat cut in a Spanish slaughterhouse. Their purpose was to elicit support for the RSPCA and I suppose it may have had that effect on some people. In my own case, its effect was simply to make me feel very hungry. I have never understood why horsemeat is not eaten in Britain, or why people show such aversion to the idea. It is just as good as beef and rather healthier, having less fat.

Perhaps it is thought that horses are more intelligent than cattle, making it crueller to kill them. I doubt this is the case. Horses are unbelievably stupid. For my own part, I hope to celebrate European integration with a horse barbecue under the equestrian statue of the Grand Old Duke of York in Waterloo Place. If the health authorities forbid it, we can always eat raw horse cut in thin slices with a gingery sauce, in the Japanese manner. Europe must learn to look outwards.

VOICES IN THE VOID
(Daily Telegraph, 25 March 1991)

Great hurt and great anger have been occasioned among the nation's cellular telephone users by the chancellor's new tax on their instruments. Although all such machines have been banned on this column since long before their invention, I do not feel I can bring myself to support any new tax, however admirable its purpose. Extra money in the hands of the government can cause nothing but mischief. When I come to power I think I will abolish this tax, as, indeed, I will abolish most taxes, but I will pass a new law requiring anyone using a portable telephone in a public place – whether train, restaurant or in the street – to wear a dunce's cap for the duration of his call.

SHORT ORDER
(Daily Telegraph, 10 April 1991)

The latest theory about Peter Sutcliffe, the Yorkshire Ripper, is that he may have turned into a mass murderer because he was forced to wear short trousers as a twelve-year-old. His father, John Sutcliffe, appeared on a late-night Channel 4 chat show to explain what happened. 'We were very unjust,' he said. 'He was the only kid in short pants, and he was very shy and self-conscious about his thin legs.' Short trousers are horrible garments on men, I agree, but I doubt whether this really explains Peter Sutcliffe's subsequent behaviour, which was strange, even by Yorkshire standards. But it seems to me that his reluctance to wear shorts might be put to some use. If people convicted of violent crime could be sentenced to wear short trousers for the rest of their lives, this would not only act as a punishment but also enable potential victims to be on their guard before the trouble started. Other people could continue to wear short trousers if they wished, of course. But perhaps fewer would be tempted.

WELL HELD
(Daily Telegraph, 27 March 1991)

Many will sympathise with the Princess Royal and her estranged husband, Captain Phillips, in their reported difficulties over the division of the 1500 wedding presents which, by convention, are given to couples jointly. It gives me some satisfaction to think that I have not added to their problems. At the time of the Royal Wedding in November 1973, I could not make up my mind between some transparent ovenproof Pyrex dishes and a slightly more ambitious set of ramekins for baking eggs, which were decorated with pictures of baby rabbits.

In the end, I more or less decided on the Pyrex dishes. But, having watched the young couple walk down the aisle, I thought I would hold on a bit and see how things worked out. At times they must have wondered at the long delay. Seventeen and a half years later, I am glad to see that my caution was justified. I have not only saved myself a considerable sum of money, I have also spared the couple any possibility of further friction at this difficult moment in their lives.

HARD TIMES
(Daily Telegraph, 24 April 1991)

Winston Churchill's poor academic record at Harrow, now exposed as an untruth by his biographer, Martin Gilbert, has had a most deleterious effect on the whole of English educa-tion. Whenever I told my children that if they did not work at school they would end up as lavatory cleaners or have to marry some fat and revolting man, they replied by pointing to Sir Winston, who ended up as Lord Warden of the Cinque Ports and much else besides. In fact it appears that the young Winston was a tremendous swot, doing very well in maths and coming top in his history division. It is easy to see why he put around this untruth. The English have no time for swots. Churchill would never have become such a popular figure if people had thought he was brainy. The myth of the late developer should be exposed. Practically no one does well in later life who did not do well at school, although some of them lie about their school records afterwards.

DEFENCE CUTS
(*Daily Telegraph*, 27 May 1991)

Further to my suggestion that certain units of the British armed forces should be reserved for homosexuals, I hear proposals for an extension of the ethnic principle in regimental designations from a colonel in the West Country. As he points out, we already have regiments of Welsh, Irish and Scots Guards. Why not a regiment of Black Guards? This would serve as a worthy focus for pride among our fellow citizens who happen to be black, and would also remove the constant niggling allegations about colour prejudice in the Brigade. It is an excellent suggestion. I am always pleased to hear from anybody in the armed forces above the rank of major. But when my correspondent suggests that the new regiment should be equipped with white bearskins, made from the pelts of polar bear cubs, I feel he is going over the top. Not only would white bearskins be too conspicuous, they would also be much too expensive.

Those of us who have lived and worked among the Masai in East Africa will remember how Masai warriors frequently spend four days at the hairdresser's before an important parade or military engagement. They achieve an effect which, although by no means similar to the bearskin in shape, is certainly comparable to it in magnificence. I would suggest that the new regiment dispense with bearskins altogether, thereby achieving an important economy in the new spirit of defence cuts. This may or may not be a logical response to the apparent relaxation of tension in the Cold War.

LOOSEN THE TIES
(*Daily Telegraph*, 3 June 1991)

South Korea, which has been agitating for reunion with its socialist northern half for the last forty-six years, seems to have experienced a change of mind. After a glance at the appalling cost to West Germany of taking on the moribund East German economy and unemployable East German workforce, South Koreans are beginning to wonder whether they can really afford unity. A gradual, controlled easing of tension and slow expansion of business and other links may be what the doctor ordered, they feel. I confess I feel rather the same about the socialist northern parts of England – the People's Republic of Liverpool, the Nuclear Free Zones of Derbyshire and Sheffield, etc. Of course one remains emotionally attached to the inhabitants in various ways, and many southerners admire them for their warm-heartedness and the unusual way they sing. But it is tremendously expensive for the rest of us to keep them in the style to which they have become accustomed.

SAFETY FIRST
(*Daily Telegraph*, 3 July 1991)

Even if it is true that 100 lives will be saved every year by the compulsory wearing of seat belts in the back seats of motor cars, I wonder whether anyone in the government has really considered whether it is a good idea to save so many lives. Those who travel in the back seat of a car are often the least important passengers. Many of them may be retired, or unemployed, or too young to be employed (and very probably unemployable). Few backseat passengers make any important contribution to the Gross Domestic Product and, of those that do, a fair number may well be employed by the government in some redundant and parasitic capacity or other, as social workers, health inspectors or lecturers in peace studies.

Some of these people might enjoy living dangerously. Since there is no law against suicide, why should they face a fine of £100 for refusing to truss themselves like chickens every time they are taken for a drive? What business is it of the government's to force them to live longer, whether they want to or not? I suppose the answer to these questions is to be found elsewhere, in the danger such people might present to other, possibly more important parties, sitting in the front seat.

It is all very well for backseat nonentities to fly around unrestrained by sensible harnesses, and crash into windows and doors, but what happens if they crash into the passenger in the front seat? It is by no means unknown for really quite important people to travel in the front seats of cars: Members of Parliament, junior ministers, even ministers of transport. Unless passengers behind can be securely tied to their seats at all times, an accident might occur which would threaten the sort of tragedy from which the nation might never recover.

A TERRIBLE RISK
(Daily Telegraph, 18 January 1992)

Many patriots will have been alarmed to see photographs in the vulgar newspapers of the Princess of Wales queuing with Prince William, unnoticed, in a crowded hamburger bar in Kensington High Street. We are told that Her Royal Highness ordered a £4.76 takeaway meal of two hamburgers, six chicken McNuggets, regular french fries, a cola and an apple pie. Our alarm did not concern itself so much with the evidence of penury which the incident affords. Many Princes of Wales have gone through patches of poverty, and it is always the wives and children who suffer. If there was no food at Kensington Palace, or no one there to serve it, then it was perfectly reasonable for the Princess and her son to seek nourishment in a neighbouring restaurant.

What is disturbing is the food she bought. Of course there

is no reason to associate hamburgers, chicken McNuggets and cola with the dreaded American disease[8] which threatens all human life in five continents, but I refuse to believe that diet is not a factor in what one can only call the American phenomenon. Anti-Europeans who rail against German dominance in Europe do not take cognisance of the only alternative, which is political, economic, cultural and intellectual absorption by the United States. The German influence is at least diluted by French, Italian, Spanish and other influences, as well as being reduced by linguistic incomprehension. The American takeover is more total, and more deleterious. Few people would take such a strict view as to say it was high treason to be caught feeding American food to the heir to the throne. But I am sure there is a decent pizza bar somewhere in the neighbourhood.

NOT IN THEIR SOCKS
(Daily Telegraph, 16 March 1992)

I try to believe everything I read in the newspapers, but I had difficulty with the account of the London vagrant who was found, after death, to be carrying £1500 in small change in his socks. My reason for doubting the story is that I, too, like to carry small change in my socks, but I have found that with more than £15 or £20 worth it becomes impossible to walk.

The English have tended to assure each other that it is wrong to give money to beggars because most beggars are tremendously rich, and only pretending to be poor, but I would like to think that the origins of this false rumour are more metaphysical. It used to be believed that every toad carried a precious jewel in its head. Many millions of toads were killed by ignorant people searching for this jewel. I myself have never much liked toads, but I have the greatest respect for those who do like them. They are said to make excellent companions.

The jewel rumour was intended to be taken symbolically, suggesting that an ugly exterior may hide a beautiful nature, or brilliant intellect. Again, I am not sure that this is universally true. Ugly people, in my experience, are no less likely to be stupid, and possibly more likely to be unpleasant, than attractive ones. Perhaps the message was intended to be that we should not close our minds to the possibilities of paradox.

No doubt the story of the London vagrant with £1500 in his socks was also intended to be taken symbolically. It would be a sad thing if the new wave of street dwellers from unhappy homes in the north of England took it literally, and started cutting the feet off older London vagrants in a vain search for their hidden treasure.

MERRIE ENGLAND
(*Daily Telegraph*, 15 April 1992)

I did not see the London Marathon this weekend, and so cannot complain about it too loudly, but my heartfelt sympathy goes out to those who found themselves confronted by 25,000 runners, all anxious to show how good-hearted they were and what fun they were having. From photographs I see that some were dressed as chickens, some as rabbits, some as Indian statesmen. Many wore cushions under their shirts or put on false breasts, whether in emulation or mockery of the gentler sex.

There are those who will argue there is no harm to this, it is all for charity; my objection is not moral but aesthetic. It is not true to say that anything is justified in a good cause: vulgarity, exhibitionism and ugliness are things to be avoided. There is no excuse for inflicting them on your fellow citizens by saying it is done in a good cause. The pains of living in an overcrowded island are apparent enough for those who have to travel inside it. But if the torture is to be compounded by organised mass merrymaking, life will soon become unendurable.

When Disney's Euro park was first mooted I, too, saw it as a cultural Chernobyl and prayed that some mad French intellectual

It makes those who fall victim stupid, mad, ugly and boring. Death is seldom long delayed. In time, no doubt, it will be forbidden to drive while dieting or to diet on the London Underground; special carriages for dieters will be supplied by British Rail, with improved ventilation and nurses, morticians, etc., in attendance. But until society wakes up to the dangers, our only hope lies in education. Its risks are certainly greater than those of being blown up by an IRA bomb. I spent two and a half hours in a train stuck in a field outside Taunton station yesterday, while police and bomb experts examined a suspicious suitcase in the station. Perhaps it is too much to expect everyone to share in the spirit of the Blitz – to ignore bomb scares, merely clear up the blood and broken glass afterwards and keep things moving – but I can't help feeling it might be a better idea *not* to report suspicious packets or parcels to the authorities.

ENDANGERED SPECIES
(*Daily Telegraph*, 20 February 1993)

The case for deerhunting has always seemed to me much stronger than the case for foxhunting. If the purpose of foxhunting is simply to kill foxes, I am sure that the local sanitary inspector (or environmental health officer, as these people are nowadays called) could manage to do that efficiently enough and might even derive a certain lonely pleasure from the occupation.

Foxes, in my experience, rather resent the attention of the hunt. They are mean, self-righteous, greedy creatures, whereas deer have a certain nobility in their wild state and live for no other purpose than to be hunted, to flee the hounds. To join the hunt is to pay tribute to their autonomy and acknowledge their purpose in the scheme of creation. The real threat to wild animals comes not from the people who want to hunt, shoot, trap or skin them, but from sentimental animal lovers who want to gawp at them. Sportsmen and trappers at least ensure their supplies, whereas animal lovers literally coddle them to death, like small children with a fledgling.

HEALTH HAZARD
(*Daily Telegraph*, 12 May 1993)

As I write, Britons seem to be scaling Mount Everest like monkeys in an Indian temple. Since I described the appalling state of the mountain a few weeks ago – rather like Brighton beach after a bank holiday – further reports suggest that the situation is even worse than I thought. Within a few thousand feet of the summit, a plateau the size of a football ground is strewn with about twenty tons of the sort of rubbish I have mentioned, but also with the dead bodies of climbers and their Sherpas. There are five of them in the immediate area, but many others are thought to be scattered around out of sight.

Soon the main risk of climbing the mountain will be not from the cold, the exhaustion or the lack of oxygen, but the ever-present danger of infection from these health hazards. It is an appalling reflection on the sort of people climbing Everest these days that they are prepared to leave their Sherpas lying around like so many empty tin cans. If the Nepalese government is not prepared to do anything about this national disgrace, the very least we can do is to send an army of environmental health officers to inspect the site and issue directives. In fact I think it would be a good idea if all environmental health officers were required to climb Everest – preferably by the North Face, and without oxygen – before being issued with a licence to make a nuisance of themselves in the pubs, clubs and restaurants of England. Those who complain it might be an expensive form of training should reflect on how much money we will save if the trainees fail to return.

WEAR A BLACK NOSE
(Daily Telegraph, 30 June 1993)

A poll commissioned by Comic Relief claims that 66 per cent of adults in Britain support its Red Nose Day, a six-hour 'laughathon' broadcast on BBC 1 in aid of various charitable causes. I saw it for a few minutes and did not smile once. In fact, I was closer to weeping. The English, whatever one may say against them, have a highly developed sense of humour, but it is a subversive force in our society, opposing the vanity of those who seek to exert power, or exercise moral leadership, or wish to impress us with their wealth or importance. Above all, it is deeply sceptical of those who make a show of doing good.

Those who wish to give money to charity can do so without wearing a red nose to advertise the fact. These red noses, worn under licence from the nanny state, harnessing the spirit of Saturnalia to goody-goody causes, should be seen as a new onslaught from the diseased, humourless minority which hopes to control us. Perhaps in Essex, or somewhere of the sort, a new movement will grow up: the Black Noses, who not only insist on wearing a black nose every Red Nose Day but also make a point of punching any Red Noses they see.

DONKEYS TO THE RESCUE
(Daily Telegraph, 24 July 1993)

My letterbox has been filled for several days with letters from donkey lovers complaining about my recent piece on the Donkey Sanctuary at Sidmouth. An interesting discovery is that donkey fanciers, with one or two exceptions, are rather nice people, unlike Thatcher fanciers, anti-smokers or militant relatives of road victims. The sanctuary's administrator points out that, far from standing around with nothing to do all day, as my correspondent complained, her donkeys are regularly visited and ridden by disabled children. At Devon County Show, they give exhibitions of jumping with deaf riders, a thoroughly admirable thing to do.

My own experience of donkeys has not been happy, but I recognise in the enthusiasm and exuberance of these donkey fanciers something of my own feeling for Pekinese: donkeys are not only beautiful, brave, kind, loyal and brilliantly clever, they are also industrious, articulate, honest, thrifty and endowed with a keen sense of moral priorities. Many took exception to my suggestion that obdurate and intractable donkeys should be supplied to teacher training colleges so that the trainees could practise chastising them. Under these circumstances, perhaps I should amend my recommendation, with appropriate apologies to the donkeys of the world and their admirers. Donkeys should be sent to teacher training colleges, but not as whipping posts, to help trainee teachers learn how to deal with obdurate and intractable pupils. Rather they should go as professors to teach the elements of good manners, reading, writing, arithmetic, English, history, French and Latin, from the store of their wisdom, to the almost totally ignorant generation which seeks to educate our children now.

UNFAIR CRITICISM
(*Daily Telegraph*, 17 November 1993)

Once upon a time I might have been prepared to believe that Chairman Mao Tse-tung was a practitioner of group sex, that every Saturday evening, until he was well into his seventies, he would summon three or four young women to his bedroom for what the *Observer* nowadays calls 'sex sessions'. Or so we are to be told on a BBC TV *Timewatch* programme, which will be shown on the hundredth anniversary of Mao's birth. I might have believed this when I was an idealistic young man who wanted to think there could be some purpose to a life of politics, some hope of reward. Of course no English prime minister would ever have the same opportunities, but the dream was still there . . .

I might also have been prepared to believe these rumours because we all enjoy gossip. Nothing on earth will stop people speculating about the intimate details of their rulers' lives. A cat may not only look at a king, it can also meditate on what the king looks like without any clothes on. It is only in middle age that one becomes sceptical. Even so, I would have been happy to believe that Mao was a secret sex maniac when he was preaching family values – but then I read that the same programme is going to accuse him of condoning cannibalism, and a dreadful boredom sets in. In a long-ish journalistic career I must have accused at least a dozen Third World leaders of this crime. The charge won't stick any more. Cannibalism is a rare taste. It is no good pretending that politicians indulge it just because we disagree with their policies. I am afraid that Mao was really just another boring, self-important politician like the rest of them.

TOP DOGS
(Daily Telegraph, 23 March 1993)

An American called Stanley Coren has written a book comparing the intelligence of 133 breeds of dog. I am afraid it will cause more fisticuffs than any religious or doctrinal squabble since Henry VIII's invention of the Church of England in 1531. When I reveal that border collies are chosen as the most intel- ligent of all dogs, followed by poodles, Alsatians and golden retrievers, while Pekinese come 127 out of 133 breeds, I trust I will have said all that needs to be said.

Border collies, while amiable and pliant enough, are notori- ously stupid, while Pekinese vary from dog to dog. Of my three Pekinese, one is only fairly intelligent, I agree, but another, to judge by his wisdom and benignity as well as his appearance, might easily be a reincarnation of Confucius himself. He can understand every nuance of a conversation between three or four people; he recognises and welcomes those he has met only once three years earlier. He reads the *Telegraph* and treats the *Sunday Times* with loathing and disdain.

It may seem odd that an American should presume to judge the intelligence of dogs, but the mystery is explained when we learn that Stanley Coren judges intelligence by success in obedience tests. Pekinese may be the cleverest, most fearless and most original of dogs, but they are also the most disobedient. They will spend some time working out what you want them to do, and then do precisely the opposite. Perhaps it is an American trait to confuse obedience with intelligence. I do not know.

BATTERED HUSBANDS
(*Daily Telegraph*, 27 April 1994)

Police have expressed alarm over a claimed increase in battered husbands – the number of reported cases has doubled in five years – but I remain sceptical, fearing a repetition of the ritual child abuse fiasco. Until fairly recently, the police did not concern themselves with quarrels between husbands and wives, unless serious harm resulted. Now they have set up domestic violence units especially for the purpose.

It seems to me that any husband who allows himself to be systematically beaten up by his wife probably enjoys it. If he doesn't, he should go back to his mother. Police must not be encouraged to go barging into private houses when they should be making life difficult for car thieves, house burglars, muggers and street hooligans. Any man who turns up at a police station to complain that the woman in his life has boxed his ears, or thrown a saucepan at him, or chased him round the kitchen table with a carving knife, should be made to take lessons in unarmed combat and sent home with the laughter of the constabulary ringing in his ears.

BEAUTY CONTEST
(*Daily Telegraph*, 6 June 1994)

The Japanese, to their eternal credit, have invented a silent piano, on which they can practise for hours on end without disturbing the neighbours, the only sound emerging in the player's earphones. I wonder if British scientists might not take this idea a stage further and develop the model of a silent politician, whose fiery denunciations, pert nostrums and false promises would echo only in his own ears.

It would save those of us who live in democracies an enormous amount of irritation and boredom. We could choose our leaders by whether we liked the look of them, which is probably as good a way as any. Under that dispensation, pretty Mr Blair would undoubtedly sweep the board at the next general election, as he promises to do in any case. Since we decided to appoint him successor to nice Mr Major, I have not heard him utter anything except vapid, goody-goody sentiments. If nobody else can be found to stand against him for the leadership of the Labour Party, I think that I shall do so myself. To hold a leadership election at all will cost the Labour Party £1 million, and unless it is prepared to bribe me with £200,000 not to stand, I shall make it my platform that Tony Blair is much too young to be prime minister. The young may look prettier than we do, but they are also tremendously boring and talk nothing but rubbish.

MAKING UP THEIR MINDS
(*Daily Telegraph*, 13 June 1994)

There are certain attractions to the idea that the unemployed should risk losing their right to benefits if they refuse to work as hairdressers or chefs. But I wonder if sufficient thought has been given to the likely impact of these young unemployed people on the culinary and hairdressing scenes. Being slightly bald, and usually shorn by my wife, I might escape the worst consequences of their activities in hairdressing. But just think of the dreadful food they would serve. The same objection applies to the proposal that they should be taken into other forms of domestic service. The trouble is that since governments made domestic service the only form of employment which has to be paid out of a person's taxed income, it has more or less disappeared, and there is no longer a superstructure there to give them any training.

I suppose the answer must be to let them do what they want to do. Many, it appears, now want to be psychologists. Application for psychology-degree places reached 80,000 this year – almost as many applicants as for physics, chemistry and biology combined. In the sixties, all the stupidest candidates wanted to go into sociology. In the seventies it was English and in the eighties it was business studies. Now they presumably want to be counsellors and psychotherapists. I feel they will do less harm counselling each other and applying whatever therapy seems appropriate than trying to cook our food and cut our hair.

A NEW AGE
(*Daily Telegraph*, 27 June 1994)

I suppose Oxford University hopes to attract some favourable publicity by awarding Nelson Mandela a doctorate of civil law. What is mildly surprising is that it should have supposed an honorary doctorate was good enough for this great figure of our times. The least it could have done, I should have thought, was to rename one of the colleges after him. Better still, rename the whole university, or the whole country, as Mandelaland. This would be in tribute to his work for world peace, just as every street and every housing estate should be named after him to acknowledge his work for race relations, and to demonstrate the political correctness of the local council.

One trouble is that Britain is less important than she used to be, and nobody might notice. The best thing might be to name the new millennium after him. At present there are a lot of bad ideas around for celebrating the new millennium: the Pope hopes for a grand recantation by the Catholic Church, listing everything it has done wrong; Mr Major still dreams of street parties where everyone will eat Spam and talk to each other classlessly about football; others plan dismal festivals of modern music and poetry and painting.

The year 2000 is a time to declare an end to all that, above all an end to the Modern Movement. In recognition of the fact that few people know what the millennium means, let alone how to spell it, I feel we should forget about the previous two millennia and dub our new age the Mandela-um, after a very clever little Chinaman who managed to persuade the world he was a black African, against all the odds.

AN INSPECTOR CALLS
(Daily Telegraph, 6 July 1994*)*

For St Swithin's Day I was hoping to sit down to a dinner of roast ostrich, rather as Americans eat turkey at Thanksgiving. I first ate it when I visited South Africa to judge a wine competition some years ago, and decided it would be a good thing to eat on St Swithin's Day, as Swithin was tutor to Ethelwulf, son of Egbert, the first king to unite England (in 829). It had been planned to give everyone a chance to eat ostrich this St Swithin's day, but now an inspector from the Ministry of Agriculture, Fisheries and Food has put a stop to it. The inspector flew out to South Africa and cancelled the entire scheme because, he said, the ostriches were plucked while still alive. This is not acceptable to our Charter on Animal Welfare.

I wonder how on earth you set about plucking a live ostrich. You would need to be very brave and very fast on your feet. It occurs to me that our charter must be extraordinarily thorough if it lays down specific rules about the plucking of ostriches, and we must care a lot if we can send food inspectors all the way to South Africa to ensure they do things in the right order. It makes one proud to be British. Now the South Africans will have to breed featherless ostriches. Ostriches don't really need feathers as they can't fly, and South Africa is quite warm enough for them to manage without.

GÖTTERDÄMMERUNG
(Daily Telegraph, 9 July 1994)

A recent study in the *Journal of Epidemiology and Community Health* is devoted to attempts made in Nazi Germany to discourage smoking. Hitler was always politically correct in these matters, being a vegetarian, teetotaller and non-smoker, as well as bitterly opposed to hunting and shooting. He was the anti-smoking campaign's greatest supporter, appearing with other celebrities and national personalities to extol the benefits of refraining from the habit. The methods were almost exactly the same as those being used now. Popular newspapers and magazines were charged with carrying the message: advertising was strictly controlled, no information in favour of smoking was permitted and there were laws against making smokers look manly. The oddest thing is that the campaign did not work. Nobody paid any attention, and smoking levels continued to rise as much in Nazi Germany as everywhere else at that time.

If there had been evidence that German tobacco consumption fell during the Hitler period, I would have had to address the question of whether or not this might have contributed to the fact that Germany lost the war. I have not seen any scientific proof that smoking makes human males more manly, but the anti-smoking fanatics are so anxious to prevent anyone making the suggestion that one cannot help wondering if there is any truth in it. There seems to be a general decline in manliness among the new generation of non-smokers, but perhaps that is because smoking has become an act of defiance, as it was in Nazi Germany.

A CHARITABLE VIEW
(Daily Telegraph, 7 December 1994)

Clergy have taken a dim view of Oxford University Press's new Bible, specially translated into multi-racial feminish to make it acceptable to Americans. The Bishop of Wakefield even went so far as to attribute a commercial motive to the publishers, which many will find shocking. One may agree that the attempt to change the language to protect the sensitivities of women, racial minorities, disabled and left-handed people may invite a certain amount of ridicule from those less sensitive.

But I take the charitable view. In the last century missionaries in savage and remote heathen territories often took simplified versions of the Bible story with them so that they could woo the natives. If this mad baby language is the only way the clergy can communicate with Americans, so be it. The book will not circulate in this country or anywhere else in European Christendom. In the United States, the Oxford American Bible might easily bring a chink of light into minds darkened by endless television and constant exposure to unsafe levels of hamburger gas. Christians must believe that Americans, too, have immortal souls. If we cannot make that act of faith, at least there is no harm in making a little money from them.

STOP THE ROT
(Daily Telegraph, 13 February 1995)

Some months ago I drew attention to a Westminster councillor who had announced his intention to crack down on the display of prostitutes' cards in public telephone boxes, and wondered why. It costs tens of thousands of pounds every month to send a new brigade of public employees around taking them down as fast as the 'card boys' can put them up. My conclusion was that the only people attracted to government or to local government are those who wish to throw their weight around and make a nuisance of themselves. Most of us can protect ourselves against them by the simple device of refusing to answer their letters, but by long tradition prostitutes are people who can be insulted and pushed around at will.

Now we spend even more public money prosecuting the card boys, some of whom work incredibly hard distributing a thousand cards a day in the Marylebone area alone. The statute found to support their persecution is a clause in the incompetent and oppressive Environmental Protection Act, which forbids leaving litter in the open air. When, on appeal from the magistrates' court, the card boys point out that the interior of a telephone box is not in the open air, they usually win. I wonder if this is why councils are so keen to replace the handsome old red telephone boxes with ugly new contraptions that don't work. The purpose is to save London schoolchildren from being offended by the sight of a prostitute's telephone number. It would be simpler to ban anyone under the age of eighteen using a public telephone. They are seldom up to much good, these teenage telephonists.

LESSONS FROM SPIDERS
(*Daily Telegraph*, 29 April 1995)

Scientists seldom have anything of interest to tell us, and most of it is, I suspect, untrue or tendentious, partial and slanted, but anybody with the slightest intellectual curiosity will have been fascinated by those photographs of spiders' webs produced under the influence of different drugs. The NASA experiments, reported in *New Scientist*, showed how the spider on marijuana never bothers to finish the job; on Benzedrine, its web is erratic and full of holes. Caffeine, the active ingredient of tea and coffee, produces a totally random collection of filaments through which any insect can fly with impunity; while under the influence of chloral hydrate, an old-fashioned sleeping draught, the spider scarcely bothers to start.

All of which is fine so far as it goes. Perhaps one has to be absurdly suspicious of scientists and their motives to observe that while they tested drugs as common as tea, pot and speed, and as rare as chloral hydrate (practically unused nowadays), they do not appear to have tested cigarettes or alcohol. This seems inexplicable. The more one broods about it, the more likely it appears that they did indeed test many brands of cigarette and almost every form of alcohol known to man, but decided for some reason not to publish the results of their findings. Can this be because, under the influence of nicotine and alcohol, spiders make webs of such precision and beauty as put their normal efforts to shame? It would be as much as any scientist's job was worth even to hint at such a truth.

SHEEP OPPORTUNITIES
(Daily Telegraph, 9 March 1996)

Many wise old heads were shaken over the news that scientists have managed to produce two identical sheep by cloning. When applied to humans, we are assured, this will surely lead to a Fascist dictatorship, rather than produce a new breed of attractive, amiable, intelligent, healthy people. Before we decide, I feel there are many experiments, not to say practical jokes, which should be tried on these two sheep. At present they look pretty well alike, but would they look the same after they had been in a field for a couple of years? More particularly, would they be the same after they had been put in different fields?

All arguments about the rival influences of heredity and environment will be settled if one of these sheep is sent to live as the pet of a duchess, frisking on the lawns of some stately home during its holidays from Eton; the other is sent to live in a run-down council estate in Liverpool. Will the Scouse sheep develop unexpected musical talents, or have motivational problems in school? Will the Etonian develop a charming, self-confident manner and a certain vagueness about whose turn it is to pay for the next round of drinks? I feel we are on the verge of great discoveries. This is no time to turn back.

A NATIONAL INSULT
(*Daily Telegraph*, 13 March 1996)

National No Smoking Day was always celebrated at the Academy Club, Beak Street, by the supply of free cigarettes to members and their guests. Two things make smoking a virtuous habit. In the first place, the smoker, by paying billions of pounds in tobacco duty, pretty well pays for the entire hospital service. In the second place, by dying on average five years younger than the non-smoker, the smoker reduces the burden of old age on society as a whole. I can understand that some people might not wish to smoke – not all of us are called to virtue in the same way – but I cannot understand the passion for stopping other people from smoking.

For some time it has been a feature of home life that brainwashed children try to persuade their parents to give up the habit. I always assumed that it was affection for their parents which drove them to this behaviour. Now we know differently. They are worried about the effect it will have on their own health, according to a gigantic new survey by the Health Education Authority. There seems no end to the untruths and exaggerations deployed against smoking. We are told that smoking costs the NHS extra money, whereas the opposite is the truth.

Endless falsehoods are deliberately put around about the dangers of passive smoking. We are told there is no demand for smoking compartments in trains. Next, they will start blaming tobacco for the longevity that threatens to destroy all social advances of this century. George Burns, the American comedian who died at 100 last week, was reported as attributing his longevity to fifteen cigars a day. 'The doctor who told me to stop is dead.'

TRY ALMOST ANYTHING ONCE
(*Daily Telegraph*, 25 March 1996)

Many people will have been shocked by the story of Philip Hall, the ornithologist who made a long trek to the banks of the Niger in search of the incredibly rare Rufous Fishing Owl, only to be shown the remains of one which had been eaten by the villagers the night before. I hope he took the opportunity to ask if he could nibble at the remaining leg. Ornithology is a respectable science, and gives many people pleasure, but gastronomy is the more important of the two, affecting, in its way, the whole human race.

If the Rufous Fishing Owl proved exceptionally delicious, it might be worthwhile to mount an expedition to secure a pair and breed them up for the table. Somebody always has to try these things first or we would never know, for instance, that rabbits are good to eat, rats are not. Being a bird-lover should be no impediment. It may not be completely true that every man eats the thing he loves, but I, who am founder, president and only known member of the Dog Lovers' Party of Great Britain (and a patron of the Canine Defence League) once ate dog in Manila. My attempts to eat giant panda in China were frustrated and I caused grave offence once in Adelaide by asking where it was possible to eat koala, but I think one has a duty to try everything.

The answer to our present beef crisis is obviously ostrich. I ate ostrich several times in South Africa and liked it, while mentally taking off my hat to the person who tried it first. Another suggestion is that we should eat alligators from Florida.

I ate crocodile once in Cuba – it tasted halfway between lobster and pork – but am not sure I would welcome its cousin from Florida. There are times when we have to allow health considerations to come first.

BANQUO'S GHOST
(*Daily Telegraph*, 18 May 1996)

It was not a good idea for Buckingham Palace to publish the guest list and seating arrangements for the state banquet on Tuesday night to welcome President and Mrs Chirac. Although there were one or two stars present, the guests were for the most part a dreadfully dull lot. It must be a depressing thought for the younger generation that at the top of the ladder in this country nothing awaits one but boredom.

My own complaint is more specific. Seeing that I was not on the list of those attending, many of my friends assumed I must be ill. All this week, my telephone has been ringing with their tender enquiries and condolences. Others observed that the Princess of Wales was absent, too, and supposed I was dining tête-à-tête with her. Would that it had been so. No, the simple truth is that on Tuesday evening I dined quietly in my club, perhaps brooding about an empty chair only a few hundred yards away in the Palace ballroom. It is a sad day when we can't even organise a state banquet without the invitations going astray.

A WISE DECISION
(*Daily Telegraph*, 3 July 1996)

Nobody should be too surprised that the British Medical Association voted to retain its prohibition on sexual intercourse with patients. Few doctors have the energy for that sort of thing, and to have to refuse patient after patient can only do harm to the crucially important doctor-patient relationship. Others may have been frightened by the suggestion that any change would involve repealing the law which makes it a criminal offence for unqualified people to impersonate a doctor. This might have been acceptable in the field of sexual opportunity – as I say, few doctors have much energy to spare – but what would it do to their livelihood?

Contemporary history is full of examples of completely untrained people who have practised successfully as doctors, even surgeons, for years, with no harm done. A profession without secrets is scarcely a profession at all. I think they have decided wisely. If they want a bit of the other thing, they can always join the amateur dramatic society.

SAVING THE KOALA
(*Daily Telegraph*, 23 September 1996)

News that London is emerging as one of the richest places in Britain for wildlife – not just rabbits, hedgehogs and deer, but rare creatures such as water voles, dormice and marsh warblers – must have some social significance. In the old days, these animals were caught and eaten by the poor. Just show a water vole or a marsh warbler to your average old-fashioned Cockney, and he would pop it straight into his mouth. This may seem cruel, but at least it kept the numbers down. Nowadays we are constantly told that under nice Mr Major the poor are poorer than they have ever been, so I can attribute the present plague of water voles and marsh warblers only to the fad of vegetarianism.

Australia is facing a similar problem with koalas, whose numbers have increased up to ten times in some places, threatening the survival of the very eucalyptus trees whose leaves are the only thing they eat. One proposal, to cull 2000 of them in South Australia, created an outcry from animal lovers. Now the state of Victoria proposes to vasectomise as many as possible of the males, but I am doubtful about this. Roger Martin, a research fellow at Monash University in Victoria, points out that vasectomy won't work because 'koalas are highly promiscuous animals. You only have to miss one and he will fertilise all the females right through the summer.'

Strangely enough, it never seems to have occurred to anyone to eat them. On my first visit to Adelaide, my hostess asked if there were any Australian delicacy I fancied. I said I would like to try a koala. They all fainted in horror. Now I know that koalas are an ecologically responsible thing to eat, the Australians should produce them at official receptions for visiting grandees like the Prince of Wales. This might produce an incentive for those of us who really want to know what they taste like to work a little harder and try to get invited.

MAN'S BEST FRIEND
(*Daily Telegraph*, 1 February 1997)

As an honorary patron of the Canine Defence League, I do not think I should let the recent remarks of the Chelmsford coroner, Dr Malcolm Weir, go without comment. He was speaking at the inquest of a couple who had died trying to save their dog, which had ventured on to thin ice: 'If anything comes out of this tragedy, perhaps the message can be got to people not to attempt to save their animals.' On the contrary, I would say that dog owners who lay down their lives for the dog they love have one of the noblest forms of death available. We must all die eventually. Why should we prefer an ignoble death – enfeebled old age, a burden on the community – to a noble one?

Another consideration is that if people stop trying to save their dogs, there will soon be nothing of interest to report in the newspapers. Since the end of the Cold War and the collapse of socialism in domestic politics, too, we can only write about the Royal Family, slimming, etc. Dr Weir pointed out that there had been six such dog-rescuing episodes over the Christmas holidays. That is one of the most reassuring statistics about Britain I have seen for a long time.

CREATING NEW JOBS
(Daily Telegraph, 8 February 1997)

Job Centres have been forbidden to offer work in what is nowadays called the sex industry, we learn, after an incident in Sheffield where a constituent of Helen Jackson, the MP for Hillsborough, was interviewed for a job advising on the services available in a massage parlour. The reason given for this is not so much any sudden access of prudishness, or old-fashioned morality, or family values, as these things are now called. It is not even that the Department of Employment might find itself in trouble with the law, which is strange and capricious but sometimes quite savage on the subject of pimping, recruiting of prostitutes and that sort of thing. Unemployed people have expressed fears that they will lose their job seeker's allowance if they turn down work in massage parlours, escort agencies and strip clubs. That is the reason given for the ban, and it seems fair enough, if it is true. This idea of our beloved welfare system forcing young people into prostitution is not what Lord Beveridge[9] had in mind.

On the other hand, there may be a significant minority among the young people of today who would welcome a break from the long hours of watching television in the afternoon. There is something unbearably poignant in the BBC's claim that 3.5 million people regularly watch a low-budget mid-afternoon cookery programme called *Ready, Steady, Cook.* I don't suppose many of these young people do much cooking as a result. Some might easily be prepared to overcome their natural horror of work by giving the sex industry a try. One must doubt whether they would be any good at it. Massage needs skill and concentration. Even striptease requires a certain desire to please, while the idea that any of these goofy, speechless young people could act as an 'escort' in any meaningful sense is too bizarre to contemplate. It is one of the great sustaining myths of our society that the young are good at sex. The best hope, as I never tire of arguing, is that they should be taught how to polish shoes.

QUIS CUSTODIET?
(*Daily Telegraph*, 24 January 1998)

As editor of a literary magazine, I spend large parts of my time correcting other people's spelling. Nothing they say about the inability of Oxford undergraduates to spell can surprise me. There are those who proclaim that spelling does not matter, it is élitist, it can all be done with digital spell-checkers. In fact, spell-checkers can only make a wild guess at what you are trying to say, and often get it wrong. Even if the spell-checkers worked perfectly, the question would arise: *quis custodiet?* Who will check the spell-checkers? There must obviously be some model of correct spelling, or we will eventually lose all ability to communicate with each other through the written word. Some people spell easily, others don't. There is no need for anyone who is good at spelling to feel conceited about it. Those whose job it is to correct other people's spelling are not paid very well for it. Even so, one can't help feeling that correct spelling should be encouraged, and that education might play a part in this.

Our children may be becoming more and more difficult to teach, but I can't help feeling we should try. When I read that Britain's youngest father had been allowed the day off school to attend his baby's birth, I almost despaired. It may have been reasonable to allow the fifteen-year-old mother a day off to have her baby, although this is her school's third pregnancy in eighteen months – but to allow a twelve-year-old boy off school to attend his child's birth seems frivolous. How will our children ever learn the rudiments of spelling if they are always being given time off to have babies? Soon they will be asking for days off to conceive and beget them. I am sorry to sound old-fashioned, but there must be a moment when spelling comes first.

THE GUIDANCE WE NEED
(*Daily Telegraph*, 6 July 1998)

The Pope did not send me a copy of his apostolic letter, Motu Proprio Ad Tuendam Fidem, so I have not read it and cannot really comment on it, although I think I may be coming round to his view on women priests. I do not take it amiss that he neglected to send me a copy. He is a very busy man and must have many people on his list. Or perhaps he was ashamed of his rather babyish Latin. Now we learn he has written a second pastoral letter, Dies Domini. This will simply urge us all to go to church on Sundays, as popes, bishops, priests and deacons have always done. They would, wouldn't they?

Perhaps he does not expect replies to these pastoral letters, but if he has sent me one, I shall answer that it would be much easier to go to church on Sunday if he, as Pope, had put a stop to the ghastly Mickey Mouse liturgy instituted by his two pred-ecessors. It is one thing to argue that modern congregations do not understand Latin. In fact, they never did. They always took it on trust, for the most part, that the priest was saying the right thing, whatever that may have been. It is quite another to expect congregations to watch grimacing celebrants and listen to feeble, patronising jokes designed for five-year-olds of moderate intel-ligence. This is as bad as watching television.

Television, as we all know, not only increases your blood pres-sure, makes you blind and gives you cancer. It is also destructive of morals. If the Pope really wishes to offer guidance to the modern world, he should forbid Catholics from owning or watching a television set. I will happily compose an encyclical for him to that effect.

THREAT TO BABIES
(*Daily Telegraph*, 12 August 1998)

People in Hampshire have been warned against leaving babies and small pets unattended after the Animal Liberation Front released up to 6000 mink from a mink farm in Ringwood, but I do not think that hatred of babies or small pets was among their motives for this curious act. Mink are not really interested in babies. Their chief delight is to kill songbirds and eat their eggs. Perhaps it was hatred of songbirds which drove the Animal Liberationists to this desperate remedy. It certainly was not love of mink. These farm-bred Canadian predators are unlikely to survive for long in the English countryside, where they will be hunted down and die miserable, lonely deaths, having no joy even in being hunted, unlike the wild deer of Exmoor who were created by God for this purpose.

If hatred of songbirds explains it all, I can almost sympathise. For many years I used to be irritated by the deafening dawn chorus which these creatures would set up every morning through spring. Some claimed to like it, but there was a gloating triumphalism in the birds' approach to every new day which seemed to undermine the rules of neighbourliness and the rights of property. Under this country's oppressive laws, we could only shake our fists at them impotently. But in the last couple of years there seem to be fewer birds around and the nuisance has abated. I do not think I would set mink on the survivors, particularly if it meant accepting these unpleasant animals as part of the scene, requiring endless supervision of Pekinese, grandchildren, visiting babies, etc.

The only encouraging result of this dreadful act may be to give our young people something to do. Nearly one in five of our university students drops out after failing to complete the university course, according to the Department of Education, and very few of those who complete their courses are fit for subsequent employment. Mink-hunting requires no educational qualification, no social awareness, no appreciation of English literature. In fact, it requires none of the things which our young people so conspicuously lack. When I was a boy, the village policeman would pay a shilling for a squirrel's tail. If we paid these young people two pounds per mink's tail, it should buy them the occasional pizza veggieburger treat, and make their lives worth living.

QUALITY TIME
(*Daily Telegraph*, 19 October 1998)

Publicans are furious at the suggestion by Bass, the brewers, that some of the company's pubs should stay open on Christmas evening. They say that it is the only moment in the year when they can put their feet up and spend time with their families. We should think hard before denying them this annual treat. When I was a child I noticed that some of the most disagreeable and unhelpful people I ever met were the owners of sweet shops. This seemed odd because at that age I could think of no employment more agreeable or useful than selling sweets. Later, I rationalised the phenomenon. Before being allowed to sell sweets, they had to make themselves hideously sick by deliberately stuffing themselves on sweets so that they never wanted to eat one again. The sweet seller's unpleasant demeanour was explained by being denied one of life's greatest pleasures, and being constantly reminded of it.

When I grew up, I made the same discovery about publicans, but did not attribute their surly manners and grudging service to drinking too much. Practically none of them drinks too much, and they are liable to lose their licences if they do. The reason they were so unpleasant, I decided, was that British licensing laws made theirs a comparatively idle job. They spent too much time at home with their feet up, I thought. It is well known that an idle job creates resentment against having to do any work at all. Now we learn they are among the hardest-working people in Britain, if not the world. Any abruptness of manner is due to exhaustion. They should be delighted to 'work' on Christmas evening, helping others to escape from the tyranny of family television. I expect their wives and children will clap, too, to see them gone.

SNORING ON
(*Daily Telegraph*, 12 June 2000)

The magistrate who dozed off while a defendant was giving evidence has all my sympathy. With every month that passes, I thank my lucky stars that I have not been called to jury service. Would it be an acceptable excuse that you very much doubt your ability to stay awake?

Perhaps it is the result of listening to sermons as a boy at Downside, but I find that as soon as anyone starts making a speech on any subject, my mind switches off and if they persist I am asleep within four minutes. The courts are infinitely worse. After a few minutes, everybody knows exactly what everybody is going to say before they have said it; then they repeat it four, five or six times. At least lawyers are paid handsomely for taking part in the ritual, but I never understand how jurors manage to stay awake. On one memorable occasion, in a civil action, I found I had fallen asleep while actually giving evidence. Luckily, nobody noticed.

Chapter Eighteen
The Last Word

My grand philosophical conclusion at the end of the day is that humanity does not divide into the rich and the poor, the privileged and the unprivileged, the clever and the stupid, the lucky and the unlucky or even the happy and the unhappy. It divides into the nasty and the nice.[1]

Waugh was pessimistic about his prospects for posterity. He was disparaging about his five novels and dismissed his journalism as transitory. Of his ten non-fiction books, he regarded his second collection of the *Private Eye* Diary, *A Turbulent Decade*, as his masterpiece, but he believed that even this *tour de force* would be incomprehensible within a decade. I trust this selection shows he was wrong. Like Pepys or Swift, his work naturally needs the odd footnote, but although the objects of his satire were transient, his wit, like theirs, has lasted. Hogarth and Gillray are still remembered long after their targets have been forgotten, and Waugh will be remembered, above all, for his humour, which transcends the people he wrote about, and the papers he wrote for. Like all good satirists, he ridiculed the strong rather than the weak, but although he was provocative and outspoken, he mainly wrote for the sheer fun of it, and that is why his writing will endure. Like Montesquieu, he regarded gravity as the joy of imbeciles. 'The boy lives for pleasure and is thought a great wit by his contemporaries,'[2] wrote Evelyn Waugh, when Auberon was still only six. It was an acute summary of his son's character, as a child and as a man. Some sixty years later, when he died, after a life lived for pleasure (and the abiding pleasure of others), he was rightly regarded as a great wit by millions of his contemporaries. And in the end, it's hard to think of a better accolade than that.

'I don't fear death myself, but the thought of it makes me angry,' Waugh told Naim Attallah. 'I don't want to die but I see I'm going to have to, which makes me furious, not frightened. What I find repugnant about death is the thought of not being able to know what's going on with the children, not being able to read the gossip columns. I find it completely against reason that an intelligence just dies out like that.'[3] Yet one of the consolations of a writer's life is that as long as people continue to read their work, that intelligence doesn't quite die out. As Waugh said in the week before his death, in answer to a question about the purpose of his life, 'Well, I suppose I have made a few intelligent people laugh.'

*

IN DEFENCE OF JOURNALISTS
(*Spectator*, 17 April 1982)

A large part of my time seems to have been spent defending journalists. There is an ineradicable suspicion of them in England which I find hard to explain except in terms of sexual guilt. Everybody, or nearly everybody, in England has a dirty secret, usually sexual but sometimes referring to some other habit or indulgence. This passion for secrecy is glorified by the name of privacy and fiercely defended by a whole apparatus of ingenious arguments: mothers and wives will be upset; worst of all, children will have their feelings hurt. In one memorable case, it was announced that somebody's *kids* had cried on the way home from school.[4] Yet despite these frightful *faux pas*, I have always maintained that the practice of journalism – and especially gossip journalism – is a genial one, adding to the gaiety of the nation, on balance, rather than subtracting from it. People should be able to laugh at themselves and their curious habits: if they can't, it is their own fault. Wives are frequently miserable for no reason. Children's tears are quickly dried. Journalists, in my experience, are generally easy-going, unpompous people whose chief concern is to unravel good stories from the tangled skein of everyday monotony and pass them on.

Notes

INTRODUCTION

1. In an article in the *Spectator* (9 September 1989) advo-
cating the legalisation of cocaine, Waugh cited the
liberal philosopher John Stuart Mill (1806–73): 'The only
purpose for which power can be rightfully exercised
over any member of a civilised community against his
will is to prevent harm to others. His own good, either
physical or moral, is not a sufficient warrant' (*On Liberty*,
1859).
2. *Spectator*, 22 August 1987
3. *Guardian*, 19 January 2001
4. Naim Attallah, *Singular Encounters* (Quartet Books, 1990)
5. *Sunday Telegraph*, 19 July 1998. When Waugh published *A
Turbulent Decade – The Diaries of Auberon Waugh 1976–1985*
(Private Eye & Andre Deutsch, 1985) he declared that
any bookshop which did not stock it should likewise be
burned down.
6. For a revealing (yet remarkably civil) confrontation
between the writer of this letter and Auberon's eldest
son, Alexander, see *Fathers & Sons*, Alexander Waugh's
excellent documentary, made for BBC 4 in 2004 to
accompany his book of the same name.
7. *Guardian*, 24 January 2001
8. *New Statesman*, 29 January 2001
9. *Daily Telegraph*, 31 July 1992
10. Auberon Waugh, *Another Voice – An Alternative Anatomy
of Britain* (Sidgwick & Jackson, 1986)
11. *Spectator*, 2 December 1989
12. *Ibid.*, 14 June 1980

13. *Daily Telegraph*, 24 July 1995
14. 'A classless society, in the English context, means a society led by the bossiest, loudest and usually the most incompetent elements of the old lower middle class.' (*Ibid.*, 13 November 1991)
15. *Ibid.*, 30 January 1999
16. Waugh's motorcycle martyr was Fred Hill, who died in prison in 1984 while serving sixty days for refusing to wear a helmet, his thirty-first sentence for this offence. Waugh commemorated the anniversary of his death in his various columns every year.
17. Waugh also founded the Venerable Society for the Protection of Adulterers (of which he was the president and only member) not to actually promote adultery, but to expose the hypocrisy of our prudish and prurient gutter press. 'Under my Family Protection Act it will be a civil tort to announce or hint of any living person that he or she has committed adultery in the past twenty years,' he wrote in the *Daily Telegraph* on 8 June 1994. 'It would be no defence to plead that the calumny was true.'
18. *Spectator*, 4 July 1987
19. 'My own eyes were opened to the fact that she was no longer a fit person to run the country at the time of the Gibraltar shootings.' (*Ibid.*, 18 November 1989) In 1988, the SAS killed three suspected IRA 'terrorists' in Gibraltar, sparking a fierce debate about whether they could or should have been arrested instead.
20. 'The simplest and most fundamental tenet of social morality is that you don't kill people or have them killed because they are inconvenient to you,' wrote Waugh, in the *Spectator* on 10 December 1994. 'If we lose sight of that, we have lost sight of everything.'
21. 'We will be much better off inside a Europe with open frontiers and a single currency. The whole concept of national sovereignty, as brandished by our politicians, is a deliberate deception. It covers the government's right

to screw up the economy once every four years in a cynical attempt to be re-elected, and we would be better off without it.' (*Daily Telegraph*, 26 June 1991)

22. *Spectator*, 25 May 1985
23. *Books & Bookmen*, March 1974
24. 'Too little happens in a columnist's life for any of it to be wasted.' (*Spectator*, 3 October 1992)
25. 'The only two pieces of news which will make me take down my shotgun from the wall will be when I hear that *Oz* has been suppressed or that the fun people from Upper Clyde Shipyards are taking control of the country,' wrote Waugh, in a feature for the magazine.
26. In this respect, Waugh was a lot like his father. Despite his staid public image, Evelyn Waugh admired artistic innovators like T. S. Eliot and Stanley Spencer, both considered rather daring in their day.
27. *Spectator*, 14 October 1978
28. *Ibid.*, 30 April 1983
29. *Viz – The Documentary*, Channel 4, 1990
30. Auberon Waugh, *Another Voice – An Alternative Anatomy of Britain* (Sidgwick & Jackson, 1986)
31. Auberon Waugh, *Will This Do?* (Century, 1991)
32. *Daily Telegraph*, 18 January 2001
33. 'Children of divorced parents are a nuisance,' wrote Waugh, in the *Spectator* on 28 October 1995. 'They can be highly inconvenient to their parents, denying them the fresh start which is what the sacrament of divorce promises.'
34. Waugh, *Another Voice*
35. *Daily Telegraph*, 16 December 2000

CHAPTER ONE: UNWILLINGLY TO SCHOOL

1. *Spectator*, 5 August 1978
2. *New Statesman*, 4 July 1975
3. *Private Eye*, 11 August 1974
4. *Spectator*, 6 May 1989

5. *Books & Bookmen*, March 1974
6. To Auberon Waugh, 27 January 1955; Mark Amory (ed.), *The Letters of Evelyn Waugh* (Weidenfeld & Nicolson, 1980)
7. *Books & Bookmen*, June 1978
8. *Private Eye*, 5 March 1976
9. Auberon Waugh, *The Last Word – An Eye Witness Account of The Trial of Jeremy Thorpe* (Michael Joseph, 1980). Waugh was wary of Thorpe from the start, on account of Thorpe's penchant for double-breasted waistcoats, which his prefects had worn at school.
10. *Spectator*, 28 February 1981
11. *New Statesman*, 28 February 1975
12. The fictional names of classmates in this piece have all been taken from Waugh's novels *Foxglove Saga* and *Path of Dalliance*.
13. Anthony Crosland (1918–77): Labour politician who held several cabinet posts under Harold Wilson. Author of *The Future of Socialism* (1956). Died of a brain haemorrhage while serving as foreign secretary under James Callaghan.

CHAPTER TWO: ARMS AND THE MAN

1. *Spectator*, 3 November 1984
2. To Auberon Waugh, 11 February 1956; Mark Amory (ed.), *The Letters of Evelyn Waugh*, (Weidenfeld & Nicolson, 1980)
3. *Spectator*, 21 November 1987
4. To Ann Fleming, 27 April 1958; Amory (ed.), *Letters of Evelyn Waugh*
5. Auberon Herbert (1922–74): Waugh's maternal uncle (and namesake).
6. Auberon Waugh, *Will This Do?* (Century, 1991)
7. Some gossipmongers subsequently spread the rumour that Waugh had been machine-gunned from behind by his own men, others that he had succeeded in shooting off both his testicles. Both stories were untrue.

8. *Spectator*, 10 June 1978

9. Waugh's editor at *Isis* was David Dimbleby.

10. Reluctance to believe what one is told may be a handicap for an aspiring economist but it is an excellent qualification for a journalist.

11. Lord Gowrie (Grey Hore-Ruthven, born 1939, 2nd Earl of Gowrie, 1955): Conservative politician, member of the cabinet (1984–5) as chancellor of the Duchy of Lancaster and minister for the arts. Waugh never forgot his amorous defeat by Gowrie, and baited him throughout his life.

12. Recounted by Mark Amory, literary editor of the *Spectator* and editor of *The Letters of Evelyn Waugh*, in the *Spectator*, 17 September 1994.

13. John Betjeman (1906–84, knighted 1969): 'Your father was one of the only great people I ever knew,' he wrote, in a letter to Waugh after his father's death. 'You have his genius and he recognised it.' Waugh returned the compliment: 'The only poet who writes with passion and sincerity about the times we live in,' he wrote in *Private Eye*, when Betjeman was appointed poet laureate, in 1972.

14. Malcolm Muggeridge (1903–90): journalist and broadcaster. Although 'St Mugg' was generous (to a fault) about *The Foxglove Saga*, Auberon objected to his obituary of Evelyn Waugh in the *Observer*.

CHAPTER THREE: VIVE LA FRANCE

1. *New Statesman*, 1 August 1975

2. Auberon Waugh, *Will This Do?* (Century, 1991)

3. *Ibid.*

4. *Ibid.*

5. *Ibid.*

6. *Spectator*, 30 August 1980

7. Anthony Barber (1920–2005, baron 1974): Conservative politician, chancellor of the Exchequer, 1970–74.

CHAPTER FOUR: IN MY VIEW

1. *Daily Telegraph*, 26 June 1993
2. Auberon Waugh, *Will This Do?* (Century, 1991)

CHAPTER FIVE: THE ABC OF BEAUTY

1. *New Statesman*, 28 September 1973
2. Auberon Waugh, *Will This Do?* (Century, 1991)
3. *Ibid.*
4. *Sunday Mirror*, 10 July 1966
5. *Daily Mirror*, 9 May 1966
6. Waugh, *Will This Do?*
7. *Sun*, 17 November 1966
8. *Ibid.*

CHAPTER SIX: HP SAUCE

1. *Evening Standard*, 8 September 1973. 'Politicians are not people who seek power in order to implement policies they think are necessary,' wrote Evelyn Waugh, in his diary, on 18 July 1961. 'They are people who seek policies in order to attain power.'
2. 'To my slight shame, I took advantage of the moral high ground occupied by orphans and widows to write what I would probably now see as a petulant and intemperate reply to the encircling enemies,' recalled Waugh, in his autobiography, *Will This Do?* (Century, 1991). 'I am glad I was not able to trace a copy.'
3. *New Statesman*, 14 March 1975
4. *Literary Review*, April 1988
5. Christopher Sykes subsequently wrote Waugh's authorised biography (*Evelyn Waugh – A Biography*, Collins, 1975).
6. 'To secure for the workers by hand or by brain the full fruits of their industry and the most equitable distribution thereof that may be possible upon the basis of the

common ownership of the means of production, distribution and exchange, and the best obtainable system of popular administration and control of each industry or service.'

7. Alan Brien (1925–2008): journalist, whose diary in the *Sunday Times* subsequently inspired Auberon Waugh's Diary in *Private Eye*.

8. Harold Macmillan (1894–1986): Conservative MP, foreign secretary 1955, chancellor of the Exchequer 1955–7, prime minister 1957–63, Earl of Stockton 1984. The publishing firm Macmillan was founded by his grandfather, Daniel Macmillan (1813–57).

9. Waugh kept his word. 'Like many wise old birds he attracted the attention of ornithologists from all over the world,' he wrote, in the *Daily Telegraph*, when 'Saint Mugg' died in 1990, at the age of eighty-seven. 'Now he has finally dropped off his perch, they will have to go away. There is nothing to be said about him which he has not said himself many times over.'

10. Nigel Lawson (born 1932, baron 1992): journalist and Conservative MP for Blaby, Leicestershire (1974–92), chancellor of the Exchequer (1983–9). 'By far the cleverest person I have ever worked with,' wrote Waugh, in *Will This Do?*.

11. *Ibid.*

12. *Spectator*, 13 September 1986

13. *Ibid.*, 14 March 1987

14. Roy Jenkins (1920–2003, life peer 1987): Labour politician, home secretary (1965–7 and 1974–6), chancellor of the Exchequer (1967–70), president of the European Commission (1977–81). One of the founders (and the inaugural leader) of the Social Democratic Party (SDP).

15. To Lynn Barber, *Independent on Sunday*, 17 February 1981

16. *Ibid.*

17. George Gale (1927–90): journalist, editor of the *Spectator* (1970–73). 'George had a slight drink problem

at the time,' wrote Waugh, in *Will This Do?*, 'but the main reason for my intrusion was that his article made some facetious reference to the Waughs which I thought cheeky.' Yet when Gale died, Waugh was kind. 'He was a genial, warm hearted, kindly man, who did not take himself too seriously and never sued a colleague for libel,' he wrote, in his 'Way of the World' column. 'His views were said to be those of the ordinary man in the street, but I doubt it. There was nothing ordinary about George.' (*Daily Telegraph*, 7 November 1990)

18. Auberon Waugh, *Another Voice – An Alternative Anatomy of Britain* (Sidgwick & Jackson, 1986)

19. *Spectator*, 4 May 1985

20. *New Statesman*, 13 September 1974

21. *Daily Telegraph*, 22 June 1996.

22. Peter Hall (born 1930, knighted 1977): theatre director who ran the Royal Shakespeare Company (1960–68) and the National Theatre (1973–88).

23. Ian McKellen (born 1939, knighted 1991): actor.

CHAPTER SEVEN: STREET OF SHAME

1. *Spectator*, 28 May 1988 and 4 July 1981

2. *Ibid.*, 19 June 1976

3. Auberon Waugh, *Will This Do?* (Century, 1991)

4. Jill Tweedie (1936–93): *Guardian* journalist, most famous for her long-running column 'Letters from a Fainthearted Feminist'. Her third husband was Alan Brien, whose *Sunday Times* diary inspired Waugh's diary in *Private Eye*.

5. Before newspaper production was computerised, the *Guardian* was renowned (whether unfairly or otherwise) for its typographical errors.

6. Waugh and *Private Eye* were being sued for libel by Nora Beloff, political correspondent of the *Observer*. The barrister was Mary Claire Hogg, daughter of the

lord chancellor, Lord Hailsham. Waugh lost the case. Beloff was awarded damages of £3000.

7. George Best (1946–2005): arguably Britain's greatest ever footballer, most notably for Manchester United (1963–73). He became increasingly renowned in the latter stages of his playing career for his colourful life off the pitch. 'I spent 90 per cent of my money on women, drink and fast cars,' he reflected. 'The rest I wasted.'

8. Ivy Compton-Burnett (1884–1969, DBE 1967): novelist, best remembered for *Pastors and Masters* (1925) and *Brothers and Sisters* (1929).

9. Max Beerbohm (1872–1956, knighted 1939): writer and caricaturist, author of *Zuleika Dobson* (1911).

10. George Bernard Shaw (1856–1950): Anglo-Irish playwright, critic and socialist. Awarded the Nobel Prize for Literature in 1925.

11. Herbert George Wells (1866–1946): writer of science fiction – *The Time Machine* (1895), *The Invisible Man* (1897), *The War of the Worlds* (1898); and other novels, including *Kipps* (1905) and *The History of Mr Polly* (1910).

12. Tony Benn (born 1925): Labour MP, minister of technology (1966–70), secretary of state for industry (1974–5), secretary of state for energy (1975–9).

13. Paul Foot (1937–2004): campaigning investigative journalist; at Shrewsbury School with Richard Ingrams, Willie Rushton and Christopher Brooker, with whom he subsequently worked on *Private Eye*. A columnist for the *Daily Mirror*, and a committed socialist, he was a close friend of Waugh's.

14. Nora Beloff (1919–97): journalist, political reporter; married Clifford Makins, sports editor of the *Observer*, in 1977.

15. Benazir Bhutto (1953–2007): subsequently prime minister of Pakistan (1988–90 and 1993–6); assassinated.

16. Waugh had just returned from his annual summer sojourn in the Languedoc, France.

17. After his annual summer sojourn in the Languedoc.
18. Home of Auberon Waugh, and his father before him. Comparable riots in Brixton and Toxteth may have been provoked by these Combe Florey atrocities.
19. The American actor Charles Bronson starred in three *Death Wish* films – *Death Wish* (1974), *Death Wish II* (1982) and *Death Wish III* (1985) – all directed by Michael Winner, about a mild-mannered liberal businessman who becomes a violent vigilante after his wife and daughter are brutally raped in New York.
20. The England football team were competing in the World Cup Final in Spain, followed by their enthusiastic supporters.

CHAPTER EIGHT: IN THE LION'S DEN

1. Auberon Waugh, *In The Lion's Den* (Michael Joseph, 1978)
2. Auberon Waugh, *Will This Do?* (Century, 1991)
3. Auberon Waugh, *In The Lion's Den*
4. *Private Eye*, 31 December 1974
5. *Ibid.*, 10 January 1975
6. Waugh's political opinions are hard to summarise, but the following mini manifesto isn't such a bad place to start: 'When I come to power I will sack one in three public employees. I will demand O level Latin as a condition of employment at any grade in the Civil Service. I will decriminalise drugs. I will abolish the higher levels of taxation and I will allow the wages of domestic servants to be deducted from an employer's taxable income.' (*Spectator*, 13 May 1995)
7. Edward Gibbon (1737–94): author of *The History of the Decline and Fall of the Roman Empire*. 'It was at Rome, on the 15th October 1764, as I sat musing amidst the ruins of the Capitol, while the barefoot friars were singing vespers in the Temple of Jupiter, that the idea of writing the decline and fall of the city first started to my mind.'

8. From 'Elegy Written in a Country Churchyard', a.k.a. Gray's Elegy, by Thomas Gray (1716–71). Given the subject of this article, Waugh may have been mindful that another of Gray's most popular poems was 'Ode on the Death of a Favourite Cat, Drowned in a Tub of Gold Fishes'.

9. Sydney Smith (1771–1845): clergyman and wit, leading member of the Holland House set and one of Waugh's heroes.

CHAPTER NINE: ANOTHER VOICE

1. *Spectator*, 10 October 1987
2. Waugh and Chancellor eventually became related by marriage, when Waugh's son Alexander married Chancellor's daughter, Eliza.
3. Auberon Waugh, *In The Lion's Den* (Michael Joseph, 1978)
4. Auberon Waugh, *Will This Do?* (Century, 1991)
5. Auberon Waugh, *Another Voice – An Alternative Anatomy of Britain* (Sidgwick & Jackson, 1986)
6. Alan Brien (1925–2008): journalist, whose diary in the *Sunday Times* inspired Auberon Waugh's Diary in *Private Eye*. Brien married the journalist Jill Tweedie (1932–93) whose column, 'Letters from a Fainthearted Feminist', ran in the *Guardian* from 1969 to 1988.
7. Prince Charles and Lady Diana Spencer were married at St Paul's Cathedral that summer.
8. Arnold Goodman (1913–95): lawyer, chairman of the Arts Council (1965–72), director of the Royal Opera House (1972–83). Uniquely, made a peer by a Labour prime minister (Harold Wilson) and a Companion of Honour by a Conservative prime minister (Edward Heath).
9. Waugh stood for the Dog Lovers' Party against Jeremy Thorpe, the Liberal MP for Devon North, in the 1979 general election. Waugh polled seventy-nine votes. Thorpe lost his seat.

10. Department of Health and Social Security, formed in 1968 when the Department of Health and the Department of Social Security were merged. These two departments were devolved again in 1988.

11. The oldest gentleman's club in London, founded as a chocolate house in 1693. Auberon's father, Evelyn, was a member. During the eighteenth century, it was renowned for reckless gaming. From the early nineteenth century onwards, it became a respectable Tory rendezvous.

12. Randolph Churchill (1911–68): journalist, only son of Winston Churchill, Conservative MP for Preston (1940–45). In 1942, Evelyn Waugh dedicated his novel *Put Out More Flags* to Randolph but their relationship, though close, was complex. 'Randolph Churchill went into hospital to have a lung removed,' wrote Waugh, in his diary in 1964, recalling a conversation with a friend at White's. 'I remarked that it was a typical triumph of modern science to find the only part of Randolph that was not malignant and remove it.'

13. *Spectator*, 3 February 1996

CHAPTER TEN: COUNTRY TOPICS

1. *Daily Telegraph*, 25 February, 1991
2. *Ibid.*, 26 October 1991
3. Auberon Waugh, *Country Topics* (Michael Joseph, 1974)
4. *Spectator*, 2 April 1988

CHAPTER ELEVEN: OTHER PLACES

1. Auberon Waugh, *Will This Do?* (Century, 1991)
2. *Daily Telegraph*, 4 August 1990
3. *Spectator*, 27 September 1986
4. *Daily Telegraph*, 14 October 1991
5. *Independent on Sunday*, 17 February 1991
6. Auberon Waugh, *Will This Do?*

7. Waugh was similarly thwarted in his ambition to eat giant panda. 'In the course of five weeks' travelling around China, I never found anyone prepared to cook one for me. China, for all its disgusting regime, is quite liberal in its dietary laws, but I was told that cooking giant panda carried the death penalty.' (*Daily Telegraph*, 10 June 1992)

8. Ibid., 13 May 1998

CHAPTER TWELVE: OTHER PEOPLE

1. *Spectator*, 5 June 1976
2. *Daily Telegraph*, 22 January 1997
3. Greene described this friendship in *Getting to Know the General* (Bodley Head, 1984).
4. Oswald Mosley (1896–1980, baronet 1928): Conservative MP (1918–22), Independent MP (1922–4) and Labour MP (1926–31). In 1932 he founded the British Union of Fascists. In 1936 he married Diana Mitford, a close friend (mainly by correspondence) of Auberon's father, Evelyn. Both Oswald and Diana were interned for three years during the Second World War.
5. Nicholas Mosley, *Rules of the Game* (Secker & Warburg, 1982)
6. *Spectator*, 20 September 1980
7. 'At about this time, meeting a group of literati at the Cheltenham Literary Festival, I discovered they were all receiving letters from him at the rate of one or two a day. What brought us closer, and singled me out as his favourite correspondent, was probably an incident which occurred around Christmas that year. He wrote to me describing an enormous meal he had prepared for his aged mother – I think it may have been her Christmas luncheon – and I wrote back to say I thought it was rather a large meal for such an old lady and hoped it would not kill her. A few days later a rather brusque note arrived: she had indeed taken to her bed

immediately afterwards, gone into a coma and died.'
(*Ibid.*)

8. Contributors to *Books & Bookmen* included Sir John
   Betjeman, Melvyn Bragg, Michael Foot, Diana Mosley,
   Enoch Powell and the Prince of Wales.

9. Kathleen Tynan, *The Life of Kenneth Tynan* (Weidenfeld &
   Nicolson, 1987)

10. Auberon Waugh, *Will This Do?* (Century, 1991)

11. Paul Foot, *Words as Weapons: Selected Writings 1980–90*
    (Verso, 1990)

12. Michael Wharton (1913–2006): journalist and satirist,
    creator of Peter Simple, fictional narrator of 'Way of
    the World' in the *Daily* (and, for a shorter time) the
    Sunday Telegraph. The first volume of his autobiography
    was *The Missing Will* (Chatto & Windus, 1984)

13. Wharton wrote the 'Way of the World' column in the
    Daily Telegraph for more than thirty-three years, from
    1957 to 1990, when he took Peter Simple to the *Sunday
    Telegraph* and bequeathed this sacred space to Waugh.
    Simple later returned to the *Daily Telegraph*, eventually
    racking up nearly half a century on both titles.

14. Alan Patrick Herbert (1890–1971, knighted 1945): writer,
    campaigner and wit; novelist (*The Water Gipsies*, 1930)
    and contributor to *Punch*. MP for Oxford University
    (1935–50).

15. Randolph Churchill (1911–68): journalist, Conservative
    MP for Preston (1940–45) only son of Winston
    Churchill, friend and wartime comrade of Evelyn
    Waugh. Evelyn said he belonged to two London clubs
    so that if Randolph was at one of them Evelyn could
    go to the other.

16. Lady Pamela Berry (1914–82): daughter of the 1st Earl
    of Birkenhead, friend of Evelyn Waugh, wife of the
    Hon. Michael Berry, 1st Baron Hartwell, editor-in-chief
    of the *Daily* and *Sunday Telegraph*.

17. John Betjeman (1906–84, knighted 1969): poet, jour-
    nalist, broadcaster, educated at Marlborough and

Oxford. Poet laureate from 1972. A good friend of
Evelyn and, subsequently, Auberon Waugh.
18. Unlike a lot of commentators, who castigated Diana
during her lifetime and then showered her with posthumous praise, Waugh was entirely consistent in his
admiration and affection for the Princess. His previous
Sunday Telegraph column, written just before she died,
was entitled 'Why I Love Her More Than Ever'.
19. Like his friends and colleagues, Richard Ingrams and
Paul Foot, Willie Rushton was educated at Shrewsbury
School.

CHAPTER THIRTEEN: BOOKS & BOOKMEN

1. *Spectator*, 19 March 1977
2. Alan Jenkins, *The Rich Rich* (Weidenfeld & Nicolson,
1978)
3. *Books & Bookmen*, April 1978
4. *Ibid.*, July 1975
5. Pelham Grenville Wodehouse (1881–1975, knighted
1975): Britain's greatest humorous writer died on
Valentine's Day, shortly after receiving a (belated)
knighthood for his services to literature.
6. Alan Alexander Milne (1882–1956): Scots author, most
famous for his children's books, *Winnie The Pooh* (1926)
and *The House at Pooh Corner* (1928) and his collections
of children's verse, *When We Were Very Young* (1924) and
Now We Are Six (1927).
7. Malcolm Bradbury (1932–2000, knighted 2000): author,
academic and pioneer of the innovative creative-writing
course at the University of East Anglia, whose gradu-
ates include Ian McEwan and Kazuo Ishiguro.
8. Bevis Hillier, *Young Betjeman* (John Murray, 1988)
9. *Sunday Telegraph*, 2 April 2000
10. *Ibid.*

CHAPTER FOURTEEN: FROM THE PULPIT

1. *Literary Review*, July 1993
2. See 'Death of A Publisher', *Books & Bookmen*, p. 204.
3. *Literary Review*, April 1986
4. *Spectator*, 3 May 1986
5. Not everyone shared Waugh's enthusiasm for conventional verse. 'It's terribly damaging to allow people to think that these absurd little ditties are poems,' the *Times Literary Supplement*'s poetry editor, Alan Jenkins, was reported as saying, in the *Daily Telegraph*. 'Waugh's taste in poetry obviously stops short at nursery rhymes.'
6. *Literary Review*, November 1990
7. *Spectator*, 3 May 1986
8. *Literary Review*, August 1994
9. *Ibid.*, February 1989
10. 'Members who have the misfortune to be sent to prison will not be expected to pay subscriptions while inside, and may resume the unused part of their subscription on release.'
10. *Spectator*, 9 December 1989

CHAPTER FIFTEEN: RAGE

1. *Spectator*, 31 May 1986
2. Auberon Waugh, *Will This Do?* (Century, 1991)
3. *Spectator*, 22 March 1986
4. *Ibid.*
5. Harry Thompson, *Richard Ingrams – Lord of the Gnomes* (William Heinemann, 1994)
6. Waugh also invested £12,000 in the magazine.
7. *Spectator*, 17th August 1991 (Ingrams was teetotal).
8. *Daily Telegraph*, 28 March 1992
9. *Ibid.*, 3 April 1993
10. *Daily Telegraph*, 16 October 1991

CHAPTER SIXTEEN: WAVIANA

1. *Bottom of Form*
2. Naim Attallah, *Singular Encounters* (Quartet Books, 1990)
3. *Books & Bookmen*, October 1975
4. *Ibid.*, October 1973
5. *Literary Review*, May 1992
6. Christopher Sykes, *Evelyn Waugh – A Biography* (Collins, 1975)
7. Auberon inherited his father's enduring distaste for sentimentality. In his column in the *Spectator* (9 December 1995) he cited James Baldwin to support his case. 'Sentimentality, the ostentatious parading of excessive and spurious emotion, is the mark of dishonesty, the inability to feel.' (*Notes of a Native Son*, 1955)
8. Alec Waugh (1898–1981): novelist and travel writer, most notably *Island in the Sun* (1956) and *The Loom of Youth* (1917), which caused controversy in public schools (especially Waugh's *alma mater*, Sherborne) with its depiction of life in an English boarding school. Evelyn Waugh's elder brother, and eldest son of Auberon's grandfather, Arthur Waugh, Alec also created the cocktail party to fill the awkward gap between high tea and dinner.
9. Evelyn Waugh worshipped at Farm Street when he was in London.
10. A student film made by Evelyn Waugh in 1924. Evelyn wrote the script and played the villain. His elder brother Alec played an old woman. Auberon was joking when he described it as an epic, but it does deserve a footnote in movie (as well as literary) history. The leading lady, Elsa Lanchester (1902–86), appearing in her first film role, subsequently became a famous actress, married Charles Laughton and went with him to Hollywood. Evelyn and Alec had met her in a drinking club in London's Charlotte Street.

CHAPTER SEVENTEEN: 'WAY OF THE WORLD'

1. *Daily Telegraph*, 3 February 1999
2. Auberon Waugh, *Way of the World* (Arrow, 1995)
3. 'It has long been my contention that the Royal Society for the Protection of Birds is one of the most sinister organisations in this country, second only to the drugs department of Customs & Excise in the vicious self-righteousness with which it applies its altogether excessive powers.' (*Spectator*, 12 August 1989)
4. Auberon Waugh, *Way of the World*
5. Auberon Waugh's final home (and his father's final home before him) was a handsome eighteenth-century country house with a sixteenth-century gatehouse. Pevsner wrote approvingly of its staircase. One of its most attractive features is the local red sandstone from which it was made.
6. England had played – and narrowly beaten – Cameroon 3–2 in the quarter-finals of the 1990 World Cup.
7. John Major (born 1943, knighted 2005): banker, cricketer, Conservative prime minister (1990–97). During his premiership, he offered the nation no guidance on matters of circumcision. History does not record whether he was a Roundhead or a Cavalier.
8. AIDS, or American Immune Deficiency Sickness, to give it the full name that Waugh bestowed on it.
9. William Beveridge (1879–1963) chaired the Committee on Social Insurance and Allied Services, whose eponymous report, in 1942, with its proposals for a social security programme for the ill, the elderly and the unemployed, became the basis of the Welfare State after 1945.

CHAPTER EIGHTEEN: THE LAST WORD

1. Auberon Waugh, *Will This Do?* (Century, 1991)
2. Naim Attallah, *Singular Encounters* (Quartet Books, 1990)
3. Evelyn Waugh to Nancy Mitford, 5 January 1946; Mark Amory (ed.) *The Letters of Evelyn Waugh* (Weidenfeld & Nicolson, 1980)
4. Clive James once remarked that *Private Eye* 'sent people's children crying home from school'.